File for Divorce in Maryland, Virginia or the District of Columbia

Second Edition

James J. Gross
Michael F. Callahan

Attorneys at Law

SPHINX® PUBLISHING
AN IMPRINT OF SOURCEBOOKS, INC.®
NAPERVILLE, ILLINOIS
www.SphinxLegal.com

Second Edition: 2006

Published by: **Sphinx® Publishing, An Imprint of Sourcebooks, Inc.®**

<u>Naperville Office</u>
P.O. Box 4410
Naperville, Illinois 60567-4410
630-961-3900
Fax: 630-961-2168
www.sourcebooks.com
www.SphinxLegal.com

This publication is designed to provide accurate and authoritative information in regard to the subject matter covered. It is sold with the understanding that the publisher is not engaged in rendering legal, accounting, or other professional service. If legal advice or other expert assistance is required, the services of a competent professional person should be sought.

From a Declaration of Principles Jointly Adopted by a Committee of the American Bar Association and a Committee of Publishers and Associations

This product is not a substitute for legal advice.

Disclaimer required by Texas statutes.

Library of Congress Cataloging-in-Publication Data
Gross, James J.
   File for divorce in Maryland, Virginia or the District of Columbia / by
James J. Gross and Michael F. Callahan.-- 2nd ed.
      p. cm.
   Rev. ed. of: How to file for divorce in Maryland, Virginia, and the
District of Columbia. 1st ed. 2003.
   Includes index.
   ISBN-13: 978-1-57248-536-5 (pbk. : alk. paper)
   ISBN-10: 1-57248-536-1 (pbk. : alk. paper)
 1. Divorce suits--Maryland--Popular works. 2. Divorce
suits--Virginia--Popular works. 3. Divorce suits--District of
Columbia--Popular works. I. Callahan, Michael. II. Gross, James J. How to
file for divorce in Maryland, Virginia, and the District of Columbia. III.
Title.

KF505.5.Z95G76 2006
346.75201'66--dc22   2006002283

Printed and bound in the United States of America.
SB — 10 9 8 7 6 5 4 3 2 1

To our wives,
Holly Gross and Madelyn Callahan,
who make it easy to stay married.

Contents

Section 3: Court Procedures

Section 9: Virginia

Section 10: District of Columbia

Using Self-Help Law Books

Before using a self-help law book, you should realize the advantages and disadvantages of doing your own legal work and understand the challenges and diligence that this requires.

The Growing Trend

Rest assured that you will not be the first or only person handling your own legal matter. For example, in some states, more than 75% of the people in divorces and other cases represent themselves. Because of the high cost of legal services, this is a major trend, and many courts are struggling to make it easier for people to represent themselves. However, some courts are not happy with people who do not use attorneys and refuse to help them in any way. For some, the attitude is, "Go to the law library and figure it out for yourself."

We write and publish self-help law books to give people an alternative to the often complicated and confusing legal books found in most law libraries. We have made the explanations of the law as simple and easy to understand as possible. Of course, unlike an attorney advising an individual client, we cannot cover every conceivable possibility.

Cost/Value Analysis

Whenever you shop for a product or service, you are faced with various levels of quality and price. In deciding what product or service to buy, you make a cost/value analysis on the basis of your willingness to pay and the quality you desire.

When buying a car, you decide whether you want transportation, comfort, status, or sex appeal. Accordingly, you decide among choices such as a Neon, a Lincoln, a Rolls Royce, or a Porsche. Before making a decision, you usually weigh the merits of each option against the cost.

When you get a headache, you can take a pain reliever (such as aspirin) or visit a medical specialist for a neurological examination. Given this choice, most people, of course, take a pain reliever, since it costs only pennies; whereas a medical examination costs hundreds of dollars and takes a lot of time. This is usually a logical choice because it is rare to need anything more than a pain reliever for a headache. But in some cases, a headache may indicate a brain tumor, and failing to see a specialist right away can result in complications. Should everyone with a headache go to a specialist? Of course not, but people treating their own illnesses must realize that they are betting, on the basis of their cost/value analysis of the situation, that they are taking the most logical option.

The same cost/value analysis must be made when deciding to do one's own legal work. Many legal situations are very straightforward, requiring a simple form and no complicated analysis. Anyone with a little intelligence and a book of instructions can handle the matter without outside help.

But there is always the chance that complications are involved that only an attorney would notice. To simplify the law into a book like this, several legal cases often must be condensed into a single sentence or paragraph. Otherwise, the book would be several hundred pages long and too complicated for most people. However, this simplification necessarily leaves out many details and nuances that would apply to special or unusual situations. Also, there are many ways to interpret most legal questions. Your case may come before a judge who disagrees with the analysis of our authors.

Therefore, in deciding to use a self-help law book and to do your own legal work, you must realize that you are making a cost/value analysis. You have decided that the money you will save in doing it yourself outweighs the chance that your case will not turn out to your satisfaction. Most people handling their own simple legal matters never have a problem, but occasionally people find that it ended up costing them more to have an attorney straighten out the situation than it would have if they had hired an attorney in the beginning. Keep this in mind while handling your case, and be sure to consult an attorney if you feel you might need further guidance.

Local Rules   The next thing to remember is that a book which covers the law for the entire nation, or even for an entire state, cannot possibly include every procedural difference of every jurisdiction. Whenever possible, we provide the exact form needed; however, in some areas, each county, or even each judge, may require unique forms and procedures. In our state books, our forms usually cover the majority of counties in the state or provide examples of the type of form that will be required. In our national books, our forms are sometimes even more general in nature but are designed to give a good idea of the type of form that will be needed in most locations. Nonetheless, keep in mind that your state, county, or judge may have a requirement, or use a form, that is not included in this book.

You should not necessarily expect to be able to get all of the information and resources you need solely from within the pages of this book. This book will serve as your guide, giving you specific information whenever possible and helping you to find out what else you will need to know. This is just like if you decided to build your own backyard deck. You might purchase a book on how to build decks. However, such a book would not include the building codes and permit requirements of every city, town, county, and township in the nation; nor would it include the lumber, nails, saws, hammers, and other materials and tools you would need to actually build the deck. You would use the book as your guide, and then do some work and research involving such matters as whether you need a permit of some kind, what type and grade of wood is available in your area, whether to use hand tools or power tools, and how to use those tools.

Before using the forms in a book like this, you should check with your court clerk to see if there are any local rules of which you should be aware or local forms you will need to use. Often, such forms will require the same information as the forms in the book but are merely laid out differently or use slightly different language. They will sometimes require additional information.

Besides being subject to local rules and practices, the law is subject to change at any time. The courts and the legislatures of all fifty states are constantly revising the laws. It is possible that while you are reading this book, some aspect of the law is being changed.

In most cases, the change will be of minimal significance. A form will be redesigned, additional information will be required, or a waiting period will be extended. As a result, you might need to revise a form, file an extra form, or wait out a longer time period. These types of changes will not usually affect the outcome of your case. On the other hand, sometimes a major part of the law is changed, the entire law in a particular area is rewritten, or a case that was the basis of a central legal point is overruled. In such instances, your entire ability to pursue your case may be impaired.

Introduction

Divorce is a confusing and complicated business. Nothing about it is easy, whether you are the one who is leaving or the one who is being left. We wrote this book to make divorce less difficult.

This is not a legal treatise and it cannot substitute for three years of law school, the bar exam, and expertise that comes from years of trying cases. However, we will explain the law and process of divorce in plain English in the jurisdictions where we currently practice law—Maryland, Virginia, and the District of Columbia.

The law is constantly changing, as legislatures pass new laws and the courts decide new cases. Also, every case is different. We do not know the specific facts of your particular case, so we cannot give you legal advice. We can only give you information about the law that will make you more knowledgeable as you go through the process.

We were inspired to write about divorce by Larry Rice, another divorce lawyer. We have adapted some of his ideas from *About Divorce in Tennessee* to Virginia, Maryland, and the District of Columbia. These ideas are reprinted with the permission of his copyright holder, the American Bar Association.

This book is set up in sections. The first section describes what you need to know and do before you start the process of divorce. The second section explains how to settle out of court. (You should know that most cases settle out of court.) The third, fourth, and fifth sections describe the litigation process for uncontested and contested divorces. The sixth and seventh sections discuss children, financial issues, and procedures you will encounter after or while you are obtaining a divorce.

Each chapter in the book describes a different topic, and the chapters are more or less in the order that you might encounter these topics in your divorce. Several chapters contain general information that is common to all jurisdictions. However, there are significant differences in the laws of each jurisdiction. Therefore, in the chapters where there are differences, we give you the specific details for each jurisdiction. In the section covering uncontested divorces, the procedures are so different that we devoted a whole chapter to each jurisdiction.

Following the main text of the book, there is a separate section for each jurisdiction. Within each of these sections, we provide separate appendices of blank forms and legal resources.

You can use the forms in this book for your divorce, but we recommend you also make copies. You will have to get a few of the forms from the court because they are a certain color or tri-part, and those forms are indicated. Usually, the court will require that you fill them out with a typewriter, but some just have boxes to check, which can be done by hand.

Each county will have different forms, but they will be similar to the ones in this book. There will always be a particular clerk or judge who will not accept the forms in this book for one reason or another. Just be patient, do not get frustrated, and ask the court clerk for current forms specific to your county. We have summarized the most important laws that govern divorce in each jurisdiction in the appendices.

Finally, if you want to do additional research on your own, or are in need of additional help, the appendices also contain resources, including reading materials, websites, agencies, and summaries of laws.

We would like to hear from you, especially if this book helps you and you are able to use it successfully to obtain your divorce. On the other hand, if you get stuck or stumped while filling out one of the forms, if something we say is confusing or unclear, or if a clerk gives you a hard time, please tell us about your experience. We will incorporate your feedback into future editions of this book to help others going through a divorce.

Thyden Gross and Callahan
4601 Willard Avenue
Chevy Chase, MD 20815
301-907-4580
Fax: 301-907-4588
www.mddivorcelawyers.com
tgclawyers@smart.net

We hope this book makes your divorce less difficult, less confusing, and less painful. Things will eventually get better. Good luck with your new life.

chapter 1

Marriage and Divorce

We all get married till death do us part and for better or worse. We have hopes and dreams of a long future together. No one expects to get divorced when they get married. As it turns out, the odds of your getting divorced are about one in two. This chapter introduces you to some of the general legal concepts about marriage, separation, annulment, and divorce.

MARRIAGE

Unless you had a *prenuptial agreement*, you entered into a contract when you signed your marriage license that you probably did not even know existed. The contract consists of hundreds of pages of law and cases for the jurisdiction where you live. It is a major undertaking that involves children, support, and property. You are presumed to know all of the terms of this contract, because you will be held to them.

The contract is not very intuitive. It is different from any other contract you may have signed. For example, your paycheck is no longer *your* paycheck, but becomes *marital property*, which is distributable by the court upon divorce. If you start a business during your marriage, and it becomes successful solely through your efforts, you will probably have to buy out your spouse's marital interest upon divorce. If your spouse breaks the contract and wants a divorce, he or she may still get half, and you may have to pay your own attorney's fees as well as your spouse's.

This stealth contract may never affect you, as long as you stay married, but it will govern if you ever get divorced.

COMMON-LAW MARRIAGE

The District of Columbia recognizes *common-law marriages,* which are legal marriages without a ceremony or license. The requirements for a common-law marriage in the District of Columbia are that both parties:

- ✪ must be free to marry;

- ✪ intend to be married;

- ✪ tell other people they are married; and,

- ✪ have sexual relations and live together in a state that recognizes common-law marriages.

There is no time limit for a common-law marriage in the District of Columbia. Maryland and Virginia do not recognize common-law marriages.

MARRIAGE COUNSELING

Even though we are divorce lawyers, we are still in favor of marriage. When a client shows up at our offices seeking a divorce, we ask first if they have tried reconciliation. We encourage them to talk to their spouses and confront the problems in their marriage head-on. If that does not work, we refer them to marriage counselors. *Marriage counselors* are social workers, psychologists, psychiatrists, and other therapists who deal with relationship issues. You can find a good counselor by word of mouth, searching the Internet, or looking in the telephone directory.

DIVORCE

Even if you are the best husband or wife in the world, you may still end up in a divorce. Although it takes two people to get married, it takes only one to get a divorce. It may take longer to get a divorce if only one person wants it, but it is inevitable.

Divorce is a way of ending a marriage. You have to go to court to get a divorce. In Maryland and the District of Columbia, you can have an *absolute divorce*, which means a final and permanent divorce. In Virginia, you can have a *divorce a vinculo matrimonii*, which means a divorce from the bonds of matrimony, or final divorce.

A final divorce allows you to get remarried again; resolves all issues of custody, support, and property; and, may allow the court to award use and possession orders for family property. It also allows the court to enter an award to adjust equity, permits the sale or retitling of property (depending on the jurisdiction), and permits a wife to resume a former name. All of these issues are explained in detail in later chapters.

LEGAL SEPARATION

There is a procedure in each jurisdiction for obtaining legal recognition of the spouses' separation, and support and other relief when you do not have grounds for a final divorce. This is called a *limited divorce* in Maryland, a *legal separation* in the District of Columbia, and a *divorce a mensa et thoro* (meaning divorce from bed and board, or limited divorce) in Virginia. The grounds for a legal separation are easier to meet than those for a final divorce. For example, any separation, even for one day, qualifies as grounds for a limited divorce (or legal separation) in all three jurisdictions.

A limited divorce or legal separation permits you to establish custody, visitation, and support until you qualify for a final or absolute divorce. If you do not need to establish those matters, then you may not need to incur the additional costs of this extra proceeding. You do not have to file for a limited divorce or legal separation first in order to get a final or absolute divorce.

PENDENTE LITE RELIEF

The court can also award *pendente lite* support. *Pendente lite* is Latin for "pending the litigation," so it means temporary support until the divorce trial. There are things you may need for the court to do pending the final trial. The court, upon request, can set a hearing to determine the needs of the parties and children, and the ability of a party to pay, then order support accordingly. This award is subject to rehearing at the final trial. The court can also order custody or specific visitation pending the final trial.

ANNULMENTS

Annulments are granted by the court only in certain rare cases. A divorce says this marriage is ended. An annulment says this marriage never existed. Annulments are rarely granted, and usually there has to be some kind of serious fraud involved.

For example, grounds for annulment in the District of Columbia are:

- ✪   you marry someone who is already married;

- ✪   you marry someone who is insane (except you cannot obtain an annulment if you live together after you discover the insanity);

- ✪   the marriage was obtained by fraud or force;

- ✪   you marry someone under age 16 or someone who is otherwise matrimonially incapacitated without your knowledge; or,

- ✪   you marry anyone from a list of certain relatives.

Religious annulments are easier to obtain, and you may request one even after you have a legal divorce from the court. You may want to get your spouse's agreement to cooperate in a religious annulment or divorce, but it is possible to obtain one even over your spouse's objection.

THE EMOTIONAL DIVORCE

Divorce is traumatic for the divorcing couple and their children. There are enormous currents of emotions at play during a divorce, as well as major legal and financial issues.

There is a difference between the legal divorce and the *emotional divorce*. The emotional divorce may not coincide in timing with the legal divorce. It may take years to get over your divorce and move on with your life. Discussing your emotional divorce with a good therapist can be extremely beneficial.

Anxiety

Anxiety is a common human emotion. People will find something to worry about even when times are good. When going through a divorce, you will find many things to worry about, and you will have good reason to worry.

Instead of letting your mind be consumed with worrying about how bad the situation is, you should concern yourself with what you can do to solve the problems. Outline your problems in writing—it helps you to focus clearly. (Then destroy these notes.)

Depression

Depression is another fairly common experience in divorce. If you are going through a divorce and you feel uncertain, insecure, or depressed, then you have a normal problem. You may want to obtain some counseling.

Support

There are support groups for separated and divorcing individuals. You can find support on the Internet, where there are virtual communities of separated and divorced people. There is a list of resources in Appendices C, G, and K for Maryland, Virginia, and the District of Columbia, respectively.

The support of friends and family is invaluable during divorce. However, when your family and friends offer you advice about your case, be cautious. The facts and circumstances of your marriage, divorce, children, and property are different from any other case. Often, such well-intentioned advice is not correct, and you need to take it with a grain of salt. This is not your neighbor's divorce or your Aunt May's divorce. It is *your* divorce and it is different from anyone else's.

If you are feeling depressed right now, or anxious, or crazy, you are not alone. In fact, you may be joining the majority. While this is not a particularly pleasant life lesson, you will survive it, and become much stronger and wiser in the process.

Lawyers

If you are reading this book because you are thinking about getting a divorce, then you may be asking whether you can do it yourself. This chapter helps you decide whether it is in your best interest to obtain a lawyer.

DOING IT YOURSELF

A number of divorce cases are granted by the courts each year with no lawyers involved. If you have an uncontested divorce, you should be able to complete your own divorce by following the forms and instructions in this book. If you represent yourself, you will be a *pro se* litigant. (Pro se is Latin, meaning "by yourself" or "on your own behalf.")

The chief advantage to representing yourself is that you save the expense of a lawyer. The main disadvantage is that you do not know the law. A judge may be sympathetic to a pro se litigant, but you will be held to the same rules and procedures that a lawyer would have to follow. It is easy to make a serious mistake.

NEEDING A LAWYER

You have no automatic right to a lawyer in divorce cases, and there is no law that requires you to hire a lawyer. Divorce, however, is a complicated business and most people want a lawyer. You should at least think about getting a lawyer when the case is *contested* and the stakes (such as custody, support, or property) are high. You have a contested case when you and your spouse disagree about any issue regarding your divorce.

You should also hire a lawyer if your spouse has a lawyer. That lawyer can only represent your spouse, and is required to do it in a manner that is in your spouse's favor and not necessarily fair to you.

You should hire a lawyer if you do not have the time, interest, or tolerance for the frustration sometimes encountered in the legal system.

A good lawyer will guide you through the process, help you avoid mistakes, save you time, and protect your interests. If you have a lot at stake, like alimony, children, or property, then you will probably want to hire an attorney. It is customary for divorce lawyers to have an initial conference with a client to discuss the facts of the case and the fees.

Benefits   If you have a lawyer, you can let the lawyer do all the worrying about your case. You can sleep at night. Lawyers have the training, skills, and experience for this job. Lawyers are used to dealing with the courts and know the rules, the laws, and the cases in which the courts have interpreted the laws. When you represent yourself, the judge will not give you much leeway. You are expected to know the rules, the laws, and the cases.

Two good lawyers can efficiently and effectively negotiate and draft a *Separation Agreement,* and will guide you through the divorce process. Lawyers and judges share a common language that contains lots of terms that are shortcuts for a body of law they understand.

The judge and your spouse's attorney may give more consideration to you if you have an attorney. Your spouse's attorney is not permitted to give you advice or help you.

Lawyers know what to do when there are complications in your case like not being able to serve your spouse, or difficult issues like pension plans, alimony, custody, and so forth.

Costs   The main downside to a lawyer is expense. Do not be penny-wise and pound-foolish, though. If a lawyer costs $5,000, and you and your spouse are arguing over $100,000, it makes sense to hire a lawyer. However, some people argue over $5,000 and the lawyer costs them $10,000.

There are different types of costs in divorce cases. The largest cost is usually attorney's fees, which is what is charged for the work a lawyer does on your case. Court costs are the fees that are charged by the court for the filing of the divorce papers and various other papers.

In contested cases, attorney's fees and court costs are higher, and there may be other costs for things such as depositions, private investigators, photographs, psychological evaluations, and tax consultants.

ATTORNEY'S FEES

Any discussion about what the costs or attorney's fees will be is the roughest of estimates. There are many variables in any divorce case, including some over which your lawyer has no control. Who your spouse will hire as an attorney, how complex the financial records are, or what mood the judge is in on the day of trial will affect how your case is handled, and therefore, what it will cost you.

The emotional cost of a divorce can be greater than the dollar cost. The damage of having a broken marriage examined in court is something only those who have lived through it can understand.

Sometimes one party ends up paying not only his or her own legal fees, but also some portion of the other party's. If there is a trial, the economically dominant party can be ordered to pay some of the economically dependent party's attorney's fees. The order will rarely pay the full amount. For example, if you are the wife, you are responsible for paying the agreed fee to your lawyer, who will give you credit for any payments made by your husband.

○ Divorce lawyers require a *retainer* to accept your case and to begin drawing up the necessary papers. A retainer is a set amount of money that is placed in the lawyer's trust account. The lawyer draws against it at his or her hourly rate as the work is completed. If you decide not to retain a particular lawyer, you may be charged for the initial office conference. If you retain him or her, you will sign a written contract setting out the terms of representation. The retainer is refundable to the extent not used. If the hourly fees earned exceed the retainer, the lawyer will probably ask you for more money.

FINDING A LAWYER

If you decide to hire a lawyer, try to find an experienced family lawyer who will settle or try your case in a professional manner, with a minimum of histrionics and hostility. A constructive approach toward your spouse, opposing counsel, and the court is the best way to navigate the divorce process. That way, you can end your marriage without destroying the relationships you have built with children, other family members, and friends.

Some lawyers are not good at returning telephone calls. This is important to you in the middle of a divorce. Ask about this in your initial interview. If your lawyer does not return your calls, get another lawyer.

You will save yourself a lot of frustration if you know that real time is not the same as lawyer time. Lawyers are used to the hurry up and wait scheduling of the court's crowded docket, and so a three- or four-month wait to get before a judge is fast for a lawyer.

If you decide to hire a lawyer, do your research. Here are a few ways to find a lawyer:

  ✪　check the Internet (see the appendices at the end of this book for specific recommendations);

  ✪　ask your friends who have been divorced about their experiences with their lawyers;

- get recommendations from the county bar association or the chair of the family law section of the county, state, or American bar associations;

- go to seminars on divorce; or,

- ask your therapist.

Find a lawyer with some passion for divorce law. You can find this out by looking at his or her credentials. For example, lawyers who publish books or articles, or teach other lawyers, would seem to have a passion for their work. Martindale-Hubbel maintains a website (**www.martindale.com**) that has ratings of lawyers by their peers. An "AV" rating is the highest rating.

You and your spouse cannot be represented by the same lawyer. It is against the law in Maryland, Virginia, and the District of Columbia. If you and your spouse have agreed on everything, it may be possible for one lawyer to do all the legal work, but he or she can represent only one of you. Your spouse should see a separate lawyer for advice. If you and your spouse disagree later, each lawyer can still only represent the person with whom he or she started.

Red Flags

As you are going through a divorce procedure, there will be many things to take care of. Some of the items on your list of things to do are *red flag items*. These are the first things you should think about at the beginning of your divorce.

BANK ACCOUNTS

At the bank, you may want to divide joint accounts or put them in your name. Let your spouse know as soon as possible, but not before you do it, or you may wake up and find nothing in the accounts. If you are the breadwinner, do not put your dependent spouse out in the cold without some money to get by on. This will aggravate the judge, who will make you pay anyway.

CREDIT ISSUES

Close all joint accounts and notify the banks, charge cards, and others by a certified, return receipt letter stating that you are no longer responsible for your spouse's expenses. You may want the company to reopen an account in your own name. If so, this is a good time to request it. Let your spouse know so he or she is not caught by surprise at the gas pump when the credit card does not work.

INSURANCE

If you cover your spouse or children on your insurance, do not drop them from the policy until the divorce is final. You are probably responsible for their medical bills until then anyway. Even after the divorce, the employed spouse may want to keep the spouse and children covered.

If you are paying child support, a large, unexpected medical expense for the child could be assessed against the noncustodial parent as additional child support. The same could happen with alimony and an ex-spouse. Federal law allows most employees to cover their ex-spouses for up to thirty-six months for a small additional premium. However, the employer must be notified prior to the final decree.

UTILITIES

Do not cut off the utilities on your spouse without giving him or her plenty of notice. Make sure you can prove this notice to the court, because leaving your spouse and children home without heat or light in December seldom sits well with the judge.

DATING

Do not date until you have a *Separation Agreement* or a divorce. You are still married, and your spouse can use it against you. If you are getting divorced, moving in with your lover could cause problems with custody, visitation, or alimony. If you do date, be prepared to face the problems that may arise.

WILLS

You probably need a new will now. Even though you have started the divorce process, if you were to die, your spouse would still inherit unless you have executed a new will providing otherwise. If you have given your spouse a power of attorney, cancel it as soon as possible. Until you do, your spouse has control over your property, and can sell it or give it away.

DOMESTIC VIOLENCE

If you must leave your home because of domestic violence and have no place to stay, the appendices contain lists of places that will provide you with shelter and assistance. If you are afraid that your spouse will physically harm you, take your money out of the bank, or run off with your children, then the court can enjoin or prohibit these things by issuing an injunction. *Injunctions*, or protective orders, are orders of the court that are issued to prevent harm pending further hearings.

In some cases, the court will issue an injunction when the case is filed; in other cases, the court may require a hearing before deciding on issuing the injunction. If your spouse disobeys an injunction, the court can put him or her in jail. Even if the judge does not put him or her in jail, he or she can be fined and the judge will have a hard time trusting your spouse later when he or she testifies. Also, the court can refuse to hear anything your spouse has to say if he or she is in contempt. The police will normally not get involved in problems between spouses, but if you show them an injunction, they will often remove the other party, and they have to act if you have a protective order.

In addition to filing criminal charges for abuse, you can petition the court for a civil protective order if you are harmed or threatened by an abusive spouse. File as soon as possible after the abuse occurs. The clerk's office will have the forms for you to fill out. Then you will speak with a judge and tell him or her what happened.

The judge can grant an *ex parte* order (meaning the judge has only heard one side so far), which the sheriff will serve on your spouse. The abuser will have to leave the home temporarily. The order can also prevent your spouse from contacting you at home or work, give you temporary custody of the children, and set a hearing date when you, your spouse, and witnesses can be present.

At the hearing, the judge will listen to both sides, and will either continue the protective order or dismiss your petition. The judge can give you all of the above relief in addition to ordering temporary support from your spouse.

SOCIAL SECURITY

You need to be aware of the *ten-year rule* for retirement, survivor, and disability benefits under Social Security. A marriage of at least ten years before your ex-spouse's retirement, disability, or death may entitle you to benefits based on your ex-spouse's Social Security account. Benefits are only payable to you if the benefits based on your own work record are less. There is also a family benefit cap.

Retirement or Disability

When your ex-spouse retires (or reaches age 62, whichever is first) or becomes disabled, in order to receive benefits as a divorced spouse, you must:

- ✪ have been married at least ten years;

- ✪ be unmarried (if you remarried, you will still be eligible if the new marriage ended in death, divorce, or annulment before you apply for benefits);

- ✪ be age 62 or older; and,

- ✪ have been divorced at least two years ago.

Death

If your ex-spouse dies, in order to receive benefits as the surviving divorced spouse, you must:

- ✪ have been married at least ten years;

- ✪ be at least age 60 (or age 50 and disabled) at the date of death; and,

- ✪ be unmarried (or remarried under certain conditions).

If your marriage has lasted almost ten years, you may want to wait to file your *Complaint for Divorce*, discussed in Chapter 9, after your tenth anniversary.

RED FLAG ITEMS

Red flag items to consider and take care of at the start of your divorce process include the following.

- ❏ Bank Accounts
- ❏ Credit Issues
- ❏ Insurance
- ❏ Utilities
- ❏ Dating
- ❏ Wills
- ❏ Domestic Violence
- ❏ Social Security

Get the Facts

A good way to organize the financial facts of a case is to complete a financial statement, listing assets and liabilities, income, and expenses. The courts have forms for this, and Chapter 24 explains how to fill these out in detail. Besides organizing your case, the court financial statements may be required when you file your divorce, and should be helpful in negotiating a settlement. You will need all financial information in order to complete a financial statement. Sometimes you have to search for this information. Check desk drawers, safe-deposit boxes, bank boxes, or other places where documents might be hidden. This is a good time to visit with your family banker, stockbroker, or accountant to discuss the family financial situation, although you may not want to tell him or her about the divorce. A list of the main documents that you want to gather or at least have copies of is on p.21. However, while gathering these documents, be mindful not to break any laws in the process.

SNOOPING

The *Omnibus Crime Control and Safe Street Act of 1968* makes it a federal crime and a civil tort for anyone to listen in on a telephone conversation or to record any conversation if they are not a party to that conversation or do not have permission from someone who is a party. Such recordings are not admissible as evidence. If you record your spouse's conversation with his or her paramour, you cannot use that tape in court and you could end up in a federal prison.

It is lawful for a person to record a telephone conversation or other conversation when both of the parties to the communication have given prior consent to record it. Maryland requires the consent of both parties. Virginia and the District of Columbia are *one party consent* jurisdictions—but do not risk it. You can still be sued by your spouse for invasion of privacy. That is why an answering machine is a good idea—the caller knows he or she is being taped, and by speaking, gives permission.

You can use the information on a family computer as evidence in a divorce trial. The courts will usually permit you to discover electronic information such as email or other files retrieved from computers.

DOCUMENTS TO GATHER

You will want copies of the following documents.

❏   *Income tax returns.*

❏   *Financial statements.* These are most often filed when borrowing money and are very important.

❏   *Employment contracts.* Any explanations of benefits from your or your spouse's work.

❏   *Canceled checks and charge records.*

❏   *Retirement plans.* Include IRAs, 401(k)s, etc.

❏   *Deeds and other settlement papers.*

❏   *Real estate tax bills or appraisals.*

❏   *Insurance policies.* Include life insurance, medical insurance, health insurance, and homeowners insurance.

❏   *Bank accounts and bank statements.*

❏   *Safe-deposit boxes.* You will want the bank to verify an inventory if possible.

❏   *Securities.*

❏   *Partnership agreements or corporate records.* Include all documents showing any business interests.

❏   *Any inheritance or trust interests.*

❏   *Wills by you or your spouse.*

❏   *Any written agreements or notes between you and your spouse.*

❏   *Any other evidence you have, such as photographs, letters, and emails.*

Alternatives to Trial

You do not want to have a contested divorce trial if you can help it. Trials involve enormous expense, time, and uncertainty. If you do not have an attorney, you have to take time off from work. Expert witnesses (for example, a therapist to testify about custody, an appraiser to value real estate or a business, or a vocational rehabilitation expert to help establish alimony needs) may cost thousands of dollars.

Judges are strangers to your life and marriage, and they are called upon to make a decision after hearing only a few hours or a few days of testimony about a marriage that may have lasted for years. Judges have no truth detector or justice detector at the bench, and they may not always decide the right way. They are also limited by the legislature in how they must rule.

In every trial, there is a winner and a loser. Even if you win, you may lose, because fees for attorneys, witnesses, and trustees, and division of income and property across two families, will strain your wallet. Only about 3% of divorces actually go to trial. In those cases, the lawyers have to spend 90% of their time preparing for trial.

It makes more sense for all parties involved to work together in reaching a settlement. This chapter discusses some of the ways to settle your case out of court that are common to all three jurisdictions.

TALKING WITH YOUR SPOUSE

You and your spouse can try to work out an agreement. If you try to work something out with your spouse yourself, the following are some useful tips.

- ✪ *Meet on neutral ground.* Do not meet at her office or at his mother's home, but some place where both parties will feel comfortable.

- ✪ *Set aside time.* A reasonable amount of time should be set aside to deal with the issues. If you leave to answer a telephone call just as you almost have things worked out, you may find that things have fallen apart when you get back. On the other hand, do not leave the meeting time open-ended. A meeting without a deadline will drag on and issues will not get resolved.

- ✪ *Set an agenda.* Decide what will be dealt with at the meeting. For example, "This week we will decide on custody and child support, and next week we will decide on the house."

- ✪ *Do not get caught up in disagreements.* Try to talk about what you agree on. No matter how bad it is, there are some things you agree on (such as how bad your marriage is or how cute the kids are). If you hit a point that gives you trouble, move on to something else and come back to the problem after you have resolved some other issues.

- ✪ *Reschedule as needed.* If things start to turn nasty, if someone gets angry, or if you are losing everything, reschedule the meeting for another time. It is important that both of you feel that the agreement is a good thing.

- ✪ *Keep the kids out of it.* Your children do not need to be involved in this. Do not have them around. They will interrupt you, and it will upset them. Do not discuss the divorce or complain about it to the children. Reassure them that they will be provided for—even if you are worried about it.

✪ *Start talking early*. Divorces usually either settle early on when both parties feel guilty and are not locked into a position, or after much litigation when the parties are too exhausted to fight anymore. Sometimes you can get more by talking than you can get at a trial.

✪ *Objectives*. It is good to know what you want. Write down your objectives before you start negotiating.

✪ *Priorities*. Assign priorities to your objectives, such as strong, medium, and weak interest. You also need to ask questions and learn what your spouse wants as well as what his or her priorities are.

✪ *Flexibility*. Sometimes you have to be flexible, especially on items that are a strong priority for your spouse and a weak priority for you. A good settlement is one in which each side gives up 60%—a little more than each wanted—to end up with more of what each truly wants.

This is the least expensive way to settle your case, but it is also difficult. (After all, if you could work things out with your spouse, you probably would not be getting a divorce.)

If you and your spouse work out something and you create and sign notes, this could be considered to be an agreement. If it is not correct legal language, you may be bound by something other than what you thought you agreed to, so you may want to have a lawyer review it at this point.

NEGOTIATION

You can hire attorneys to try to work out an agreement. The classic *negotiation* style involves one party making a proposal in writing (the *offer*) that covers all issues of the marriage and divorce. The other party then responds in writing to the offer with a different proposal (*counteroffer*) or with specific objections to specific provisions of the first proposal (*objections*).

These writings go back and forth, with compromises on the part of each, until agreement is reached (or not, as the case may be). Telephone calls and face-to-face meetings help answer questions or break an impasse during these negotiations.

Your attorney ought to discuss any settlement proposal with you in advance and send you copies of all counteroffers as they are received. Although your attorney may recommend certain options in settlement negotiations, you can expect to have the final say. There is no final agreement until it is put in writing and signed by you.

It costs money every time you talk to your attorney and every time he or she writes a letter. It can easily end up totaling several thousand dollars. However, if your spouse will not talk to you, this may be your only option.

MEDIATION

In *mediation*, a trained, neutral third party attempts to help the parties resolve their disputes through special techniques. The mediator does not represent either party, but guides the discussions, explores and offers options, explains the law, and facilitates an agreement. Mediators can be lawyers, psychologists, accountants, ministers, or anyone else with proper training.

Mediators charge from $50 to $200 an hour, but the fee is normally shared by both parties. You will go to the mediator's office for two or three hour-long sessions with your spouse. You will exchange financial information, and with the mediator's help, try to reach an agreement.

The agreement is not final or binding until it is put in writing and signed by both parties. You do not have to sign the agreement if you do not like it. You are encouraged to hire a lawyer to review the agreement before you sign. Once you do sign, the agreement will be binding and enforced by the court.

The advantage of mediation is usually lower cost and control over the outcome. However, you cannot use mediation unless your spouse is willing.

The court often requires litigating parties' to go to mediation. Court-appointed mediators (sometimes called *facilitators*) can recommend solutions and do a little more "arm-twisting" than their private counterparts.

COLLABORATION

In *collaborative family law*, each party hires a lawyer trained in collaborative law to be his or her advocate. There are no neutral parties like there are in mediation. The lawyers and parties sign an agreement stating that both lawyers must withdraw if the case does not settle and goes to litigation. Everyone is committed from the beginning to settle the case and not litigate it, so the focus is on the settlement and not the trial.

Collaborative family law works through a series of four-way meetings with you, your spouse, and the two lawyers. You are a full participant in the settlement process. You can speak face-to-face with everyone involved instead of having to communicate with your spouse through your lawyers.

The lawyers and parties also agree to provide full and early disclosure of all issues such as income and assets. The parties may agree to hire one or more experts (instead of the litigation model, where each party hires competing experts). For example, the parties would hire one appraiser to value the house or one therapist to design a parenting plan.

Collaborative lawyers place value on long-term relationship issues that may be overlooked in the litigated divorce, where only financial and legal issues are considered. Collaborative law works well when you both want to settle and want to control the outcome of your divorce yourselves. You each have to pay your own lawyer, although fees may be reimbursed as a result of the final agreement. Regardless, you will save money as compared to litigation. However, if one of you wants to litigate, then both lawyers have to withdraw.

ARBITRATION

You and your spouse can agree to submit your dispute to a third party for a binding or nonbinding decision in a process called *arbitration*. Arbitration works well if you need a quick decision and you are willing to take your chances with an arbitrator who is not the judge of your case. Arbitration has the advantage of speed and expense over a trial. It can also be used to decide limited issues when negotiation, mediation, or collaborative law reaches an impasse.

You can find an arbitrator through your attorney or the bar association for your city or county. The third party can be a mediator, lawyer, retired judge, or any other party.

CHILDREN

The court will make the final decision on child custody, visitation, and support. It cannot delegate this authority to the parties or a third-party mediator or arbitrator. The court can consider the opinion of the parties and third parties, and often follows these recommendations. However, the court must make its own decision based on the best interests of the child. See Chapters 21, 22, and 23 for more information on child custody, visitation, and support.

Different Types of Divorce

There are two types of divorces in Maryland, Virginia, and the District of Columbia. In all three jurisdictions, you can either have a *contested* divorce or an *uncontested* divorce. The following descriptions apply to all three jurisdictions.

CONTESTED DIVORCE

Contested divorces are those in which the parties cannot resolve one or more of their disputes, such as custody, visitation, alimony, or property division, and so the parties go to trial. Each side is entitled to examine witnesses and present evidence. The parties then ask the judge to decide. Although judges are usually experienced and wise, they are only human. They do not have truth detectors in court. A marriage of some years is compressed to a few days, and the judge makes a decision in a few minutes that affects the rest of your life. These trials take a lot of time (days or weeks) and cost a lot of money.

UNCONTESTED DIVORCE

If the parties have reached an agreement on all issues, including custody and finances, they are entitled to an uncontested divorce. This is a short hearing before the court that takes about ten minutes. The parties testify about the grounds for divorce, and ask the court to approve their agreement and grant their divorce.

LENGTH OF TIME

Uncontested divorces usually take two to three months after filing. If you need a faster divorce—say, to get remarried—then you can shorten the time it takes if your spouse cooperates. You can file your papers together at the courthouse, explain to the clerk your circumstances, and see if you can get an early hearing. Judges normally like to accommodate settled cases because there are more cases than there are judges, and settlement means one more case they can move off their desk.

Contested divorces can take up to two years or even longer in some cases. There is no right to a speedy trial in divorce cases like there is in criminal cases. The wheels of justice move slowly and even lawyers are frustrated sometimes by the time it takes to be heard by a judge.

COST

If you hire a lawyer, you can expect to pay between $2,000 and $5,000 for an uncontested case, depending on whether there are children, support, and property issues. The average contested case costs about $20,000, but could be much more depending upon the issues, your spouse, and your spouse's lawyer.

SEPARATION AGREEMENTS

More divorce cases are filed each year than there are judges to try them. However, most contested divorce cases are settled before trial with an agreement. These agreements are called by various names, such as *Voluntary Separation* and *Custody, Support, and Property*

Settlement Agreement. In this book, they will usually be referred to as *Separation Agreements* (although you do not necessarily have to be separated to have one).

The court encourages agreements and provides for ways to help you and your spouse settle during the litigation. You can propose or sign a *Separation Agreement* before you file for divorce, or you can file for divorce first and negotiations on the *Separation Agreement* can proceed on a parallel track with the divorce litigation. A case filed as a contested divorce often is amended to an uncontested divorce once a *Separation Agreement* is signed.

If you have a choice, you want an uncontested divorce. Therefore, you need a *Separation Agreement*, which is covered in Chapter 7.

Separation Agreements

Although not required by law, a written *Separation Agreement* is always recommended, even when there are little or no assets. In Virginia, *Separation Agreements* must be in writing to be enforceable by the court. Although Maryland and the District of Columbia do not require written agreements, it is always a good idea to put them in writing, because the parties usually never agree on what a verbal agreement says. This chapter describes *Separation Agreements* in general, and is applicable to all three jurisdictions.

THE ESSENCE OF DIVORCE

Because a *Separation Agreement* resolves all issues that otherwise would be resolved by the judge in a contested divorce, it is said that reaching a *Separation Agreement* is the essence of your divorce. You do not have to be separated and you do not have to have grounds for divorce to have a *Separation Agreement*. There is no waiting period. You can sign one now.

Separation Agreements usually provide that the parties may live *separate and apart* as though unmarried. Therefore, issues such as adultery will no longer have any effect at the divorce trial, because property division and alimony have already been decided. Once you both sign a *Separation Agreement*, you can date, contribute to your pension and savings, and buy property—all without worry that these things may impact your future divorce.

The *Separation Agreement* will be attached to your *Complaint for Divorce* and you will ask the court to incorporate it into your *Decree of Divorce*. Essentially, it will substitute for the judge's findings after a long trial. You will be able to tell the court that you do not need a divorce trial, because you have already resolved everything in a *Separation Agreement*.

Once you have a *Separation Agreement*, you have almost everything that a divorce will give you, so you no longer even need a divorce. The only reason that you may want a divorce is to get remarried or for tax filing status.

A *Separation Agreement* has other advantages, in that it allows the parties to decide their future rather than the judge, who is a stranger to their lives and marriage. It can be a lot more detailed than a court order, and it can also provide for things that a judge is limited by law from ordering.

WHAT TO INCLUDE IN YOUR SEPARATION AGREEMENT

You will want to include many things in your *Separation Agreement*, because it will cover all of the issues of your divorce. The items for you to cover include the following.

❑ The marital residence and other real property
  - Who is leaving?
  - Who will live where?
  - How will the mortgage and other expenses be paid?
  - Will the house be sold?
  - How will the equity be divided?
  - How will other real estate be divided?

❏ Bank accounts and stocks
  • Who gets what?

❏ Personal property
  • Who gets which car, what appliances, and what happens to the sofa in the den?
  • Who gets Rover? (You would be surprised how many people fight over the pets.)

❏ Retirement
  • What happens to any retirement benefits for either spouse that have accrued?

❏ Debts
  • Who pays what?
  • Should the debts be paid off by refinancing?

❏ Court costs and attorney's fees
  • Who pays?

❏ Alimony
  • How much?
  • How long?
  • When and how is it paid?
  • When does it start?
  • How will it be modified?

❏ Custody
  • Should the children be split up between the parents?
  • Should any aspects of custody be shared?
  • Will joint custody work?
  • How will decisions be made about doctors, schools, discipline, religious upbringing, and who will have the final say?
  • How will day-to-day decisions be made?
  • Where will the children live?
  • What will be the schedule for seeing the other parent?

❑ Child support
  • How much?
  • How long?
  • When does it start?
  • When is it due?
  • How will payment be made?
  • Is there a cost of living adjustment?
  • Who carries health or life insurance on the children?
  • Who gets to claim the children as income tax deductions?
  • Private school or public school?
  • College tuition and costs?
  • Who pays for uncovered medical expenses?
  • Who pays for day care expenses, summer camp, extracurricular activities, and baby-sitters?

❑ Visitation
  • Do you want a specific schedule or can you and your spouse be flexible and work together on it, especially as the children grow up and change?
  • What will be the schedule for visitation?
  • Daily and weekly?
  • Holidays?
  • Birthdays?
  • School vacations?
  • Summer vacations?
  • When can a parent take a child out of the state?
  • Out of the country?
  • What notice needs to be given for a change in plans?
  • How will visitation be changed if one parent moves?

❑ Life insurance
  • Who is insured?
  • Who is the beneficiary?
  • Term or cash value?
  • How much?

❑ Health insurance
  • Who is covered?

NOTE: *In many cases, an employee's spouse can be covered up to thirty-six months after the divorce by the employed spouse's insurance company for an additional premium. Sometimes one party's health coverage is cheaper than the other's, and the cost differential can be reimbursed in other ways.*

❑ Other Provisions
  • Security for obligations in the agreement, for wills, for death, and for taxes.

On the following pages is a sample *Separation Agreement*. Because every agreement is different, this agreement is not set up as a blank court form, but only as an example of what one may look like. When you draw up your own *Separation Agreement*, it may look similar to this sample, but remember that you must make your agreement work for you and your spouse.

SAMPLE

VOLUNTARY SEPARATION, SUPPORT, AND
PROPERTY SETTLEMENT AGREEMENT

THIS AGREEMENT, the original of which being executed in quadruplicate, is made this ___17ᵗʰ__ day of _January_, _2007_, by and between _____Teddie Bear_____, whose Social Security Number is _____458-90-8232_____, hereinafter referred to as "Wife" and _____Theodore Bear_____, whose Social Security Number is ___236-92-9736___, hereinafter referred to as "Husband."

WITNESSETH :

WHEREAS, the parties hereto were married on the ___5ᵗʰ___ of _March_, _1993_, in _Roanoke, Virginia_; and

WHEREAS, _2_ children were born to the parties as a result of said marriage; namely _Roberta_, born ___April 4_, _1996_; and _Roland_, born ___June 26, 1999_; and

WHEREAS, relations between the parties have been such that they have separated as of the _1ˢᵗ_ day of _November_, _2006_; and they have mutually and voluntarily determined to live separate and apart, and have mutually concluded that it is in the best interest of all concerned to live separate and apart for the rest of their lives; and

WHEREAS, in view of the foregoing, the parties desire to settle and determine their obligations to each other and to their children, including all of their property rights, the maintenance and support of the parties and their children, and all rights, claims, relationships, or obligations between them arising out of their marriage or otherwise; and

WHEREAS, each party hereto declares that he or she has had independent legal advice by counsel of his or her own selection or has been advised to obtain legal counsel; that each has made a full disclosure to the other of his or her financial assets and liabilities; that each fully understands the facts and all of his or her legal rights and obligations; and that after such advice, disclosure, and knowledge, each believes this Agreement to be fair, just, and reasonable and that each enters into same freely and voluntarily;

NOW, THEREFORE, in consideration of the premises, and the mutual covenants and agreements hereinafter contained, and in further consideration of the sum of ONE DOLLAR ($1.00), to each of the parties in hand paid by the other, the receipt whereof is hereby acknowledged, the parties hereto covenant and agree as follows:

SEPARATION

1. The parties mutually and voluntarily separated on <u>November</u> <u>1</u>, <u>2006</u>, with the intention of ending their marriage. It shall be lawful for each party at all times thereafter to live separate and apart from the other party at such place or places as he or she may from time to time choose or deem fit.

2. Each party shall be free from interference, authority, and control, direct or indirect, by the other, as fully as if he or she were single and unmarried. Neither party shall endeavor to compel the other to cohabit or dwell with him or her, nor in any manner or form whatsoever molest or trouble the other party.

3. Nothing herein contained shall be construed to bar or prevent either party from suing for divorce in any competent jurisdiction because of any past or future fault on the other party's part.

4. Henceforth, each of the parties shall own, have, and enjoy, independent of any claim or right of the other party, all items of property of every kind, nature, and description, wheresoever situated, which are now owned or held by him or her with full power to him or her to dispose of the same as fully, effectively, and effectually in all respects and for all purposes as if he or she were unmarried. Both parties agree to execute all necessary documents to carry out the terms of this Agreement.

CUSTODY AND VISITATION

5. The parties agree that it is in the best interests of the children for the Wife to have sole legal and physical custody.

6. The parties agree that it is in the best interests of the children for the Husband to have reasonable visitation, the exact dates and times to be agreed upon by the parties.

7. The parties agree to abide by the <u>Roanoke County</u> <u>Guidelines for Effective Parenting</u>.

CHILD SUPPORT

8. Commencing and accounting from <u>February 1, 2007</u>, the Husband shall pay to the Wife for the support and maintenance of the parties' children the sum of <u>one thousand</u> DOLLARS ($ <u>1000.00</u>) per month, by mail, directly to the Wife in accord with the attached Child Support Guidelines Worksheet. Said child support payments shall con-

tinue on the first day of each month thereafter until the first to occur of the following: a child dies; the Husband dies; a child marries; a child enters the armed forces; a child no longer has principal residence with the Wife; a child obtains full-time employment (other than employment during school recesses); or a child attains the age of eighteen (18), provided however, if a child has not graduated high school by his or her 18th birthday, child support shall continue until graduation or the 19th birthday of that child, whichever first occurs.

WAIVER OF ALIMONY

9. In consideration of the mutual agreement of the parties to voluntarily live separate and apart and the provisions contained herein for the respective benefit of the parties, each party releases and waives to the other any claim or right to temporary or permanent alimony, support, or maintenance, whether past, present, or future.

HEALTH INSURANCE

10. The Husband agrees to provide medical insurance coverage for the Wife until the date of divorce and for the parties' children until age 23.

LIFE INSURANCE

11. To secure the payment of child support, the Husband agrees to acquire life insurance in the face amount of at least two hundred thousand Dollars ($ 200,000.00) with the Wife as beneficiary. The Husband will provide the Wife with evidence of such coverage on January 1 of each year. If such life insurance is not in effect and the Husband dies, then the Wife will have a claim against the Husband's estate for the face amount of the life insurance that should have been in effect.

REAL PROPERTY

12. The parties own no real estate.

MISCELLANEOUS PERSONAL PROPERTY

13. Furnishings and Miscellaneous Items. It is agreed that the parties have separated all their household furnishings, clothing, jewelry, and similar items of tangible personal property to their mutual satisfaction, and all such property shall be and become the sole and separate property of the individual who has possession and control thereof.

14. Automobiles. The Wife will keep the Chevy Sedan and shall assume all financial responsibility for this vehicle. The Husband will keep the Jeep and shall assume all financial responsibility for this vehicle.

15.   Bank Accounts.   The parties have no joint bank accounts. Each party will keep the individual bank accounts that are in his or her own name.

16.   Retirement Accounts.   The parties have no retirement accounts, pension plans, profit-sharing plans, Individual Retirement Accounts, 401(k) plans, or similar retirement funds.

OUTSTANDING DEBTS

17.   The parties have no joint credit card debt.   Except as otherwise provided herein above, neither party has incurred any debts or obligations heretofore for which the other may be held liable.   The parties agree that neither will incur hereafter any liability or obligation whatsoever upon the credit of the other, or for which the other might be held liable.   Each party agrees to indemnify and hold harmless the other from any obligation, liability, or expense incurred by the other by virtue of any breach of this paragraph, including attorney's fees he or she may necessarily incur in connection therewith.

TAXES

18.   Each party may have certain tax liabilities resulting from separate returns filed by each of them.   Each party agrees to be responsible for their own tax liabilities, and indemnify and hold harmless the other from such liabilities.

19.   The Wife shall take the son as an exemption each year and the Husband shall take the daughter as an exemption each year.

LEGAL FEES

20.   Each party agrees to be responsible for his or her own legal fees in connection with the negotiation of this Agreement and any action that either of the parties may undertake for either a limited or absolute divorce in whichever jurisdiction said action is ultimately filed.   The parties also agree to divide the court costs and master's fees equally between them in connection with any subsequent suit for divorce.

21.   The reasonable cost of any legal services required in the Court enforcement of this Agreement will become the obligation of the person whose breach required the enforcement of the Agreement, provided the movant prevails and provided that the Court feels a legal fee should be awarded.

MUTUAL RELEASES

Except as otherwise provided in this Agreement:

22. Each party shall be fully released by the other from any obligation for alimony, support, and maintenance, except as hereinabove set forth, each accepts the provisions hereof in full satisfaction of all obligations for support, or otherwise arising out of the marital relation of the parties, and relinquishes any right or claim to the earnings, accumulation, money, or property of the other.

23. All property and money received and retained by the parties pursuant hereto shall be the separate property of the respective parties, free and clear of any right, interest, or claim of the other party, and each party shall have the right to deal with and dispose of his or her separate property, both real and personal, as fully and as effectively as if the parties had never been married.

24. Provided all obligations hereunder have been performed, each party hereby releases and forever discharges the other, his or her heirs, executors, administrators, assigns, property, and estate from any and all rights, claims, demands, or obligations arising out of or by virtue of the marital relation of the parties, including loss of consortium, dower rights, curtesy, homestead rights, right of election regarding the estate of the other, or to take against the Will of the other, right of inheritance or distribution in the event of intestacy, right to act as administrator of the estate of the other, and similar or related rights under the laws of any state or territory of the United States or of any foreign country, as such laws exist or may hereafter be enacted or amended. Nothing herein, however, shall constitute a waiver of either party to take a voluntary bequest or bequests under the Will of the other.

25. Except for any cause of action for divorce that either party may have or claim to have, and except for the enforcement of the provisions of this Agreement, each party does hereby release and forever discharge the other of and for all causes of action, claims, rights, or demand whatsoever, in law or in equity, which either of the parties ever had or now has against the other.

INCORPORATION IN ANY DECREE OF DIVORCE

26. The parties hereto agree that any action for Divorce between them shall be subject to and governed by the terms of this Agreement, and that this Agreement shall be presented to the appropriate court for affirmation, ratification, and incorporation in any Decree of Divorce, Limited or Final, which may be entered in any action between the parties, but this Agreement shall be independent of and shall not depend for

its effectiveness upon such affirmation, ratification, and incorporation, shall not merge in the Decree, and shall survive execution of the Decree.

FULL DISCLOSURE

27. The parties warrant that they have fully disclosed their respective assets and liabilities to the other, and that the parties have no other assets and liabilities other than what they have disclosed. They have relied on the information obtained during marriage in valuing assets and not on the representations of counsel or any other person. They have been advised by counsel of their rights to obtain discovery and to have the assets valued by expert appraisers, and they have knowingly and voluntarily waived these rights. If assets of either party are discovered after the signing of this agreement, such assets shall be divided between the parties in the following manner: forty percent (40%) of the value of each previously undisclosed asset shall be the property of the party failing to disclose the asset, and sixty percent (60%) of the value of each previously undisclosed asset shall become the property of the party to whom disclosure was not made. If liabilities of either party are discovered after the signing of this agreement, such liabilities shall become the sole responsibility of the party failing to disclose the liabilities. The parties shall do any and all acts necessary to assign their interests and financial responsibilities in said asset(s) and/or liability(ies) accordingly.

GENERAL PROVISIONS

28. The parties agree that no provision of this Agreement, except as otherwise set forth herein, shall be modifiable by any court except by agreement of the parties. Any modification or waiver of any of the provisions of this Agreement shall be effective only if made in writing and executed with the same formality as this Agreement. The failure of either party to insist upon strict performance of any of the provisions of this Agreement shall not be construed as a waiver of any subsequent default of this same or different nature.

29. Each of the parties hereto shall, from time to time, at the request of the other, execute, acknowledge, and deliver to the other party, any and all further instruments that may be reasonably required to give full force and effect to the provisions of this Agreement.

30. If any provision of this Agreement is held to be invalid or unenforceable, all of the other provisions shall, nevertheless, continue in full force and effect.

31. Failure to perform any of the obligations contained herein shall create a lien on the estate of the obligor.

32. This Agreement contains the entire understanding of the parties, and there are no representations, warranties, covenants, or undertakings of, by, or between the parties other than those expressly set forth herein.

33. This Agreement shall be construed in accordance with the laws of the State of _Virginia_ .

IN WITNESS WHEREOF, the parties being fully advised as to the matters herein set forth, have set their hands and affixed their seals on the date set forth below.

WITNESSES:

John Jones _____   *Teddie Bear* _____ (SEAL)

Bill Smith _____   *Theodore Bear* _____ (SEAL)

STATE OF ___Virginia___)

COUNTY OF _Roanoke County_) to wit:

I HEREBY CERTIFY that before me, the undersigned Notary Public, personally appeared _Teddie Bear_, known to me to be the person whose name is subscribed to the within instrument, who, after being sworn, made oath in due form of law under the penalties of perjury that the matters and facts set forth in the foregoing Agreement with respect to the voluntary separation of the parties are true and correct as therein stated and acknowledged said Agreement to be her act.

WITNESS my hand and official seal this _17_th day of _January_, _2007_.

A. Fine Notary
Notary Public
My commission expires:
__12/31/2008__

STATE OF ___Virginia___)

COUNTY OF _Roanoke County_) to wit:

I HEREBY CERTIFY that before me the undersigned Notary Public, personally appeared _Theodore Bear_, known to me to be the person whose name is subscribed to the within instrument, who, after being sworn, made oath in due form of law under the penalties of perjury that the matters and facts set forth in the foregoing Agreement with respect to the voluntary separation of the parties are true and correct as therein stated and acknowledged said Agreement to be his act.

WITNESS my hand and official seal this _17_th day of _January_, _2007_.

A. Fine Notary
Notary Public
My commission expires:
__12/31/2008__

Legal Requirements for Divorce

In this chapter, some of the preliminary legal requirements you must meet before going to court are discussed. These requirements are common to all three jurisdictions, but the details are different. You will find that most of the law, as it pertains directly to divorce, is written in four places: the United States Constitution, the various state codes, court cases, and in the various local rules. The differences for each jurisdiction are discussed and the specific grounds for divorce (both final and limited, or for a legal separation) are set forth.

CONSTITUTION

The United States and each state has a written constitution that sets forth essential rights of the people. For example, you have the right to due process of law and the right to pursue happiness. You can find these constitutions at the library or on the Internet. Lists of the Internet sites for each state are located in the appendices.

CODES

The legislature, elected by and representing the people, passes laws, also called *statutes*, each year. These are published in volumes called the *Maryland Code*, *Virginia Code*, and the *Code of the District of Columbia*.

They are called *codes* because laws are meant to codify human behavior and reflect the will of the majority in our society. They are intended to be logical and practical, but you may not always find this to be true. Laws are supposed to be consistent with the constitution of the individual state and the United States Constitution. You can find the code for each state at law libraries or on Internet sites listed in the appendices. A summary of divorce laws for each jurisdiction with code citations is also included in the appendices.

CASES

The appellate courts for each jurisdiction review the record of trial courts on a case-by-case basis when appeals are brought by the parties. The appellate court either affirms, vacates, modifies, or reverses the trial court. It usually explains its decision in writing, and many decisions are published in books called *reporters*. These cases form a precedent for later trials and appeals. The court can interpret or even invalidate laws if they are unconstitutional. While the legislature reflects the will of the majority in writing general laws, the court can look at the facts of individual cases and make exceptions for the minority when the law would work an unjust result.

RULES

There is a rules committee in each jurisdiction that passes rules for the court, which the parties and their lawyers must follow. The rules are published as Maryland Rules, Rules of the Supreme Court of Virginia, and District of Columbia Court Rules. These are very detailed and cover how pleadings must be presented and signed, time deadlines, how evidence is to be presented at trial, and many other subjects. In addition, some courts and some judges publish what are called local rules, which apply to a particular courthouse or a particular judge's courtroom. These local rules may be available only in a memorandum from the clerk or order from the judge. Finally, there are what lawyers refer to as unpublished rules, which are the customs and practices of various courts and judges, that you only know from experience.

WHERE TO FIND THE LAW

If you want to do more research on divorce law in your jurisdiction, you have many places to look. The summaries of divorce laws with citations to the codes of Maryland, Virginia, and the District of Columbia are provided in the appendices. These summaries will point you in the right direction for research if you want to know more. Usually there is a law library at the courthouse that is available to the public. Also, many laws and cases are available free of charge on the Internet.

JURISDICTION

When a court has *jurisdiction,* it has the power to hear and decide a matter, as well as bind the parties to its decision. If the court lacks jurisdiction, any order it enters in your divorce case is void and of no effect.

Subject-Matter Jurisdiction

The Maryland, Virginia, and the District of Columbia courts have *jurisdiction* over your marriage as long as one of the parties meets the residency requirements set forth in the law. In Maryland, the courts can also obtain jurisdiction if the grounds for divorce arose within the state. The power and authority to decide matters concerning your marriage and divorce is called *subject-matter jurisdiction.*

Personal Jurisdiction

The courts must also have the power to bind the parties to their decisions. This is called *personal jurisdiction.* The courts have jurisdiction over any person living in the state or served with process in the state. The court can also obtain personal jurisdiction over a nonresident by serving process outside the state in certain circumstances (known as *long-arm jurisdiction*). A person may submit to jurisdiction of the court by appearing in court or filing a pleading in the case.

RESIDENCY

You or your spouse have to live in the state for a certain period of time before you can use the courts of that jurisdiction for a divorce. You can file for emergency relief, such as custody or support, before the residency period has run in all three jurisdictions.

In Maryland, the residency requirement is twelve months. (Maryland Code, Family Law Article, Sec. 7-101(a).) You do not need to meet the twelve-month residency requirement if the grounds for divorce arose in Maryland, but at least one party must be a resident at the time the divorce is filed.

In Virginia and the District of Columbia, the residency requirement is six months. (Virginia Code, Sec. 20-97 and the District of Columbia Code, Sec. 16-902.)

If your spouse contests your residency, you can prove it with items like a lease, utility bills, driver's license, or voter registration card. Once you establish your home in a jurisdiction, it stays there—even if you temporarily move elsewhere—as long as you have the intent to remain a permanent resident.

It is only necessary that you meet the residency requirements at the time of filing for divorce. Neither party has to be a resident at the time of the divorce.

You or your spouse may meet the requirements to file a complaint in more than one jurisdiction. You may be able to get a divorce faster by moving across the state line. It is important to know the differences in the laws of each jurisdiction so you can choose the place most favorable for you to file.

NOTE: *Different residency requirements and different grounds in the three jurisdictions mean that you can move to a different jurisdiction to get divorced faster. However, you also have to consider the other differences in the divorce laws among the three jurisdictions when making the decision to move.*

VENUE

You may file a divorce in the county where you live or where your spouse lives or works. This is called *venue* (the place where you may properly bring a lawsuit). The parties may consent to a different venue. In Maryland or Virginia, if you file in the wrong county and your spouse objects on the basis of venue, you may simply ask the court to transfer venue to the right county. In the District of Columbia there is only one court.

GROUNDS FOR DIVORCE

In order to file for a divorce, you must have good reasons for wanting a divorce, which are called *grounds*, and you have to prove these grounds to the court at your divorce trial. You must plead and prove your grounds even if your divorce is uncontested. It used to be that the only grounds for divorce were fault grounds, like adultery or cruelty. Now Maryland and Virginia accept *no-fault grounds*, such as separation for a certain period of time, in addition to fault grounds. The District of Columbia has abolished fault grounds altogether and only has no-fault grounds. If you allege a *fault ground*, such as adultery, you will have to provide evidence of the adultery, and that evidence must prove the adultery took place. That is why so many now file for divorce using a no-fault ground. However, you still must prove that you meet the separation time limits the no-fault ground requires.

Defenses to Grounds   There are certain defenses to the various grounds for divorce that may be raised by your spouse in any of the three jurisdictions. For example, *condonation* and *recrimination* are sometimes raised in response to allegations of adultery. Condonation means forgiveness, and is usually shown by sexual relations between spouses after the adultery is disclosed. Condonation and recrimination are no longer absolute defenses to adultery, but may be taken into consideration by the court when adultery is raised as grounds for divorce.

The following sections discuss the grounds for divorce and legal separation in each jurisdiction.

MARYLAND GROUNDS

In Maryland, the grounds for an *absolute divorce* are as follows.

- *A one-year voluntary and mutual separation.* The parties must live under separate roofs for twelve consecutive months, without cohabitation or sexual relations. The time starts over if you have sexual relations, live together, or even spend one night under the same roof. The separation must be mutual and voluntary with the intention of ending the marriage, and there can be no reasonable expectation of reconciliation. A separation that begins as involuntary on the part of one spouse can become voluntary at a later date. A *Separation Agreement* can corroborate voluntariness if signed before a *Complaint for Divorce* is filed.

- *A two-year involuntary separation.* The parties must live under separate roofs for twenty-four consecutive months, without cohabitation or sexual relations.

- *Adultery.* Adultery means sexual intercourse with a person other than your spouse. Adultery is grounds for an immediate divorce and no separation is required. You can prove adultery by direct evidence, such as the admission of your spouse and the deposition or affidavit of the paramour. You can also prove adultery by circumstantial evidence indicating opportunity and predisposition. *Predisposition* means your spouse and another person act romantically. *Opportunity* means a specific chance to have sex with that person. Circumstantial evidence could be the testimony of a private detective who saw your spouse holding hands with another person, and watched them enter a hotel and stay for a period of time.

- *Desertion for a year.* Desertion can be either *actual* or *constructive.* Actual desertion is when your spouse leaves the marital home without legal justification, and ends cohabitation or sexual relations. The desertion must be for at least twelve months and be the deliberate and final act of the deserting party, and there must be no reasonable expectation of a reconciliation. Constructive desertion means that the behavior of your spouse is so harmful to your physical or mental well-being that you are forced to leave. Again, the constructive separation must be for twelve months, without cohabitation, sexual relations, or reasonable expectation of a reconciliation. This is harder to prove because the judge always wants to know why you did not leave sooner. In other words, what happened on the day you left that made you leave at that particular time?

✪ *Insanity*. This requires the confinement of your spouse to a mental institution for at least three years, and the testimony of two psychiatrists that the insanity is incurable without hope for recovery.

✪ *Imprisonment*. This requires that your spouse be in jail for one year under a sentence of three or more years.

✪ *Cruelty or excessively vicious conduct*. The cruelty may be directed at the complaining party or that party's child. There is no waiting period for this ground. There must be no reasonable expectation of reconciliation. This ground requires a pattern of conduct and one incident is usually not enough, unless it was especially violent and your spouse intended to harm you or your child. It is also hard to corroborate because often there are no witnesses besides the parties to domestic violence. Be sure you have your corroborating evidence. You do not want to get all the way through your trial and have the judge tell you that you have not made your case. (Maryland Code, Family Law Article, Sec. 7-103.)

Limited Divorce   One form of legal separation in Maryland is called a *limited divorce*. It also requires that you have grounds. The grounds for a limited divorce are different from the grounds required for an absolute divorce, and they are:

✪ *voluntary separation* without reasonable expectation of reconciliation (no minimum duration);

✪ *desertion* (no minimum duration);

✪ *cruelty* toward the complaining party or that party's child; or,

✪ *excessively vicious conduct* toward the complaining party or that party's child. (Maryland Code, Family Law Article, Sec. 7-102.)

VIRGINIA GROUNDS

In Virginia, the grounds for a *final divorce* are:

✪ a six-month separation with a written *Separation Agreement* and no children;

✪ a one-year separation with the intent on the part of at least one party that it be permanent;

✪ adultery;

✪ conviction of a felony and imprisonment for one year;

✪ cruelty continuing for one year; or,

✪ desertion or abandonment continuing for one year. (Virginia Code, Sec. 20-91.)

Limited Divorce

In Virginia, you may obtain a *limited divorce*, also called a *divorce a mensa et thoro* (from bed and board). A limited divorce also requires that you have grounds. The grounds for a limited divorce are different from the grounds required for a final divorce, and they are as follows:

✪ reasonable fear of bodily harm;

✪ desertion or abandonment (no minimum duration); or,

✪ cruelty. (Virginia Code, Sec. 20-95.)

DISTRICT OF COLUMBIA GROUNDS

In the District of Columbia, the grounds for an *absolute divorce* are:

✪ a six-month voluntary separation or

✪ a twelve-month involuntary separation. (District of Columbia Code, Sec. 16-904(a).)

In the District of Columbia, you can be separated and still live together, meaning at least separate sleeping arrangements and a lack of physical relations; however, that makes it harder to prove in court. This is different from Maryland, which defines separation as living in separate places, and Virginia, where the courts are not generally receptive to claims that spouses are living separate lives under the same roof.

Legal Separation

A *legal separation* in the District of Columbia also requires that you have grounds. The grounds for a legal separation are as follows:

✪ mutual and voluntary separation (no minimum duration);

✪ separation for one year;

✪ adultery; or,

✪ cruelty. (District of Columbia Code, Sec. 16-904(b).)

Starting the Divorce

A divorce action is started by filing a *Complaint for Divorce* in Maryland, Virginia, and the District of Columbia. You can also file a complaint for spousal support or child support without filing a *Complaint for Divorce* if you do not want a divorce. In Maryland and the District of Columbia, if you are seeking a final divorce the *Complaint* would ask for an absolute divorce. You file it with the court clerk at the courthouse in the county or city where you live or where your spouse lives. You do not have to file in the place where you were married.

THE COMPLAINT

In all three jurisdictions, your *Complaint* is essentially a letter to the judge. The *Complaint* starts with the *caption*, which states the court and the names and addresses of the parties. There is a blank space for the court clerk to assign a case number. The party that files the *Complaint* is called the *plaintiff* and the other party is the *defendant*.

No matter which jurisdiction you file in, your *Complaint* will contain certain statements, called *allegations*. First, you state the jurisdiction of the court. Then, state the facts about the parties, the marriage, the children, and the grounds for divorce, as follows:

- ✪ where you and your spouse live;

- ✪ the date, city, and state of your marriage;

- ✪ names and birthdates of any children born or adopted as a result of the marriage;

- ✪ who the children are living with now;

- ✪ that it is in the best interests of the children that they live with you or that custody be shared;

- ✪ grounds for divorce (for example, if separation is your ground, give the date of separation, that it was mutual and voluntary or involuntary, and that there is no hope or expectation of a reconciliation)—you may have more than one ground for divorce;

- ✪ your income and your spouse's income, if you are seeking support;

- ✪ the property acquired during the marriage that needs to be determined, valued, and distributed by the court;

- ✪ that the house, furniture, and automobile may be family use property, and you want use and possession of them (family use property means property that has been used during the marriage for the children and the family, such as the house, furniture, and automobiles);

- ✪ child support, including guidelines showing the needs of the children and your spouse's ability to pay;

- ✪ if there is an agreement, identify it by date, and attach a copy to the *Complaint* as an exhibit;

- ✪ ask the court to approve your agreement and make it part of the judgement or decree of divorce;

✪ you can ask the court to change your name back to your birth given name; and,

✪ if there is no *Separation Agreement*, you must ask the court to decide what you and your spouse cannot agree upon. If you do not include something in your prayer for relief (the section of the complaint where you ask the court for what you want), you may not get it—so be sure to ask for everything you want. The list may seem long to you, and the wording may seem strange, but it is a formal legal document and much of the language is required by law. If you are asking the court for spousal support or child support, you will have to attach a financial statement to the court's form that lists assets, liabilities, income, and expenses.

The *Complaint* is accompanied by an information form for the clerk. There is a filing fee and *master's fee* that ranges from $66–$95 in the District of Columbia. The clerk will start a court file and put the *Complaint* in it. The outside cover of the court file will have an index of pleadings and dates.

The clerk will give you a copy of the *Complaint* with related attachments, such as a *Summons*. These will be served on your spouse to give him or her notice of the divorce and a chance to respond. Have an extra copy of the *Complaint* for your file. The clerk will stamp it with the filing date and write the case number on it. The following sections describe how to complete the *Complaint* for each jurisdiction.

MARYLAND COMPLAINT FOR ABSOLUTE DIVORCE

To complete the **COMPLAINT FOR ABSOLUTE DIVORCE**, complete the *case caption* by filling in the city or county of the court, then both your name (as plaintiff) and your spouse's name (as defendant). (see MD–4, p.238.) Provide current addresses and telephone numbers for both. There is no specific requirement that the plaintiff supply an address on the **COMPLAINT**. If you are represented by an attorney, the court and the defendant will mail the papers to your attorney. However, if you represent yourself you must provided an address. If you are concerned about harassment or violence and your spouse does not already have your address, consider opening a post office box and using that address in the litigation. The court clerk will fill in the case number when you file the **COMPLAINT**. Complete the rest of the form as follows.

- ◈ *Line 1.* After printing your name in the space provided, fill in the month, day, and year of your marriage. In the second blank, fill in the city or county and the state where you were married. Circle whether you were married in a religious or a civil ceremony.

- ◈ *Line 2.* Check off all statements that apply in your case and fill in the blanks.

- ◈ *Line 3.* If you check off, "We have no children...," remember to skip lines 5 and 6. If you check off, "My spouse and I are the parents...," write in the full names of all the children you and your spouse had together and their dates of birth.

- ◈ *Line 4.* Fill in information about any court cases (in Maryland or outside the state) that have involved either yourself, the opposing party, or one of the children involved in this case.

- ◈ *Line 7.* Fill in the name of the person who the children listed above now live with.

- ◈ *Line 9.* Check the box for the type of custody or visitation you have agreed upon, and fill in the names of the children involved. For a contested case, you will mark the type of custody you want.

- ◈ *Line 10.* Check the appropriate box for whether or not you are seeking alimony. If you are seeking alimony, state "by agreement," or for a contested case, state why you are seeking alimony.

- ◈ *Line 11.* Skip this if you have a *Separation Agreement* and an uncontested case. For a contested case, if you are asking the court to make a decision about your property, check off the kinds of property you and your spouse have. If you or your spouse have debts, you may check the box marked "Debts" and attach a list of the debts to this form.

> **NOTE:** *Normally, the court cannot order one party to pay the debts of another. However, the court may need to know what debts you have in order to determine the value of any marital property.*

◈ *Line 12.* Check each ground for divorce that applies and fill in the blanks. You may have more than one ground. Choosing a certain ground or grounds will not necessarily result in a divorce being granted, because you must still prove and corroborate at least one ground at trial. For an explanation of each of the grounds for divorce in Maryland, see Chapter 8.

◈ On the third page of the form, in the blank space at the top, insert, "The parties have signed a Separation Agreement, dated (insert the date), resolving all issues between them."

◈ In the section that begins "FOR THESE REASONS...," insert your name change if you want it, then add after the last box, "The Separation Agreement be incorporated in, but not merged with, the Decree of Divorce." For a contested case, you will check off everything you want. If you fail to ask for alimony or property before the divorce, you will never be able to get it. However, the court will not necessarily give you what you asked for. You still have to prove your case and convince the master or judge.

◈ Date and sign the **COMPLAINT**.

VIRGINIA COMPLAINT FOR DIVORCE

Start your divorce by filing a **COMPLAINT FOR DIVORCE**, in the circuit court for your city or county. (see form VA–5, p.282.) The **COMPLAINT FOR DIVORCE** tells the court and the defendant what it is that the plaintiff (the person filing for divorce) wants, and why he or she is entitled to it.

Complete your **COMPLAINT FOR DIVORCE** as follows.

◈ Make a caption identifying the court followed by the names and addresses of the plaintiff and the defendant. There is no specific requirement that the plaintiff supply an address on the **COMPLAINT**. If you are represented by an attorney, the court and the defendant will mail the papers to your attorney. However, if you represent yourself you must provided an address. If you are concerned about harassment or violence and your spouse does not already have your address, consider opening a post office box and using that address in the litigation.

◈ Write that the court has jurisdiction, and include the facts that give it jurisdiction. For example, you can state that the defendant is an actual and bona fide resident and domiciliary of this county and state, and has been so continuously for the immediately preceding six months.

◈ Write that both parties are over the age of 18. Include each party's military or nonmilitary status.

◈ Fill in the date and place that the parties were married.

◈ Write the children's names and dates of birth, or a statement that no children were born to or adopted by the parties.

◈ Declare who has custody and that said person is a fit and proper person to have custody.

◈ State the facts constituting the grounds for divorce, generally either:

a) the parties have lived separate and apart without cohabitation (without any sexual relations and without spending a night under the same roof) and without interruption for the twelve months immediately preceding the filing of the **COMPLAINT**, with the intent to end the marriage on the part of at least one party or

b) the parties have lived separate and apart without cohabitation and without interruption for the six months immediately preceding the filing of the **COMPLAINT**, with the intent to end the marriage on the part of at least one party, no children were born to or adopted by the parties, and the parties have entered into a written agreement resolving all issues arising out of the marriage.

◈ State that reconciliation of the parties is not probable.

◈ If applicable, write that the parties have settled all matters arising out of the marriage, and have put their agreement in writing and signed it (or, if the case is not settled, allegations regarding marital property, the parties' income, and the need for and ability to pay support).

◈ Request what the plaintiff is asking the court to do. In an uncontested case, you ask the court to grant a divorce pursuant to Virginia Code, Section 20-91.9; ratify, approve, and incorporate—but not merge—the parties' agreement into the court's decree; order custody and support as requested, if applicable; and, grant the plaintiff any other appropriate relief.

DISTRICT OF COLUMBIA COMPLAINT FOR ABSOLUTE DIVORCE

The District of Columbia Bar Association has published a mark-the-box form for a **COMPLAINT FOR ABSOLUTE DIVORCE**. (see DC–3, page 326.) All District of Columbia forms must be typewritten. To prepare the **COMPLAINT**, do the following.

◈ At the top, fill in your name and address as the plaintiff and your spouse's name and address as the defendant. If you wish to keep your address secret because you believe that you will be harmed or harassed by your spouse or your spouse's family, you may provide an *in care of* name and address for someone to receive court papers for you. Check the "SUBSTITUTE ADDRESS" box.

❖ The clerk will assign the case number, which goes on the right side of the Complaint after "DR", when you file the Complaint and pay the filing fee. Underneath the case number, write the case numbers of any related cases, such as child support or domestic violence cases.

❖ After the title of the Complaint, check "yes" or "no" to indicate whether or not your case involves child support.

❖ Write your name in the first paragraph.

❖ Paragraph 1 asks for information about you and your spouse related to residency. To meet the residency requirement, either you or your spouse must be a resident of the District of Columbia and lived there continuously for six months before filing the Complaint. Check the applicable box, or both boxes if you and your spouse meet this requirement.

❖ At Paragraph 2, fill in the date and place of your marriage ceremony and check the first box. Look at your marriage certificate to make sure it says the same thing. Since the District of Columbia recognizes common-law marriage, you would check the second box if you have a common-law marriage.

❖ At Paragraph 3, state the date you and your spouse stopped living together and were no longer have sexual relations.

❖ Paragraph 4 sets forth the only two grounds for absolute divorce in the District of Columbia. The first box is for six months of mutual and voluntary separation. The second box is for twelve months of involuntary separation.

❖ Paragraph 5 asks whether or not you want the court to restore a former name you had before you were married.

❖ Paragraph 6 is about marital property. Check the first box if you have no marital property, the second box if you do not want the court to divide marital property, the third box if you have a written agreement dividing marital property, the fourth box if you want the court to divide your marital property, and the fifth box if you do not know. Attach a list of property as Attachment A if you want the court to divide it.

◈ Paragraph 7 is about marital debt, and the boxes are similar to those for property in Paragraph 6. Include the debt on Attachment A.

◈ Paragraph 8 is for temporary alimony until the divorce trial, and you check the box indicating whether you need it or not. If you do need temporary alimony, you will need to file a separate motion explaining to the court why you need it.

◈ Paragraph 9 is for rehabilitative or permanent alimony. Check one of the boxes indicating whether or not you are asking for alimony. Remember, if you do not ask for it now, you cannot ask for it after your divorce has been granted.

◈ Paragraph 10 is about custody of the children of the marriage, whether by birth or adoption. If you want the court to decide custody, then you will have to provide an Attachment B with the children's birthdates and Social Security numbers, and the names and addresses of who the children lived with for the last five years.

◈ At Paragraph 13, indicate whether you have any attachments to the Complaint.

◈ Paragraph 14 is called your *prayer for relief*. This is where you tell the commissioner what you want the court to do. The boxes follow the same pattern as the facts above; that is, that you want the court to give you a divorce; decide property, alimony, custody, and child support; include your settlement agreement in its order; and, restore your former name. Check all the boxes that are applicable.

◈ Sign your name and write your name, address, and telephone number. You may use the substitute address if you do not feel safe providing yours. Print your name in the oath and sign below the oath. The oath swears that you are making true statements in your Complaint under the penalties of making a false statement.

ANSWER

If you are served, you have to respond to a **COMPLAINT FOR DIVORCE** within:

- thirty days in Maryland, but sixty days if served outside of Maryland, and ninety days if served outside the country;

- twenty-one days in Virginia; or,

- twenty days in the District of Columbia.

If your spouse (or you if you are the defendant) does not file a timely response to the **COMPLAINT**, you (or your spouse) may be able to proceed with the divorce upon default. (see Chapter 13.)

The response is usually in the form of an *Answer*, a formal legal pleading, in which the answering party—the defendant—either admits or denies each of the allegations of the **COMPLAINT**. In an uncontested case, prepare the *Answer* as follows:

- Write the name and location of the court and the names of the parties (the parties' addresses are not necessary) at the top.

- Copy the assigned case number on the *Answer*.

- In an uncontested case, it is sufficient to state that the defendant admits the allegations of the **COMPLAINT** and does not oppose the granting of the relief requested.

- Complete the *Certificate of Service*.

- Sign the *Answer* and the *Certificate of Service*.

- File the *Answer* with the court clerk at the courthouse.

- Mail or hand-deliver a copy of the *Answer* to the Plaintiff.

If your case is still contested on one or more points, you should address each allegation of the **COMPLAINT** by admitting or denying the allegations, or stating that you do not have sufficient information to admit or deny the allegation and therefore you deny it. You can admit part of an allegation and deny the remainder. After answering the plaintiff's allegations of fact, you should say what you want the court to do. Usually, it is sufficient to ask that the court deny all relief requested by the plaintiff, and grant you any other appropriate relief.

The defendant may also file a *Counterclaim for Divorce* stating his or her own grounds for divorce and requesting relief. The same rules that apply to **COMPLAINTS FOR DIVORCE** apply to *Counterclaims*, except that a *Counterclaim* can be served by mailing it to the plaintiff. If the defendant files a *Counterclaim*, the plaintiff must then file an *Answer* in the same fashion and within the same time frame discussed above. (The Maryland out-of-state time frames do not apply, however.)

chapter 10

Information Reports

The clerk in each jurisdiction will require some form of an information report as a cover sheet to accompany your *Complaint for Divorce*. This chapter explains how to fill them out.

MARYLAND CIVIL—DOMESTIC CASE INFORMATION REPORT

To complete the Maryland CIVIL—DOMESTIC CASE INFORMATION REPORT (form MD–5, p.241), do the following.

◈ Fill in the city or county where the court is located at the top of the first page.

◈ In the first section, check the plaintiff box.

◈ The clerk will insert the *case number*.

◈ For *case name*, print your name as plaintiff and your spouse's name as defendant.

◈ Provide your name again as party, as well as your address and telephone number. This is called the *case caption*.

◈ Mark the box that you are not represented by an attorney and supply the requested information for any related cases.

◈ Indicate whether you need an interpreter or other accommodation.

◈ Indicate whether alternative dispute resolution has been tried or requested, and if so, provide details.

◈ Mark the box showing the case is uncontested (or indicate what issues are disputed if you have a contested case).

◈ Mark the box requesting an absolute divorce.

◈ You will leave the next three sections blank for uncontested divorces (and mark the appropriate issues in dispute for contested cases).

◈ On the second page (or reverse), repeat the case name and put "ten minutes" in "time estimated for a merits hearing."

◈ Print your name and address.

◈ Sign and date the report.

VIRGINIA DIVORCE CASE COVER SHEET

Several counties in Virginia require you to file a **DIVORCE CASE COVER SHEET** with the **COMPLAINT FOR DIVORCE** to give the court a summary of information about your case in a convenient format. The court clerk will tell you whether a cover sheet is required.

To complete the **DIVORCE CASE COVER SHEET** (form VA–6, p.284), follow these instructions.

◈ Enter the date of filing where indicated.

◈ The court clerk will enter the *case number*.

◈ Enter your full name and the defendant's full name where indicated.

   NOTE: *Names on the cover sheet must agree with the names on the* **COMPLAINT FOR DIVORCE.**

◈ Check the box to indicate that the case is totally uncontested, or if not, check the appropriate contested boxes.

◈ Check the *Ore Tenus* box if you want to have your divorce hearing before a judge instead of a commissioner.

DISTRICT OF COLUMBIA CERTIFICATE OF DIVORCE

The **CERTIFICATE OF DIVORCE, DISSOLUTION OF MARRIAGE, OR ANNULMENT** form (DC–4, p.334) is filed with the **COMPLAINT FOR ABSOLUTE DIVORCE.** Although a copy of the form has been provided in this book, you will need to obtain the original, three part, tri-colored form from the clerk. Type the following information to complete the form.

◈ At the top left, after "D," fill in the case number the clerk gives you for your **COMPLAINT.**

◈ In the first section, for lines 1 through 4, provide the name, address, and date of birth for the husband.

◈ In the second section, provide the same information for the wife in lines 5a through 8.

◈ At line 9, fill in the date of the marriage.

◈ At line 10, list the names of the minor children of this marriage.

❖   For line 11, check whether the husband or the wife is the Plaintiff.

❖   At lines 12 and 13, give the name and address of the plaintiff's attorney if applicable.

❖   Skip the section entitled "Decree," lines 14 through 18, which will be completed by the clerk.

❖   At lines 19 through 22, provide statistical information on race and number of marriages for the husband and wife.

Service of Process

Your spouse must have notice of your *Complaint*. This gives your spouse an opportunity to defend him- or herself and also satisfies the requirement of due process of law. It also gives the court personal jurisdiction over your spouse. This is accomplished by *service of process*, which means serving him or her with a copy of the *Complaint* and *Summons*.

After you file the *Complaint for Divorce* and pay the filing fee, the court will issue a *Summons*. The *Summons* is a notice to the defendant that a lawsuit has been filed against him or her. It is your responsibility to have the *Summons*, together with a copy of the *Complaint for Divorce*, served upon the defendant.

Service of process can be by certified mail or by handing a copy of the *Complaint* and *Summons* to your spouse. You cannot personally serve your spouse. You have to have a friend or a professional process server do it. The average cost of a process server is about $40. Once the *Complaint* is served, the process server sends you an *Affidavit of Service* to file with the court.

If your spouse avoids service or if your spouse cannot be found, you can file a motion with the court to serve him or her by alternative means, such as posting on the courthouse bulletin board or publishing in the local newspaper. Accompany your motion with an affidavit describing your unsuccessful attempts to serve. See Chapter 12 for more information.

Your spouse can voluntarily submit to jurisdiction of the court by filing an *Answer*, and then you will not have to serve the *Summons* and *Complaint*, or file an *Affidavit of Service*.

If you do not know where your spouse is, contact his or relatives and last known employer. Check the Internet, phone book, military listings, and traffic and criminal records. After a diligent search, you can ask the court to permit service by alternative means, such as publication in the newspaper or posting a notice on the courthouse bulletin board. Following are the rules and forms for service of process in each jurisdiction.

MARYLAND SERVICE

Serve your spouse with the *Complaint for Divorce*, one copy of the *Summons* (provided by the clerk when you file the *Complaint for Divorce*), the CIVIL—DOMESTIC CASE INFORMATION REPORT you completed, and a blank CIVIL—DOMESTIC CASE INFORMATION REPORT. You can serve it by certified mail, return receipt requested, or by private process server (anyone over 18 years of age, except you).

Affidavit of Service by Certified Mail

If you use certified mail, when you get the return receipt, file it with the AFFIDAVIT OF SERVICE BY CERTIFIED MAIL. (see form MD–6, p.243.) Fill in the case caption at the top and complete the rest of the form as follows.

◈ *Line 1.* Insert "Complaint for Divorce and Summons."

◈ *Line 2.* Enter your spouse's name.

◈ *Line 3.* Insert the date you mailed and the address you mailed to.

◈ *Line 5.* Fill in your spouse's name.

◈ Date, sign, and print your name, address, and telephone number on the form.

➔ Attach the original return receipt and a copy of the *Summons*.

➔ File this with the court.

Affidavit of Service by Private Process

If you serve by hand, the person you used as a process server will complete the **AFFIDAVIT OF SERVICE BY PRIVATE PROCESS**. (see form MD–7, p.244.) Fill in the case caption at the top and complete the rest of the form as follows.

➔ *Line 1*. Print your spouse's name and time served.

➔ *Line 2*. Indicate the date served and address where served.

➔ *Line 3*. Insert "Complaint for Divorce and Summons."

➔ Have the server date, sign, and print his or her name, address, and telephone number on the form.

➔ Attach a copy of the *Summons*.

➔ File this with the court.

VIRGINIA SERVICE

Service of process on a Virginia resident can be accomplished by personal service, which means handing the *Summons* (prepared by the court) and *Complaint for Divorce* to the defendant. This can be done by the sheriff or by an individual over the age of 18 who does not have an interest in the lawsuit. That is, you can have a friend or a relative serve the defendant, but you cannot serve the papers yourself.

Service is highly technical. Even if your spouse actually receives all the paperwork, if there was any mistake with how it was done, the court may make you start all over. The defendant must have been served with process in one of the ways authorized by the statute or must have formally waived or accepted process.

If a resident defendant cannot be personally served, service can be accomplished by leaving the papers with a member of the defendant's household who is at least 16 years of age, or if that is not possible, by posting the papers at the defendant's front door. The plaintiff must show by the process server's affidavit that each method was attempted in the proper order. In an uncontested divorce case, service problems are needless opportunities for delay and additional expense.

The methods of service of process on a nonresident defendant depend upon the particular basis for jurisdiction. Generally, personal service by a law enforcement official authorized to serve process in the foreign jurisdiction is sufficient. Acceptance or waiver of process by the nonresident defendant is also effective.

Return of Service   Service by the sheriff is an effective and cost-efficient means to have a resident defendant served, and should be used in most circumstances. The sheriff will file a *Return of Service* with the court.

Affidavit of Service   If you have someone other than the sheriff serve the defendant, then you must file an **AFFIDAVIT FOR SERVICE** with the court. (see form VA–8, p.289.) Complete the **AFFIDAVIT FOR SERVICE** as follows.

⬦   The name of the court, the names of the parties, and the case number must agree with those shown on other papers filed in the case.

⬦   Enter the title of this paper below the caption. The title is "Affidavit of Service of Process."

⬦   The process server should state his or her name, that he or she is over the age of 18, and that he or she is not a party to the case.

⬦   State the date and the address where the defendant was served.

⬦   State that the defendant acknowledged his or her identity, and give brief physical description.

⬦   The process server should sign the affidavit before a notary or deputy clerk of court, and have his or her signature notarized.

Acceptance/ Waiver Form   A defendant in Virginia can accept or waive service of process by signing the **ACCEPTANCE OF SERVICE OF PROCESS AND WAIVER OF NOTICE** (the

ACCEPTANCE/WAIVER FORM). (see form VA–7, p.286.) Waiver of process also dispenses with the need to formally serve the defendant with notice of the divorce hearing. The form must be signed in front of a notary or other official authorized to administer oaths, and filed with the court. Complete this form as follows.

◈ Fill in the boxes for case number, location of court, and names of parties.

◈ In item 1, check the defendant box.

◈ In item 2, check the *Summons* box and the *Complaint for Divorce* box, and write in the additional documents, if any, you are sending to the defendant with these documents (such as exhibits to the complaint).

◈ In item 3, check boxes a through e.

◈ Check the defendant box under the signature line.

◈ Send the completed ACCEPTANCE/WAIVER FORM to the defendant along with the *Summons, Complaint for Divorce*, and any other papers.

◈ The defendant then signs the ACCEPTANCE/WAIVER FORM before a notary and has his or her signature notarized.

◈ The defendant files the ACCEPTANCE/WAIVER FORM with the court and mails (or hand delivers) a copy to the plaintiff.

DISTRICT OF COLUMBIA SERVICE

Service of process in the District of Columbia may be by:

✪ certified mail, return receipt requested;

✪ hand delivery to your spouse; or,

✪ hand delivery to someone at your spouse's home of suitable age or discretion.

Personal Service

You may not personally serve the papers yourself. You can use any other person who lives or works in the District of Columbia, is over the age of 18, and is not a party to the divorce. You may use a special process server.

The process server hands the *Complaint for Absolute Divorce* and the *service copy* of the *Summons* that the clerk gave you to your spouse or someone in your spouse's home. The person in your spouse's home must be someone of suitable age and discretion, but not a young child or a visitor.

The *Summons* must be delivered within twenty days of issuance or it expires. If your *Summons* expires before you can have it served on your spouse, you can ask the clerk for a second *Summons* (sometimes called an *alias Summons*) for a fee of $10. You can have the *Summons* served anytime and anywhere (at work, home, or elsewhere).

Once the papers are served, the process server will complete the bottom portion of the *legal copy* of the *Summons* and have it notarized. The date and time of service as well as the name of the person served will be stated. File this copy with the clerk. Make a copy and have the clerk stamp it with the date for your records.

Service by Certified Mail

Instead of personal service, you can send the papers yourself to your spouse's home by certified mail, return receipt requested. When you receive the green return receipt card, attach it to the bottom of the legal copy of the *Summons*.

Prepare an **AFFIDAVIT OF RETURN OF SERVICE BY CERTIFIED MAIL.** (see form DC–6, p.340.) The **AFFIDAVIT** is your sworn and notarized statement of:

- ✪ the date you got the summons;

- ✪ the date you mailed it; and,

- ✪ the date your spouse received it.

If someone other than your spouse signed for it, you will have to state who that person is. That person must be someone of suitable age and discretion who lives with your spouse.

If you do not know the person who signed for it, you do not have good service, and you will have to try again by certified mail or have it served by hand. If you are still living with your spouse, the court will not consider it good service if you sign the receipt for him or her.

ONCE YOU HAVE SERVED YOUR SPOUSE

Once you have obtained service of process, then the defendant has to file a response or be found in *default*. Chapter 12 explains what to do if you cannot find your spouse. Chapter 13 tells you what to do if your spouse does not respond after you have served him or her with a *Complaint for Absolute Divorce*.

Finding Your Spouse

If you cannot find your spouse or your spouse is avoiding service, you will have to ask the court for alternative service. Since this will slow your case down, you should make every effort to locate and serve your spouse first. The courts in Maryland, Virginia, and the District of Columbia will require a good faith effort on your part, and records of your attempts to locate your spouse. Here are the procedures and forms for alternative service of process in each jurisdiction.

ATTEMPTS TO LOCATE YOUR SPOUSE

To attempt to locate your spouse, you need to make diligent efforts. Keep copies of documents, correspondence, receipts, and all other records of your attempts to locate your spouse. Diligent efforts may be made if you:

❂ serve by certified mail at the last known address;

❂ send letters to relatives and friends;

❂ write to the last employer;

✪   hire a private investigator to find him or her;

✪   use a telephone directory, directory assistance, and the Internet;

✪   call the Motor Vehicle Administration in your state for a current address;

✪   use the **MILITARY SERVICE LOCATORS** (form MD–9, p.248) to see if he or she is a member of the armed forces (you can also use this form in Virginia and the District of Columbia);

✪   ask former neighbors;

✪   contact the local child support enforcement agency for any records of whereabouts; and,

✪   use any other method you can think of.

MARYLAND ALTERNATIVE SERVICE

If you have tried all the previously mentioned means to locate or serve your spouse and are still unsuccessful, then you are ready to file a **MOTION FOR ALTERNATE SERVICE**. (see form MD–8, p.245.) First, fill in the top section with the caption of your case. Then, complete the rest of the form as follows.

◈   *Line 1.* Print your name.

◈   *Paragraph 1.* Write "Complaint for Divorce," the city or county of the court, and the date you filed.

◈   Date and sign the form.

◈   On the *Affidavit* portion of the form, put in the county where you are signing.

◈   Print your name where indicated.

❖ *Line 1.* Write "Complaint for Divorce," the city or county of the court, and the date you filed.

❖ *Line 2.* Check off all the boxes that indicate your attempts to locate or serve your spouse and attach supporting documents.

❖ *Line 3.* Indicate the last date you saw your spouse and check the appropriate boxes to indicate what you know about his or her whereabouts.

❖ Sign the form in front of a Notary Public and have the Notary complete the notarization part of the form.

❖ Fill in the case caption of the Order for Alternative Service. The judge will complete the rest.

❖ Fill in the case caption of the *Notice*. The clerk will complete the rest.

File all of these documents with the clerk. There will be another filing fee for this motion. If the judge grants your motion and orders service by posting, the clerk will arrange to have the notice posted, usually on the bulletin board at the courthouse. If the judge orders service by publication in the newspaper, you will have to check to see whether the clerk will arrange this or if it is your responsibility. In either event, you will have to pay the newspaper for publication.

VIRGINIA ALTERNATIVE SERVICE

If your spouse is not a Virginia resident or you cannot locate your spouse after following the steps previously described, you can use the procedures for service by publication. The steps for service by publication are as follows.

Affidavit for Service by Publication

Complete and file an **AFFIDAVIT FOR SERVICE BY PUBLICATION**, stating the reasons you are seeking to serve by publication. (see form VA–13, p.294.) Complete the affidavit by doing the following.

◈ Complete the *caption* as usual.

◈ Enter your name on the plaintiff line.

◈ Enter the your spouse's name on the defendant line.

◈ Check the appropriate box to indicate whether the basis for publication is that your spouse is a nonresident, cannot be found, or cannot be served by the sheriff, or if there is another reason (and state the reason, if applicable).

◈ Fill in your spouse's name and last known address where indicated.

◈ State any other information that is relevant to the need for an *Order of Publication*.

◈ Sign where indicated in the notarizing officer's presence.

◈ Have your signature notarized by a notary or deputy clerk of court.

Order of Publication   Complete and file an **ORDER OF PUBLICATION** as follows. (see form VA–14, p.295.)

◈ Fill in the caption.

◈ Check the appropriate box to indicate whether the basis for publication is that your spouse is a nonresident, cannot be found, or cannot be served by the sheriff, or if there is another reason (and state the reason, if applicable).

◈ Fill in your spouse's name and last known address where indicated.

◈ Sign where indicated and fill in your address and telephone number.

◈ If the judge signs the **ORDER OF PUBLICATION**, the clerk's office will arrange for publication of the order.

◈ Pay the clerk's office the cost of publication, or your pro rata share if two or more orders are combined in one publication.

DISTRICT OF COLUMBIA ALTERNATIVE SERVICE

If you do not know where your spouse is, you may ask for service by publication or posting.

Motion to Serve by Publication

Prepare a **MOTION TO SERVE BY PUBLICATION OR POSTING** (form DC–7, p.342), together with **POINTS AND AUTHORITIES** (form DC–9, p.355) and an **AFFIDAVIT OF RETURN OF SERVICE BY CERTIFIED MAIL** (form DC–6, p.340). This affidavit states your true belief that your spouse has lived outside the District of Columbia for the last six months and describes your diligent search for your spouse, including relatives, last known employer, telephone book, military listings, and traffic and criminal records. Attach an **ORDER OF PUBLICATION—ABSENT DEFENDANT**. (see form DC–8, p.354.) Sign the **AFFIDAVIT OF SERVICE** in front of a notary. Then, file all of these documents together with the clerk. It will be up to you to arrange for publication.

Default Divorce

If your spouse fails to file an *Answer* or other pleading within the required time, or after the time passes that is set forth in the judge's *Order for Alternative Service*, you may seek a divorce by default in any of the jurisdictions in which you filed your *Complaint for Divorce*.

MARYLAND DEFAULT

If your spouse has failed to answer the *Complaint* in the required time in Maryland, file a **REQUEST FOR ORDER OF DEFAULT**. (see form MD–10, p.249.) To complete the **REQUEST**, fill in the case caption at the top and then do the following.

♦ Print your name on the first line.

♦ Print your spouse's name on the second line.

♦ On the third line, write "Complaint for Divorce."

♦ Insert your spouse's last known address on the fourth line.

◈ Sign and date the **REQUEST**.

◈ On the *Non-Military Affidavit* portion of the form, put your spouse's name, and sign and date the *Affidavit*.

◈ On the next page, fill in the case caption on the *Order of Default* and the judge will complete the rest.

Once you receive an **ORDER OF DEFAULT**, you will need to contact the court clerk to schedule an uncontested divorce hearing.

VIRGINIA DEFAULT

If your spouse fails to file an *Answer* or other pleading within twenty-one days of service of process, or after the time passes that is set forth in the judge's *Order for Alternative Service*, you may seek a divorce by default.

Count the time by counting the first day after the day of service as day one and counting each calendar day thereafter. If day twenty-one falls on a weekend or holiday, then the defendant has until the next business day to answer.

The default procedures contain safeguards to ensure that the defendant is given notice and an opportunity to appear and defend. The safeguards create potential for mistakes by the plaintiff that will prevent entry of the *Decree of Divorce* until the plaintiff goes back and corrects the mistake.

In short, like service of process problems, the default procedure is full of opportunities for needless expense and delay. If the parties to an uncontested divorce want to obtain a divorce without needless delay and expense, the defendant has to file a timely answer.

You proceed on default by obtaining an *ore tenus* hearing or a hearing before a commissioner. In addition to the usual requirements for obtaining a hearing, you will have to file an **AFFIDAVIT REGARDING MILITARY SERVICE**. (see form VA–21, p.306.)

Once the hearing date has been set, have the notice of hearing served on the defendant in the same manner that the original *Summons* was served, and make sure an affidavit of service or return of service (by the sheriff) is filed.

If the defendant is on active duty in the Armed Forces of the United States, you cannot proceed by default.

DISTRICT OF COLUMBIA DEFAULT

If you file and serve the *Complaint* properly, but the defendant does not file an *Answer* within twenty days, you can ask the court to enter a default against the defendant and to set a hearing for *ex parte* proof. *Ex parte* means one-sided; that is, you get to tell your side of the story and the defendant does not.

Praecipe for Default and Ex Parte Hearing

First, file a **PRAECIPE FOR DEFAULT AND EX PARTE HEARING** asking the court to determine whether it is necessary to appoint an attorney for the defendant. (see form DC–10, p.356.) If the court determines it is not necessary to appoint counsel for the defendant, file a **PRAECIPE** asking the court to enter a default and set a hearing.

Affidavit in Support of Default

File your **AFFIDAVIT IN SUPPORT OF DEFAULT** with the **PRAECIPE**. (see form DC–11, p.357.) Complete it as follows.

◈ Fill in the case caption and case number at the top.

◈ Print your name on the first line after the title.

◈ Fill in the date of service of process and the date proof of service was filed.

◈ Sign the **AFFIDAVIT** before a notary or a clerk at the courthouse.

Soldiers and Sailors Affidavit

You will also need to complete and file an **AFFIDAVIT IN COMPLIANCE WITH THE SERVICEMEMBERS CIVIL RELIEF ACT** (form DC–12, p.359) with your **PRAECIPE FOR DEFAULT** in order to affirm that you spouse is not a member of the military. Complete the caption, insert your name, check the appropriate box, and sign the **AFFIDAVIT** before a notary. Use the last two pages of the form in your military search.

Default Order   Finally, attach to the **PRAECIPE FOR DEFAULT** a proposed **DEFAULT ORDER** for the judge to sign after your hearing. (see form DC–13, p.363.) Complete the proposed order as follows.

⬦   Fill in the case name and number.

⬦   Fill in the day your spouse was served.

⬦   Fill in the day you are filing the **PRAECIPE FOR DEFAULT**.

⬦   Fill in your spouse's name.

⬦   The judge will complete the rest.

You have six months from the time you file the *Complaint* to process your default or bring the case to issue (meaning an *Answer* is filed by the defendant). Otherwise, the court will dismiss your case and you will have to start over by filing a new *Complaint*.

Maryland Uncontested Divorce

You can file a **COMPLAINT FOR ABSOLUTE DIVORCE** in Maryland if you or your spouse meets the residency requirement of one year prior to filing, or the grounds for divorce (such as adultery) arose within the state. You must also have one of the grounds for either an absolute or limited divorce that were described earlier. A case is uncontested if you have a comprehensive *Separation Agreement* in writing and signed by both parties. In other words, to have an uncontested case, you and your spouse must be in agreement on grounds, custody, child support, alimony, and property distribution.

If you have any negotiations left to do on any issue, you do not have an uncontested divorce. However, you can do your arguing before the trial and reach a comprehensive *Separation Agreement* to present to the court, thus becoming an uncontested divorce. If you do your arguing before the judge or master, you have a *contested* divorce, discussed in Chapters 19 and 20.

REQUIRED FORMS

To begin an uncontested divorce in Maryland, you'll need to file the following with the court clerk.

✪ **CIVIL—DOMESTIC CASE INFORMATION REPORT** (form MD–5, p.241);

✪ **COMPLAINT FOR ABSOLUTE DIVORCE** (form MD–4, p.238);

✪ *Separation Agreement*; and,

✪ filing fee.

If you are seeking alimony or child support, you will also be required to file a **FINANCIAL STATEMENT** (form MD–1, p.225). Later you will file a **JOINT REQUEST TO SCHEDULE AN UNCONTESTED DIVORCE HEARING** (form MD–11, p.251). At the final hearing you will need:

✪ a **REPORT OF ABSOLUTE DIVORCE** (the "Blue Form" for statistical information) (sample form MD–12, p.252);

✪ a copy of your marriage license (or witness present at your marriage);

✪ *Child Support Guidelines* (if there are children);

✪ witness identification information;

✪ *Separation Agreement* (if you did not file it with your *Complaint*); and,

✪ **SUBMISSION FOR JUDGMENT OF DIVORCE** (for waiving appeals) (form MD–13, p.253).

The following sections will describe the uncontested divorce process and the required forms.

FILING A COMPLAINT

File your **COMPLAINT FOR DIVORCE** (form MD–4, p.238) and **CIVIL—DOMESTIC CASE INFORMATION REPORT** (form MD–5, p.241) with the clerk's office at the courthouse in the county where you live or where your spouse lives. If you are requesting alimony or child support, you also have to file a **FINANCIAL STATEMENT**. (see form MD–1, p.225.) There is a filing fee of about $105, depending upon the county where you are filing. The clerk will process your **COMPLAINT**, give it a case number, open the court's file, and return it to you with two copies of a *Summons*.

SERVICE OF PROCESS

Serve the **COMPLAINT** and *Summons* on your spouse by certified mail or by personal service. Remember that you cannot personally serve your spouse. You must have a friend or a professional process server do it. Once the **COMPLAINT** is served, file the **AFFIDAVIT OF SERVICE** with the court. (forms MD–6 or 7, p.243 or p.244.)

ANSWER

Once served, your spouse has to respond to your **COMPLAINT** with an *Answer* or other pleading within thirty days (sixty days if served outside Maryland and ninety days if served outside of the United States), or he or she will be found in default.

JOINT REQUEST TO SCHEDULE AN UNCONTESTED DIVORCE HEARING

Once an **AFFIDAVIT OF SERVICE** or an *Answer* has been filed, the court will send you *Notice of a Scheduling Conference*. The court will also send you, attached to the *Notice*, a **JOINT REQUEST TO SCHEDULE AN UNCONTESTED DIVORCE HEARING**. (see form MD–11, p.251.) If your spouse answers and admits all the allegations of your **COMPLAINT**, the divorce is uncontested. You may file a **JOINT REQUEST** signed by both of you.

To complete the **JOINT REQUEST**, state your grounds for divorce—usually one-year voluntary separation or two years' separation in an uncontested divorce. Then check the following items, if applicable.

◈   Check line 1b if custody and visitation have been agreed to.

◈   Check line 2 if child support has been established in compliance with the child support guidelines.

◈   Mark line 3 if all parties speak English.

◈   Mark line 4 if there are no pension or any pension rights have been waived.

◈   Check line 5 if there are no support or property rights to be adjudicated.

◈   Attach a completed **CHILD SUPPORT WORKSHEET**. (see forms MD–2 or 3, p.234 or p.235.) This is required for an uncontested hearing if you have minor children of the marriage. (Child support is discussed in Chapter 23.)

Once you file the **JOINT REQUEST**, the scheduling conference will not be held and you will not be scheduled for any other hearings except your divorce hearing.

Go to Chapter 17 for information on how to prepare for your uncontested divorce hearing.

Virginia Uncontested Divorce

Once you meet the residency requirements and have grounds for divorce, you may file for an uncontested divorce in Virginia.

Residency in Virginia means that one party is an actual and bona fide resident and domiciliary of the state for at least six months before filing the *Complaint*. This means someone has established a residence in the state with the intent to remain indefinitely. Special statutory provisions cover military personnel. Anyone in the military who is stationed in Virginia for six months is presumed to be a Virginia resident and domiciliary.

Once you meet the residency requirement so the court has subject-matter jurisdiction over your marriage, the court has the power to grant you a divorce. However, if you want the court to decide custody, support, or property, it will have to have personal jurisdiction over the defendant. The court will have personal jurisdiction if the defendant is properly served with process and:

- he or she is a Virginia resident at the time the suit for divorce is filed;

- the parties lived in Virginia at the time of the separation that is the grounds for divorce;

- ✪ the defendant lived in Virginia at the time the grounds for divorce arose;

- ✪ the defendant maintains a marital home in Virginia at the time the suit is filed;

- ✪ the defendant executed an agreement in Virginia to pay support to a Virginia resident;

- ✪ the defendant has previously been ordered to pay support by a Virginia court that had jurisdiction over him or her; or,

- ✪ the defendant fathered or conceived a child in Virginia.

REQUIRED FORMS

To begin an uncontested divorce, you will need to file the following with the court clerk.

- ✪ **COMPLAINT FOR DIVORCE** (form VA–5, p.282);

- ✪ **DIVORCE CASE COVER SHEET** (if required) (form VA–6, p.284);

- ✪ *Separation Agreement* (if you have one); and,

- ✪ filing fee.

Later, you will file:

- ✪ **AFFIDAVIT FOR SERVICE** (unless the sheriff serves the papers on the defendant) (form VA–8, p.289); or,

- ✪ **REQUEST FOR ORDER OF PUBLICATION** (form VA–9, p.290); and,

- ✪ **AFFIDAVIT IN SUPPORT OF ORDER OF PUBLICATION.** (form VA–10, p.291, form VA–11, p.292, or form VA–12, p.293—whichever is appropriate to your situation.)

You will also file a **PRAECIPE** requesting an uncontested divorce hearing.

The defendant will file these two forms:

- ✪ **ACCEPTANCE/WAIVER FORM** (form VA–7, p.286) and

- ✪ *Answer*.

At the final hearing you will need:

- ✪ a **REPORT OF DIVORCE OR ANNULMENT (FORM VS-4)** (form VA–16, p.297);

- ✪ a copy of your marriage license (or witness present at your marriage);

- ✪ *Child Support Guidelines* (if there are children);

- ✪ *Separation Agreement* (if you did not file it with your **COMPLAINT**);

- ✪ corroborating witness; and,

- ✪ **FINAL DECREE OF DIVORCE**. (see form VA–19, p.300, or form VA–20, p.302.)

The following will describe the uncontested divorce process in Virginia and explain the required forms.

FILING YOUR COMPLAINT FOR DIVORCE

File an original and one copy of the **COMPLAINT FOR DIVORCE** at the clerk's office at the courthouse. (see form VA–5, p.282.) Bring an extra copy for you to keep. The clerk will stamp it "filed" and note the case number on it. Pay the filing fee of $66, plus an additional $19 if a change of name is required. You will also have to pay for the cost of service of process if you want the sheriff to serve it.

REQUEST FOR ORE TENUS HEARING

Once the defendant has filed an *Answer*, or been placed in default, the case is *at issue* and the clerk's office will schedule a hearing upon request.

You can have a hearing scheduled by filing a request, called a **REQUEST FOR ORE TENUS HEARING**. An Ore Tenus hearing is before a judge, as opposed to a hearing before a commissioner in the office of a commissioner. In some counties, you will also be required to file a completed **REPORT OF DIVORCE OR ANNULMENT (FORM VS-4)** (form VA–17, p.297) and a **FINAL DECREE OF DIVORCE**. (see form VA–19, p.300, or form VA–20, p.302.)

Complete the **REQUEST FOR ORE TENUS HEARING** as follows. (see form VA–15, p.296.)

⬥ Enter the name of the court, the names of the parties, the case number, and the title of the paper (*Request for Ore Tenus Hearing*) as usual.

⬥ Fill in your name and check plaintiff.

⬥ Fill in your address and telephone number.

⬥ Check the appropriate attachments and list any other attachments to your request.

⬥ Send a copy of the **REQUEST FOR ORE TENUS HEARING** to the defendant, and complete and sign the *Certificate of Service* if the defendant has not filed an **ACCEPTANCE/WAIVER** in the case. (see form VA–7, p.286.)

Go to Chapter 17 for information on how to prepare for your uncontested divorce hearing.

District of Columbia Uncontested Divorce

You can file a **COMPLAINT FOR ABSOLUTE DIVORCE** in the District of Columbia if you or your spouse meets the residency requirement of six months prior to filing, and if you have one of the grounds for either an absolute divorce or legal separation that were described in Chapter 8.

A case is uncontested if you have a comprehensive *Separation Agreement* in writing and signed by both parties. In other words, to have an uncontested case, you and your spouse must be in agreement on grounds, custody, child support, alimony, and property distribution.

If you have a *Separation Agreement* with your spouse and you are both cooperating, it is possible to obtain an uncontested divorce in the District of Columbia in three to six weeks.

REQUIRED FORMS

To begin an uncontested divorce, you will need to file the following with the clerk:

- *Vital Records Collection Form*;

- *Intake / Cross-Reference Sheet*;

- **Certificate of Divorce, Dissolution of Marriage, or Annulment** (form DC–4, p.334 is a sample);

- **Complaint for Absolute Divorce** (form DC–3, p.326);

- *Separation Agreement*;

- **Financial Statement** (if you are seeking alimony or child support) (form DC–1, p.323);

- *Notice of Hearing* and *Order to Appear* (if child support is contested); and,

- filing fee.

Later you will file a **Praecipe for Uncontested Divorce**. (see form DC–14, p.364.) At the final hearing you will need:

- a certified copy of your marriage license;

- *Child Support Guidelines* (if there are children);

- *Separation Agreement* (if you did not file it with your **Complaint**);

- **Consent to Have Proceedings Conducted by Hearing Commissioner** (form DC–15, p.365);

- **Findings of Fact, Conclusions of Law and Judgment of Absolute Divorce** (form DC–16, p.366); and,

- **Joint Waiver of Appeal.** (see form DC–17, p.372.)

The court in the District of Columbia runs a free divorce clinic, which you can register for with the clerk. The clerk also has forms for an *Answer*, an **Uncontested Praecipe**, and the **Vital Statistics Form**; however, the clerk does not have packages of forms for a contested divorce or for a *Separation Agreement*. Be sure to ask the clerk for a copy of the court's divorce booklet. If your spouse cooperates, you can file all of these forms at once to expedite your divorce. Be sure to let the clerk know that you have an uncontested divorce and are filing the **COMPLAINT**, *Answer*, and **UNCONTESTED PRAECIPE** at the same time. The following sections will describe the uncontested divorce process, explain the required forms, and give you instructions for completing the forms.

FILING YOUR COMPLAINT

File your **COMPLAINT FOR ABSOLUTE DIVORCE** (form DC–3, p.326) and the associated documents with the clerk of the Domestic Relations Branch of the Family Court.

Clerk of Domestic Relations Branch
Family Court
Room 4230
District of Columbia Superior Court
Moultrie Courthouse
500 Indiana Avenue, NW
Washington, DC 20001

Business hours are from 9:00 a.m. to 4:00 p.m., Monday through Friday. There is a filing fee of $80. The clerk will process your **COMPLAINT**, give it a case number, open the court's file, and return it to you with two copies of a *Summons*.

SERVICE OF PROCESS

Serve the **COMPLAINT** and *Summons* by certified mail to your spouse or by hand delivery to your spouse or someone of suitable age and discretion living at your spouse's residence. Remember that you cannot personally serve your spouse. You have to have a friend or a professional process server do it. Once the **COMPLAINT** is served, file the **AFFIDAVIT OF SERVICE** with the court.

ANSWER

Once served, your spouse has to respond to your **COMPLAINT**, with an *Answer* or other pleading, within twenty days, or he or she will be found in default. There is no form *Answer* for a contested divorce. If you are the one served with a **COMPLAINT**, and you want to contest it, you will have to prepare your own *Answer* admitting the statements in your spouse's **COMPLAINT** you agree with, and denying those you do not. You may also bring to the court's attention facts in your *Answer* that you think your spouse omitted in the **COMPLAINT**.

PRAECIPE FOR UNCONTESTED DIVORCE

If your spouse is cooperating, both of you can file a **PRAECIPE FOR UNCONTESTED DIVORCE**. (see form DC–14, p.364.) A *praecipe* is a letter to the clerk asking him or her to do something. In this case, you are asking the clerk to set a hearing date on your divorce as soon as possible, since it is uncontested. Complete the form as follows.

- ◈ Put the case number where it says "Jacket No." and fill in the date at the top of the form.

- ◈ Fill in the names of the plaintiff and defendant as they appear on the **COMPLAINT** on the next lines of the form.

- ◈ Provide names, addresses, telephone numbers, and signatures at the bottom. The plaintiff completes the box on the left and the defendant completes the box on the right.

To speed things up, the **COMPLAINT**, *Answer*, and **PRAECIPE FOR UNCONTESTED DIVORCE** can all be filed at the same time. You should draw the clerk's attention to the fact that the **COMPLAINT**, *Answer*, and **PRAECIPE** are being filed, and that the case is ready to be scheduled for an uncontested divorce.

Go to Chapter 17 for information on how to prepare for your uncontested divorce hearing.

Preparing for the Uncontested Divorce Hearing

There are certain things you need to know and forms you must fill out before your uncontested divorce hearing in each jurisdiction. This chapter explains the steps you must take before your hearing.

MARYLAND UNCONTESTED DIVORCE

In an uncontested divorce case in Maryland, the plaintiff needs to appear in court to testify. The defendant may appear, but is not required to be present, unless the defendant is a spouse who wants to change her name back to her maiden name. Uncontested divorces are usually heard by a *family law master*. At the hearing for an uncontested divorce, you must have the following items.

- ✪ *Witness Information Form.* Have your witness print his or her name and address on it, and mark whether the witness is for the plaintiff or defendant. Get this form from the court clerk.

- ✪ **REPORT OF ABSOLUTE DIVORCE OR ANNULMENT OF MARRIAGE.** This is statistical information for your divorce. (see form MD–12, p.252.) The form is reproduced in this book for your information, but the court will not accept a copy, because the original is blue in color. You must obtain an original blue form from the court. Because the form says it must be typewritten, you need to request it before the hearing. Complete this form as follows.

◈ Lines 1–4. Write the husband's name, address, birthplace, and age.

◈ *Lines 5–8.* Provide the same information for the wife, as well as her maiden name.

◈ *Lines 9–10.* Place and date of marriage.

◈ *Line 11.* Write the date of separation.

◈ *Line 12.* Indicate the number of children you have together.

◈ *Line 13.* Indicate whether the husband or wife is the plaintiff.

◈ *Line 14.* Write the name and address of the plaintiff's attorney, if applicable.

◈ *Line 15.* Explain how custody is being awarded.

◈ *Line 16.* Write the grounds for divorce.

◈ *Line 17.* Include the title and county of court.

◈ *Lines 18–23.* This section will be completed by the clerk.

◈ *Lines 24–26.* Include the number of marriages, date of divorce of previous marriages, race, and education for husband and wife.

✪ *Separation Agreement* (if you did not file it with the **COMPLAINT**).

✪ *Marriage License.* You will need a certified copy of your marriage license or you must present a witness who was present at your wedding.

✪ **SUBMISSION FOR JUDGMENT OF DIVORCE**. If you and your spouse want to waive the ten-day period for filing exceptions so that your divorce becomes final earlier, you can file a **SUBMISSION**. (see form MD–13, p.253.) Complete the **SUBMISSION FOR JUDGMENT OF DIVORCE** by filling in the case caption and signing it as plaintiff or defendant. Both parties must sign for this form to be accepted, so if your spouse will not be present at the hearing, you must obtain his or her signature in advance.

Corroborating Witness

Whenever you must prove something in court, you need witnesses. In divorce cases, you need to have *corroboration* (support) of your proof, even if your spouse is not disputing the grounds. Corroboration usually means a witness other than your spouse in addition to yourself. You can corroborate the wedding with a copy of the marriage certificate or a witness who was present at the wedding. A notarized *Separation Agreement* dated prior to the filing of the *Complaint for Divorce* is corroboration that the separation was mutual and voluntary. You need to prove and corroborate every allegation in your *Complaint*.

You can request a *subpoena for witnesses* from the court clerk. The subpoena will help the witnesses get time off work to appear in court. If the witnesses do not appear in court, and you did not subpoena them, you cannot necessarily have the case put off until you can get them to appear in court. Your case could be dismissed.

MARYLAND UNCONTESTED DIVORCE

❏ *Witness Information Form.* Have your witness print his or her name and address on it and mark whether the witness is for the plaintiff or defendant.

❏ **REPORT OF ABSOLUTE DIVORCE OR ANNULMENT OF MARRIAGE.** This is statistical information for your divorce. (see form MD–12, p.252.)

❏ *Separation Agreement* (if you did not file it with the **COMPLAINT**).

❏ *Marriage License.* A certified copy of your marriage license or a witness present at your wedding.

❏ **SUBMISSION FOR JUDGMENT OF DIVORCE.** If you and your spouse want to waive the ten-day period for filing exceptions so that your divorce becomes final earlier, you can file a **SUBMISSION.** (see form MD–13, p.253.)

VIRGINIA UNCONTESTED DIVORCE

Unlike other lawsuits, even an uncontested divorce in Virginia requires a hearing at which the plaintiff must prove the essential facts of the case in order to show that he or she is entitled to a divorce. The hearing can be in front of a specially appointed commissioner or in front of a judge (referred to as an *ore tenus hearing*). To conduct your uncontested divorce hearing in Virginia you will need the following documents.

NOTE: *While it is possible to obtain a divorce by taking testimony of witnesses at a deposition, divorce by deposition is not recommended.*

✪ **DECREE OF REFERENCE.** (see form VA–17, p.298 or VA–18, p.299.) If a hearing before a commissioner is desired and available, the plaintiff should file a **DECREE OF REFERENCE.** The commissioner procedure requires the payment of the commissioner's fee and the court reporter's fee, which will usually total several hundred dollars. Complete this form as follows.

⬧ Enter the name of the court, the names of the parties, and the case number.

⬧ Enter the title of the pleading, "Decree of Reference."

⬧ The first paragraph states the procedural history of the case to date, that is, that the plaintiff filed a **COMPLAINT FOR DIVORCE** and served it upon the defendant, and the defendant filed an *Answer*.

⬧ The second paragraph states that the court concludes that the case has matured and can be referred to a commissioner in chancery.

⬧ The next paragraph is the court's order. Leave the space for the commissioner's name blank.

◉ **REPORT OF DIVORCE OR ANNULMENT (FORM VS-4)** Form VS-4 gathers statistical information about divorces. (see form VA–16, p.297.) Complete the form using a typewriter or printing in black ink as follows.

⬧ *Line 1.* Enter the court location.

⬧ *Lines 2–8.* Enter the husband's full name, Social Security number, place of birth, date of birth, race, number of this marriage for husband, number indicating husband's highest educational level attained, and husband's home address.

⬧ *Lines 9–15.* Enter the wife's full name, Social Security number, place of birth, date of birth, race, number of this marriage for wife, number indicating wife's highest educational level attained, and wife's home address.

⬧ *Line 16.* Enter the place of the marriage.

⬧ *Line 17.* Enter the date of the marriage.

⬧ *Line 18.* Enter the number of children under age 18 in the family.

⬥ *Line 19.* Enter who was awarded custody of the children, or how many to each spouse, if appropriate.

⬥ *Line 20.* Enter the date of separation.

⬥ *Line 21.* Check box to indicate who is the plaintiff.

⬥ *Line 22.* Check box to indicate to whom the court granted the divorce.

⬥ *Line 23.* State the grounds (for example, "one-year separation").

⬥ *Line 24.* Sign where indicated, enter your name and address, and check the "Petitioner" box.

✪ **FINAL DECREE OF DIVORCE**. (see form VA–19, p.300 or form VA–20, p.302.)

The decree is the court's decision and order granting your divorce. When a party files a proposed decree, the party prepares the decree to say what he or she wants the court to rule. In your divorce case, there are certain findings and decisions you want the judge to make, and there are certain things that the law requires to be in the decree. If you and your spouse have children, there are very specific statutory requirements the decree must meet with respect to the child support provisions.

Complete the **FINAL DECREE OF DIVORCE** as follows.

⬥ The **DECREE** has a caption, style of the case, case number, and heading like other court papers.

⬥ The text of the **DECREE** begins with an introductory statement that explains what happened in the case before the hearing, such as "a complaint for divorce was filed, and properly served (or service was accepted or waived), and an answer was filed."

❖ The next part of the **DECREE** sets forth the judge's findings of fact. It is traditionally introduced by the phrase "IT APPEARING THAT." This section relates the statements of fact in your **COMPLAINT** regarding residency, age, Social Security or DMV number, military status, date and place of marriage, children's names and dates of birth, date of separation, that at least one party intended that the separation be permanent, that there is no reasonable likelihood of reconciliation, and that the parties entered into a written agreement, if applicable.

❖ In cases involving child support or spousal support, the law requires that detailed notices and information be in the **DECREE**. This section should be reproduced and filled in exactly like form VA–20 on p.302 in the Virginia forms appendix. Do not paraphrase or summarize. All required information must be set forth even if it seems to be inapplicable to your case. However, for good cause, such as fear of violence or harassment, you can withhold your address. Complete this portion of the **DECREE** as follows.

◈ At paragraph 3, list the required information regarding children.

◈ At paragraph 4, name the person responsible for paying support and list all the information regarding both spouses' employment (or state none), even though only one spouse is responsible for paying support.

◈ At paragraph 5, fill in the information regarding occupational licenses or check the line indicating neither party holds such license.

◈ At paragraph 7, check the appropriate line.

❖ The next section is the court's decisions and orders in the case. Each paragraph contains one decision or order and is introduced by the (traditionally) capitalized word "ORDERED." In an uncontested divorce, there will be at least two such ordering paragraphs, one granting the divorce, and one affirming and ratifying the agreement and incorporating it into the decree.

❖ The last section of the **Decree** informs the clerk's office whether the case should be closed or held open for further proceedings.

❖ There is a signature line for the judge.

❖ At the bottom left, the **Decree** has signature space for the party seeking the decree or both parties below the phrase "ASK FOR THIS." If the defendant has not waived service of process and will not be at the hearing, it is important that he or she endorse the proposed decree. If not, the plaintiff must serve notice of the divorce hearing upon the defendant in the same manner as original process is served.

VIRGINIA UNCONTESTED DIVORCE

❏ **Decree of Reference**. (see form VA–17, p.298 or VA–18, p.299.) If a hearing before a commissioner is desired and available, plaintiff should file a **Decree of Reference**.

❏ **Report of Divorce or Annulment (form VS-4)**. Form VS-4 gathers statistical information about divorces. (see form VA–16, p.297.)

❏ **Final Decree of Divorce**. (see form VA–19, p.300 or form VA–20, p.302.)

DISTRICT OF COLUMBIA UNCONTESTED DIVORCE

Usually, *commissioners* preside over uncontested divorces in the District of Columbia. However, both you *and* your spouse must sign a **Consent Form** agreeing to have your case heard by a commissioner instead of a judge.

✪ **Consent Form.** You will both need to appear at the hearing where the clerk will give you a **Consent Form**, or if only one of you will be there, you need to bring the **Consent Form** to the hearing signed by both of you. (see form DC–15, p.365.) You will also need the original or a certified copy of your marriage certificate. The court clerk will ask for these documents together with **Findings of Fact** (see following paragraph) just before the hearing. If you do not have them, you probably will have to come back another day.

✪ **Findings of Fact, Conclusions of Law and Judgment of Absolute Divorce.** This will become your *Final Judgment of Divorce* after you give your testimony and evidence to the commissioner at the uncontested divorce hearing, and prove all the statements in your **Complaint**. The court will mail you a copy signed by the commissioner after the clerk enters it in the court files. Complete the **Findings of Fact, Conclusions of Law and Judgment of Absolute Divorce** (form DC–16, p.366) as follows.

⟡ Use the same names, addresses, and case number as the **Complaint**, and include Social Security numbers for you and your spouse, to fill in the top section of the form.

⟡ The first part of the form is entitled "FINDINGS OF FACT." These are the facts about your marriage and divorce that the commissioner will find to be true from your testimony and evidence. The commissioner will fill in the blanks in the first paragraph with the date of the hearing.

⟡ At paragraph 1, either you or your spouse must have been a resident of the District of Columbia when you filed the **Complaint**, and must have lived there continuously for the previous six months. If you or both of you meet this requirement, write "Plaintiff." If only your spouse meets the requirement, write "Defendant."

⟡ At paragraph 2, fill in the date and place of your marriage, making sure it matches your marriage certificate.

❖ At paragraph 3, state the date you and your spouse stopped living together and were no longer having sexual relations together.

❖ At paragraph 4, fill in the number of children born or adopted to you and your spouse together (but not children from other relationships), and list their names and birthdates.

❖ At paragraph 5, if there have been any earlier orders concerning the children, such as custody, visitation, or child support orders, provide the case numbers, dates, and what the orders stated.

❖ At paragraph 6, if the children are living with you, insert "Plaintiff." If they are living with your spouse, and that is what you have agreed, write "Defendant."

❖ At paragraph 7, if your spouse has visitation with the children, write "Defendant." If you have visitation, write "Plaintiff." Write the agreed-upon visitation schedule, or if you have not agreed, you may leave this blank for the commissioner to complete.

❖ Paragraph 8 states the terms of any agreement you have reached with your spouse about child support. Fill in who pays whom. For example, if your spouse has agreed to pay you, then fill in the blanks to show that the "Defendant" will pay. Then, put the amount and how often it will be paid.

❖ Paragraph 9 states that there are no property rights for the court to decide. If you have a *Separation Agreement,* add to the end of this sentence "because the parties have entered into a written Agreement dated [insert date] settling all issues between them."

❖ Paragraph 10 states that there is no reasonable prospect of your getting back together with your spouse.

❖ Fill in paragraph 11 if you want the court to restore your birth name or prior name.

❖ The second part of the form is entitled "CONCLUSIONS OF LAW." This is where the court finds you are entitled to a divorce based upon the "FINDINGS OF FACT."

❖ The third part of the form is entitled "JUDGMENT." These are the orders of the court concerning your divorce. The commissioner will fill in the dates in the first paragraph.

❖ Paragraph 1 grants your divorce. Fill in the present married names of you and your spouse, which should be the same as the caption of the **COMPLAINT**.

❖ Paragraph 2 orders custody and visitation. Fill in whether you (Plaintiff) or your spouse (Defendant) will have custody. List your children's names and then the party having visitation. If the party with custody is you (Plaintiff), then your spouse (Defendant) will have visitation. Set out the visitation schedule if you have a *Separation Agreement*, or leave it blank if you do not.

❖ Paragraph 3 orders child support. Fill it out the same as you did paragraph 8 in the "FINDINGS OF FACT" section. If your spouse is paying you child support, put "Plaintiff" in the last blank. Put "Defendant" if you are paying your spouse child support.

❖ Paragraph 4 does not require anything.

❖ If you want a name change, fill in paragraph 5 the same way as you did paragraph 11 in the "FINDINGS OF FACT" section. Otherwise, leave it blank.

❖ The judge will sign the form.

❖ Under "Copies to," fill in the names and addresses for you and your spouse.

DISTRICT OF COLUMBIA UNCONTESTED DIVORCE

❏   **CONSENT FORM**. You will both need to appear at the hearing, where the clerk will give you a **CONSENT FORM**, or if only one of you will be there, you need to bring the **CONSENT FORM** to the hearing signed by both of you. (see form DC–15, p.365.)

❏   **FINDINGS OF FACT, CONCLUSIONS OF LAW AND JUDGMENT OF ABSOLUTE DIVORCE**. This will become your *Decree of Divorce* after you give your testimony and evidence to the commissioner at the uncontested divorce hearing, and prove all the statements in your **COMPLAINT**. (see form DC–16, p.366.)

The Uncontested Divorce Hearing

Court is a formal place. This chapter discusses some general rules for appearing your best in court in any of the three jurisdictions. Courtroom procedures for each jurisdiction are also discussed.

COURTROOM BEHAVIOR

Dress neatly, modestly, and nicely for all court appearances. It is unfortunate that people judge others by the clothes they wear, but they do. If you want the master to think you are one of the "good guys," then dress like a good guy. Women should wear little or no makeup or jewelry. Men should wear suits and ties.

Do not chew gum or smoke. Walk and stand erect. Do not slouch in the witness stand or slur your words. Be serious and forceful but not aggressive. Do not cover your mouth or avert your eyes.

Look at the master, commissioner, or judge when you talk. Remember, you are trying to convince the master, commissioner, or judge to give you what you want, so talk to him or her—not to your spouse or your spouse's attorney.

Be polite. It makes a good impression on the court. Answer "yes sir" or "madam," and address the master, commissioner, or judge as "your honor."

PUBLIC RECORDS

All papers filed in your case and all testimony in your case are theoretically matters of public record, and the public has a right to see or hear it. However, the only people you are likely to see at court are other people who are getting divorced themselves that day, and they are far more concerned with their own problems than with your case. Following are the specific courtroom procedures for each jurisdiction.

MARYLAND HEARING

The master's clerk will call your case by name and number. You and your witness will come forward to the tables in front of the master's bench.

The master will ask you to introduce yourselves and then raise your right hands to be sworn in. The master will ask you to prove, and your witness to corroborate, by your testimony and documents, the allegations in your *Complaint*.

At the end of the hearing, the master will give his or her findings and recommendations that you be divorced. Once these are signed by the judge, they become your *Decree of Divorce*. It will be entered on the court docket and mailed to you a couple of weeks later.

VIRGINIA HEARING

The clerk's office can tell you whether there are commissioners appointed to hear divorce cases in your county. Where it is available, the commissioner procedure has several advantages. One advantage of this procedure is early and easier scheduling. Another advantage is that many commissioners will conduct the hearing and ask all the questions. If so, the plaintiff only has to appear with the witness and listen to the questions and answer them truthfully.

Once the commissioner is appointed, call his or her office to schedule the hearing and find out whether the commissioner will conduct the examination of the witness. If not, you have to prepare your questions in advance. The hearing is usually in the commissioner's office, not in court.

After the hearing, the commissioner will prepare and file a written report and send you a copy. If all has gone as expected, the commissioner will report facts entitling the parties to a divorce.

Be sure to review the report carefully to make sure that the essential facts are correct. Check spellings of names and dates of marriage, birth, and separation. If there is a problem, contact the commissioner's office and request that it be corrected. If it is not corrected several days before the objection period runs, you may file an objection to the report. After the commissioner's report is filed and the objection period has run, file the proposed *Final Decree of Divorce* with the clerk of the court. (see Chapter 15.)

Appearing Before a Judge

When no commissioner is appointed, you have more work to do in preparing for and conducting the divorce hearing. First, you should prepare a proposed **FINAL DECREE**. (see form VA–19, p.300 or VA–20, p.302.) The facts that the **FINAL DECREE** recites as "APPEARING" are the facts to be proven at the hearing. You and your witness will testify to these facts. Also, write out a list of questions for which those facts are the answers.

The facts must be proven by the testimony of the plaintiff and a corroborating witness, not the defendant. In selecting a witness, the plaintiff should choose an adult who can testify to all the essential facts from personal knowledge. Pick a person who will take the matter seriously, listen carefully to you before and at the hearing, appear on time, and testify truthfully.

Be sure to ask the corroborating witness all these questions before the hearing so that you know what the witness will answer. If the witness does not know the answer or remembers the events differently from you, check to make sure your memory is correct and refresh his or her memory before the date of trial, or if necessary, find another witness.

In addition to witnesses, two exhibits are generally required—the marriage certificate and the *Separation Agreement*.

You can give your own testimony in short declarative sentences. You can write these out, or if you are comfortable with it, use a copy of the **Final Decree** as your talking points for your testimony. Be careful not to leave out any essential facts.

Arrive at the courthouse well before the time your hearing is scheduled and take care that your witness does so as well. If you are late and miss your call, you will have to sit through the entire docket before your case is called again. In some courts, this could include sitting through hearings on contested motions or even trials of contested cases. Go into the courtroom and observe a few cases if possible.

When your case is called, go to the appropriate table or lectern or approach the judge's bench, depending on what you have observed. When you address the judge, be serious and respectful. State your name and that you are the plaintiff in the case. You will be sworn in and then may proceed with your case. Tell the judge you are your first witness. The judge may or may not direct you to the witness seat. In either case, give your testimony in a serious, businesslike way.

You should look at the judge when you give your testimony, but you can refer to the proposed decree or other prepared notes. Identify the agreement and the certificate of marriage by telling the judge what they are. When testifying, try to remember that you are a witness and not the person conducting the case. When you are through testifying, indicate this to the judge and return to your role as the person conducting the case. Ask the judge to accept the agreement and the certificate of marriage into evidence. Then, call your corroborating witness to testify.

Ask the witness the questions in the order you asked them before court, and use the same words. If the witness is nervous and cannot remember something, you can probably get away with what lawyers call *leading questions*. A leading question is one that suggests the answer, such as "Isn't it true that...." When you are finished with your questions to the corroborating witness, tell the court that concludes your case.

Ask the court to grant your divorce and to ratify and approve the agreement and incorporate but not merge it into its decree. If appropriate, ask the judge to restore you to the use of your birth given name.

Final Decree of Divorce

After the judge gives his or her ruling, thank the judge. In most counties, the judge will sign the **FINAL DECREE OF DIVORCE** at the conclusion of the hearing if the divorce is granted. You may be able to walk the file to the clerk's office and leave with two certified copies of the **FINAL DECREE OF DIVORCE** that day. Ask the clerk's office prior to the hearing whether you can do this. If so, ask the judge after he or she signs the **FINAL DECREE OF DIVORCE** for it to be taken to the clerk's office. Once the **FINAL DECREE OF DIVORCE** is signed by the judge and entered into the court's records, you are divorced.

DISTRICT OF COLUMBIA HEARING

You will receive a notice of the hearing date in the mail. The plaintiff has to move the case forward and provide evidence, so he or she needs to be there. The defendant is invited to the hearing, but does not have to attend.

No Corroborating Witness

You do not need a corroborating witness in the District of Columbia, but you must prove your case. The plaintiff can testify to prove his or her six months' residency in the District of Columbia, but if the **COMPLAINT FOR ABSOLUTE DIVORCE** is based on the defendant's residency in the District of Columbia, you may need a witness to corroborate that if the defendant is not present. (see form DC–3, p.326.) The marriage license can corroborate your marriage. If you do not have it, then you need a witness who was at your wedding. The plaintiff can prove the other issues, such as the separation, through his or her testimony. You do not need to have the *Separation Agreement* at court, but a copy is usually introduced as an exhibit to corroborate your testimony. If there are no children, alimony, or property issues to be decided by the court, you can simply say so.

Hearing

The commissioner's clerk will call your case by name and number. Come forward to the tables in front of the commissioner's bench. The clerk will ask you to raise your right hand and be sworn in. The commissioner will ask you to introduce yourself. The commissioner will ask you questions and you will give testimony to prove the allegations in your **COMPLAINT**.

The commissioner will then give his or her findings, usually reading from the proposed order that you have submitted. The commissioner will sign the order, and you are divorced. A copy will be mailed to you after the clerk enters it in the court records.

Preparing for a Contested Divorce Trial

A contested case begins the same way as an uncontested divorce in all three jurisdictions—with a *Complaint*, service of process, and an *Answer* by your spouse. If the *Answer* from your spouse denies any allegation in your *Complaint*, then you have a contested case. Preparing for a contested divorce trial is similar in the three jurisdictions, and the differences are pointed out in this chapter.

SETTLEMENT NEGOTIATIONS

As you read this, keep in mind that settlement negotiations can go on simultaneously with litigation, and over 90% of contested cases settle and turn into uncontested cases before trial. While it is not impossible for you to try a contested case without a lawyer, this is the time to consider hiring one.

Scheduling Conference

The court will notify you of a *scheduling conference* in Maryland and Virginia, or an *initial conference* in the District of Columbia, as soon as the *Affidavit of Service* or *Answer* has been filed. At the scheduling conference, the court will set various dates for your trial. The court will not hear argument about your case at this point.

Custody Disputes

If custody is disputed, the court may divide the case into two trials and give you two schedules. The first trial will be the custody trial, and it will determine all issues related to the children, such as child custody, visitation, and support. The other trial will be the merits trial, and it will determine everything else, including the remaining financial issues, such as alimony and property division, as well as grounds for divorce.

Parenting Classes

The court may order *parenting classes* if custody is contested. These are usually taught by mental health professionals for two evening sessions in a classroom setting.

Custody Mediation

The court will order two sessions with a custody *mediator* if custody is contested. The mediators are mental health professionals on the court staff, and they have a high rate of success in settling custody cases.

Alternative Dispute Resolution

The court may also require you to participate in *alternative dispute resolution* (ADR) unless there has been domestic violence or you both agree that it would be futile. ADR facilitators are experienced family lawyers who will attempt to help you settle the financial issues in your case.

Pendente Lite Hearing

If you need temporary support, you will need to work with the master or commissioner to set a *pendente lite hearing*. The lawyers and master or commissioner may refer to this as a *p.l. hearing*. Be sure to tell the master or commissioner the temporary relief you need, such as visitation, child support, spousal support, expert witness fees, or attorney's fees.

Scheduling Order

At the end of the scheduling conference, the clerk will usually give you several papers about your case, including a scheduling order. Check the scheduling order before you leave the courtroom to make sure that everything you asked for is listed.

The scheduling order will also set dates for identification of expert witnesses, cutoff of discovery, and a pretrial hearing. You will need to tell the other side—in writing—the names, addresses, and telephone numbers of your expert witnesses, and what they will be testifying about.

Pendente Lite Relief

The master or commissioner may send you to an attorney facilitator at the scheduling conference to see if a settlement can be reached as to pendente lite relief. If you can settle with the facilitator, you can avoid the pendente lite hearing.

Experts

Expert witnesses may be desirable in many contested cases. For example, a vocational expert can testify about potential earning ability of a spouse seeking alimony. An appraiser may testify about the value of a house, furniture, or a business (although an owner may testify as to his or her opinion of values too). An appropriate therapist may testify as to grounds for divorce or custody and visitation. A financial planner or accountant may testify as to financial needs.

Discovery

Discovery can be described as interrogatories, document requests, requests for admissions, and depositions. These must all be concluded within a certain time, typically three to six months, unless extended by the court. You have to ask for discovery. Then, if your spouse fails to respond to discovery or responds inefficiently, you may ask the court for an order compelling your spouse to respond. If your spouse still fails to respond, you can ask for sanctions, such as striking your spouse's pleadings or payment of attorney's fees if you have an attorney.

Each party may discover information about the other party's case. Discovery responses are due within thirty days from when they are served in Maryland and the District of Columbia, and twenty-one days in Virginia, plus three days if they are mailed. Time is counted by counting the day after service as day number one. If the last day is a weekend or holiday, then you have until the next business day to respond.

Interrogatories. Interrogatories are written questions that must be answered under oath. Parties are limited to thirty interrogatories in Maryland and Virginia and forty interrogatories in the District of Columbia.

Requests for Documents. You can ask that your spouse produce, for your inspection and copying, documents related to the issues in your divorce. These would include bank and business records.

Requests for Admissions. You can ask your spouse to admit facts.

Depositions. You can ask oral questions of your spouse under oath. A court reporter will prepare a transcript for use in court.

Pretrial Conference

The pretrial conference is when the master, commissioner, or judge sets the trial date. The parties are required to present pretrial statements in Maryland, which inform the court about such matters as mediation, discovery, pending motions, disputes, agreements, trial exhibits, and trial witnesses. The master, commissioner, or judge will also usually ask about the possibility of settlement. In the District of Columbia, you are required to meet with the opposing counsel two weeks before the trial. You are also required to exchange copies of exhibits and an exhibit summary one week before trial.

Maryland Joint Statement of Parties Concerning Marital and Nonmarital Property. In Maryland (but not Virginia or the District of Columbia), you are required to file a **JOINT STATEMENT** at the pretrial conference. (see form MD–14, p.254.) This form is very important, because the judge will use it at trial as a checklist to divide your property.

Prepare your own version of the **JOINT STATEMENT** before the pretrial conference and mail it to your spouse. Send it with a transmittal letter inviting your spouse to sign, and keep a copy for yourself. If your spouse does not cooperate in preparing a statement, then file the one you prepared at the pretrial conference.

To complete the **JOINT STATEMENT**, you will need the information from your **FINANCIAL STATEMENT**. (see form MD–1, p.255.) Then, follow these steps.

◈ Fill in the top part of the form with the court, names and addresses of you and your spouse, and the case number.

◈ In section 1, in the first column, list all property from your **FINANCIAL STATEMENT** that you and your spouse agree is marital property. In general, this includes any property acquired during the marriage. (The exceptions are listed in section 2 of the form.) Include, if applicable, real estate, bank accounts, stock, automobiles, furniture and furnishings, jewelry, and any other property.

◈ In the second column, write how the property is titled. You may write "J" for jointly held, "H" for held in the husband's name, or "W" for held in the wife's name. There is a place for your assertion and your spouse's assertion. You can either give your opinion of value or have the property valued by an appraiser.

◈ In the third column, put your assertion of value and your spouse's assertion. It is acceptable to write "unknown" for your spouse's assertion or leave it blank if you do not know. You should place your best estimate of value in the space for your assertion.

◈ In the fourth column, fill in any debt directly attributable to an item of property (for example, the balance remaining on your mortgage goes on the line with your house, and the balance of your automobile loan goes on the line with your automobile).

◈ In section 2, list in the left-hand column all property that you and your spouse agree is nonmarital, which means any property that was:

• acquired by one of you before the marriage;

• an inheritance or gift from someone other than you or your spouse;

• excluded by agreement; or,

• directly traceable to one of these sources.

◈ For the remaining columns in section 2, follow the instructions in section 1.

◈ In section 3, list in the left-hand column any property about which you and your spouse have a dispute concerning its marital or nonmarital status.

◈ For the remaining columns in section 3, follow the instructions in section 1.

◈ Sign and date the form as plaintiff or defendant as the case may be.

TRIAL PREPARATION

To help you prepare for trial, follow these tips.

❏ Prepare a trial notebook before trial. Write out your opening statement, all your questions for witnesses, and your closing argument. You can have a section on discovery and a section on legal research. You will be glad you prepared so well when you are in trial.

❏ Review any documents you will refer to during your testimony.

❏ Review any statement you made.

❏ Visit the court before your case to make yourself more comfortable about your court appearance. After you watch a few cases, you will see that no one dies or is seriously injured when testifying. You will feel better when it is your turn.

❏ Try not to discuss your case with anyone before trial if you can help it. One of the best ways for the opposition to trip you up is to get a statement you made before trial (especially to so-called mutual friends) that does not coincide exactly with your testimony at trial.

❏ Call the court clerk a couple of days before court to make sure your case will be heard. Often, cases are continued by the court for one reason or another, and you do not want to waste a trip if it is avoidable.

chapter 20

The Contested Divorce Trial

This chapter describes the basics of a contested divorce trial. The procedures for a contested divorce trial are basically the same in Maryland, Virginia, and the District of Columbia, with the exception of the Maryland *Joint Property Statement*. However, each court and each judge will do things a little differently.

ELEMENTS OF THE TRIAL

At trial, the parties present witnesses, testimony, and documents called *exhibits*. The plaintiff goes first, and then the defendant. Each side can ask questions of the witnesses. At the conclusion of the trial, the judge will usually grant a divorce and give a decision as to custody, visitations, child support, alimony, property, and legal fees.

Rules of Evidence

The court uses the *rules of evidence* at trial. These are intricate legal rules to which volumes of books are devoted. You will generally be able to maneuver these rules in a divorce if you remember that only testimony based on personal knowledge is permitted. You cannot testify about what someone else told you—this is called *hearsay* and is not allowed.

NOTE: *An important exception to this rule is that you can testify about what your spouse said.*

Documents like letters, reports, and appraisals require special treatment at trial. They may be objected to by the other side if there is not a live witness in court to authenticate them. The proper way to handle a document is to have the clerk mark it as an exhibit (e.g., "Plaintiff's Exhibit No. 1"). Show it to the other side, ask the witness to identify it, and say to the judge, "Your Honor, I move the admission of Plaintiff's Exhibit No. 1 into evidence." The judge cannot base his or her decision on an exhibit that you fail to move into evidence.

A contested trial starts with the clerk calling the case name and number. The judge will ask both parties to introduce themselves and inquire as to whether they are ready for trial.

Preliminary Matters

Preliminary matters, which would include any unresolved motions, are addressed first. The *rule on witnesses*, which you usually must ask for to get, requires all witnesses except the parties to leave the courtroom until they are called. That is so they cannot listen to the testimony and be tempted to change their own testimony.

Opening Statements

The judge will then ask for *opening statements*. The plaintiff goes first and the defendant follows. Use the opening statement to give the judge a summary of your case. Tell him or her the important issues and what evidence you will present. Start your statements like this: "Good Morning, Your Honor. May it please the court, the evidence will show...."

The Plaintiff's Case

The plaintiff's case begins next and the plaintiff calls the first witness, usually him- or herself. The following describes a contested trial from the plaintiff's point of view.

Direct examination. You will take the stand and be sworn in by the court clerk. This is called *direct examination*. If you do not have an attorney, the judge may ask you questions or allow you to speak in a narrative and tell your story. Your testimony will generally follow this outline:

- the parties (your name, age, address, how long you have lived at that address, and occupation, and your spouse's name, age, address, and occupation);

- the marriage (date, place, and your marriage certificate);

- the children (names, birthdates, and which parent the children are residing with);

- grounds for divorce;

- your financial statement;

- the joint property statement, and your opinions on and evidence of values of property;

- your contributions to the marriage, both monetary and nonmonetary; and,

- what you want in the way of custody, visitation, child support, alimony, property division, and legal fees.

Cross-examination. The defendant or his or her attorney will then cross-examine you. They can ask you questions about your testimony and try to undermine it. Listen to the question and keep your answers short.

TIPS FOR YOUR TESTIMONY

Here are a few tips for *your* testimony.

- Stay calm and make all your remarks to the judge, not your spouse or your spouse's attorney, no matter how provoked you may be by the other side.

- Do not be a smart aleck, or appear nervous, scared, argumentative, or angry. If your adversary baits you into becoming angry, he or she is probably trying to set you up for a trap, so keep your cool. (Lose your temper, and you may lose your case.)

✪ Tell the truth. It is going to come out eventually anyway, and it is better coming from you than from the other side. (If the other side catches you in a lie, you may lose your case.)

✪ Listen carefully to all questions. Pause, make sure you understand the question, then take your time and answer that question. You cannot give a truthful and accurate answer if you do not understand the question. If you ask, the attorney will repeat the question.

✪ Do not tell the court "I think" or what it "must have been." The court does not normally care what you think or what could have happened. It wants to know what actually happened. However, if you estimate a time or a cost, make sure the court knows it is an estimate. If you make a mistake during your testimony, correct it as soon as possible. Politely say something such as, "May I correct something I said earlier?"

✪ When the other side asks you a question you do not know the answer to, say "I do not know." Witnesses are often trapped by being led into areas about which their knowledge is inadequate. They try to save face and end up making a statement that is incorrect. This gives the other side what it needs to shoot them down. You can usually avoid the problem by saying "I do not know." In cross-examinations, most questions can be answered with yes, no, or I do not know, or with a simple sentence.

✪ Do not try to play with words. When you say things like "to the best of my recollection," people may think you are getting ready to lie to them. Do not volunteer information. Do not let the other attorney pull you into testifying more than you need to by standing there looking at you, waiting for you to add material. When you are finished with your answer, stop talking.

✪ One of the oldest tricks in the book is for the other side to ask you if you have discussed the case with anyone else. If the other sides asks you, then tell the truth—you have. The other side is not asking you if you have fabricated the story, but it is asking you if you have talked about it. Only a fool would go to court without having discussed the case with his or her witnesses.

☢ Do not let the other side trick you by asking you if you are willing to swear to what you are saying. You already did when you took the oath as a witness.

Redirect examination. You can then ask the judge for permission to explain any answer you gave on cross-examination. This is called redirect examination.

Witnesses Next, you present and question your corroborating witness and any expert witnesses. Again, the other side will cross-examine your witnesses and you may conduct redirect examination.

If you are seeking support, you need to provide your spouse's income. Call the defendant as a witness and ask him or her to identify his or her financial statement or tax return.

Then, tell the judge that is all you have for your case, or say, as lawyers do, "Your Honor, that submits the plaintiff's case."

Defendant's Case The defendant will then present his or her case, and you may cross-examine the defendant and the defendant's witnesses.

Rebuttal At the close of the defendant's case, you can present witnesses to *rebut,* or contradict, anything the defendant's witnesses said.

Closing Arguments Both sides then make a *closing argument* to the judge summarizing the evidence in their favor. The plaintiff goes first, the defendant follows, and then the plaintiff can respond to the defendant's argument.

Decision The judge will usually announce a *decision* right away (*from the bench*), but he or she may need some time in more complex cases (*taken under advisement*). You may not like the judge's decision. The judge may not always believe everything you said, may not understand part of your case, or may just disagree with you. Judges are not always right, but they make the decisions. You can accept the judge's decision or you can appeal it. If you decide to appeal, contact an attorney.

Custody

During or after your divorce, you may encounter disagreement over custody. Custody cases are the cruelest and most destructive of litigations. Be sure that the children would be significantly better off with you than the other parent before you get involved in a custody fight. Custody cases are expensive in both emotional and legal costs. A custody case will automatically double your legal fees. The damage caused by winning a custody case is great; the damage caused by losing is terrifying.

LEGAL CUSTODY AND PHYSICAL CUSTODY

In Maryland, Virginia, and the District of Columbia, all parents, separated or not, have joint custody of their minor children until and unless the court orders otherwise. However, the court can determine custody and issue a custody order in a divorce. Custody consists of two parts: *legal custody* and *physical custody*. The following discussion describes custody law common to all three jurisdictions and points out where they differ. For example, the custody factors the court must consider are slightly different in each jurisdiction. Finally, custody trials and parenting plans applicable to the three jurisdictions are described.

Legal Custody   *Legal custody* means long-term parenting decisions, such as educational, medical, disciplinary, and religious decisions. Legal custody can be *joint*, meaning both parents make decisions mutually, or the court can grant one parent *sole* legal custody, which means that parent makes the final long-term parenting decisions. The District of Columbia has enacted a presumption in favor of joint legal custody, except in cases of domestic abuse. Maryland and Virginia look at various factors, such as the ability of the parties to agree on parenting issues, to determine the best interests of the child.

Physical Custody   *Physical custody* means where the child lives most of the time. It is sometimes referred to as *residential custody*. Sometimes the term is avoided altogether and it is just said that the children will have their primary residence with one of the parents.

BEST INTERESTS OF THE CHILDREN

The legal standard in deciding who will get custody is what is in the *best interests of the children*. Every judge sees it differently. There are no courts in Maryland, Virginia, or the District of Columbia where the mother has an automatic edge in litigation. Fathers win in at least half of the litigated cases, except when the children are very young.

There are also certain doctrines and presumptions in all three jurisdictions (but not inflexible rules or requirements) that aid the court in determining the best interests of the child. Some of these general factors include the following.

- *Parental rights.* Parents must be shown to be unfit before the children will be given to someone else, such as grandparents.

- *Continuity of placement.* If children are doing well where they are, judges do not like to move them.

- *Children's preference.* A judge will consider who the children want to live with. The judge may talk with the children in private. The judge is not bound by what the children want.

- *Other.* The court can consider the custodian's age, health, wealth, religious beliefs, conduct, type of home, and psychological evaluations; the location of the residences of the child's siblings; the child's school performance; or, anything else the court considers important.

Because the factors the courts in each jurisdiction will consider in determining custody are similar, but with slightly different nuances, each jurisdiction's factors are described.

MARYLAND CUSTODY FACTORS

In determining whether to award joint legal custody in Maryland, the court will consider the following factors:

- capacity of the parents to communicate and to reach shared decisions affecting the child's welfare;

- willingness of the parents to share custody;

- fitness of the parents;

- relationship established between the child and each parent;

- preference of the child;

- potential disruption of the child's social and school life;

- geographic proximity of parental homes;

- demands of parental employment;

- age and number of children;

- sincerity of parents' requests;

- financial status of the parents;

- impact on state and federal assistance;

- ❂ benefit to parents; and,

- ❂ any other factor or circumstance related to the issue. *(Taylor v. Taylor*, 306 Md. 290, 508 A.2d 964 (1986).)

VIRGINIA CUSTODY FACTORS

In Virginia, the court is required to consider the following factors in determining the best interests of a child for custody arrangements:

- ❂ the age, and physical and mental condition of the child, giving due consideration to the child's changing developmental needs;

- ❂ the age, and physical and mental condition of each parent;

- ❂ the relationship existing between each parent and each child, giving due consideration to the positive involvement with the child's life, and the ability to accurately assess and meet the emotional, intellectual, and physical needs of the child;

- ❂ the role that each parent has played, and will play in the future, in the upbringing and care of the child;

- ❂ the propensity of each parent to actively support the child's contact and relationship with the other parent, including whether a parent has unreasonably denied the other parent access to or visitation with the child;

- ❂ the relative willingness and demonstrated ability of each parent to maintain a close and continuing relationship with the child, and the ability of each parent to cooperate in and resolve disputes regarding matters affecting the child;

- ❂ the reasonable preference of the child, if the court deems the child to be of reasonable intelligence, understanding, age, and experience to express such a preference;

✪   any history of family abuse; and,

✪   any other factors that the court deems necessary and proper. (Virginia Code, Sec. 20-124.3.)

DISTRICT OF COLUMBIA CUSTODY FACTORS

In the District of Columbia, there is a rebuttable presumption that joint legal custody is in the best interests of the child, unless child abuse, neglect, parental kidnapping, or other intra-family violence has occurred. The court may order the parents to submit a written parenting plan for custody. The court will award custody without regard to a parent's sex, sexual orientation, race, color, national origin, or political affiliations, based on the following factors:

✪   the preference of the child, if the child is of sufficient age and capacity;

✪   the wishes of the parents;

✪   the child's adjustment to his or her home, school, and community;

✪   the mental and physical health of all individuals involved;

✪   the relationship of the child with parents, siblings, and other significant family members;

✪   the willingness of the parents to share custody and make shared decisions;

✪   the prior involvement of the parent in the child's life;

✪   the geographical proximity of the parents;

✪   the sincerity of the parents' requests;

✪   the age and number of children;

✪   the demands of parental employment;

○ the impact on any welfare benefits;

○ any evidence of spousal or child abuse;

○ financial capability of providing custody; and,

○ the benefit to the parties. (District of Columbia Code, Sec. 16-911(a)(5).)

CUSTODY TRIAL

If there is custody litigation in Maryland, Virginia, or the District of Columbia, you must be able to show the judge that the child is better off with you. Photographs of you and your child having a good time doing things together is useful evidence. Make sure you know the names of your children's teachers, coaches, doctor, dentist, and best friends. It does not hurt to know your children's shoe sizes, clothing sizes, favorite pajamas, and bedtime stories, because opposing counsel may ask you.

This is a good time to subscribe to publications such as *Parents* magazine. Buy some books about children, parenting, and getting children through divorce. Attend seminars, and keep the brochures and literature. The point is to do these things for your child and yourself, not just to impress the judge.

Divorce proceedings are very emotional, and parties sometimes use children to seek revenge. Try to keep the children out of this. If they must be involved, prepare them properly without poisoning their minds about your spouse. Obtain professional advice if possible, but do not try to use your child's therapist to gain an advantage in a custody battle. Tell the children that the divorce is not their fault and that they will still have both parents.

When you discuss issues like support and property division with your spouse, do not use the children as messengers. Make a special effort to spend time with your children during this difficult time. Give them your full attention. Reassure them that both parents love them. Give them extra love now—they need it.

PARENTING PLANS

Although you may be ending your relationship as husband and wife, you will still be partners in the business of raising your children for the next several years. Just like any other business, you need a plan.

You can settle custody and avoid a custody trial in any of the three jurisdictions with settlement agreements that are often called *parenting plans*. They can be a part of a *Separation Agreement* resolving your whole divorce, or they can be stand-alone agreements before you reach a global settlement.

Parenting plans are an infinitely better resolution of custody disputes than a custody trial. Parenting plans provide much more detail than a custody order from the court. Because they are designed by the parties and not the judge, they can be much more specific about plans for parenting the children.

A parenting plan includes, at a minimum, discussion of legal and physical custody, timesharing, and child support. It contains a visitation schedule, which is discussed in Chapter 22 and deals with who lives where. You may include as much detail as you want about such things as schools, doctors, religion, conduct of the parents, rules and routines at each house, and many other issues. In other words, a parenting plan resolves all issues in a divorce that concern the children.

There are Sample Guidelines for Effective Parenting starting at page 144, which can give you an idea of provisions you may want in your parenting plan. A lawyer can help you draw up a parenting plan. Once signed, the parenting plan becomes a contract enforceable by the court. If you are in litigation, it may be submitted to the court for approval either by itself or as part of your marital settlement agreement.

Visitation

If the mother and father can agree on visitation, the courts of Maryland, Virginia, and the District of Columbia will usually approve their schedule. If you are able to handle visitation without dispute, sometimes the agreement will just say *reasonable* or *liberal* visitation. However, you can avoid any future disputes by having a specific visitation schedule. This chapter describes visitation in general and discusses any differences among the three jurisdictions.

TYPICAL VISITATION SCHEDULES

The sample *Guidelines for Effective Parenting* at the end of this chapter is an example of a visitation schedule that will work in any of the three jurisdictions. The visitation schedule provides for alternating weekends, a weeknight every two weeks, two consecutive weeks in the summer, and alternating holidays. The children are also with the mother on her birthday and Mother's Day, and with the father on his birthday and Father's Day. The children alternate spending their birthdays with each parent.

The example holiday schedule works like this: In even-numbered years, the residential parent has the children for Memorial Day, Labor Day, Halloween, Christmas Eve, and Christmas morning for the winter school break. The nonresidential parent has them for President's Day, Easter, Fourth of July, Thanksgiving, and Christmas afternoon and evening through New Year's Day for the winter break. The schedule is reversed in odd-numbered years. Parents are encouraged to make other arrangements for other religious holidays.

If the parties are far apart, this pattern will not work. If the parties are more than 100 miles apart, the sample parenting plan then calls for fewer but longer visitation periods. The example schedule then becomes one weekend a month, seven weeks in the summer, and alternating Thanksgiving and spring vacations. You must also deal with who will provide or pay for transportation.

NOTE: *The sample guidelines and visitation schedules on p.144–149 are from a specific county in Maryland, but they can easily be modified for your specific needs.*

VISITATION DISPUTES

The courts of all three jurisdictions encourage visitation except in very extraordinary circumstances. Sometimes when parents fight about visitation, they are very upset about something else that they do not believe they can fight about. It may be because they feel angry at the other spouse for leaving or it may be that they feel they gave up too much in the divorce agreement. For whatever reason, they are involved in an argument about the children. Remember that the parent who visits regularly tends to be the parent who pays support regularly. Children benefit from having two parents.

If your approach does not seem to be working for you, include a provision in the parenting plan appointing a *parenting coordinator* or requiring a certain number of hours of mediation before going back to court. Many visitation disputes are minor, and the court is an expensive and cumbersome way to resolve whether your child was returned on time from visitation.

WITHHOLDING VISITATION

Withholding visitation from the children of the noncustodial parent is a very bad idea. Withholding visitation to coerce the payment of child support is illegal in Maryland, Virginia, and the District of Columbia, and it never works.

If you withhold visitation, the children may turn to the other parent's side. The children may blame you for forcing the other parent to leave. The children dream about a perfect parent, and since they do not see the absent parent, they do not see any flaws in that parent. You might win against many things, but you will lose against your children's imagination.

A bad former spouse is not necessarily a bad parent. It may be hard to remember this, but they are two separate issues. The court can find you in contempt for withholding visitation and even change custody to the other parent.

GRANDPARENT VISITATION

Grandparents can petition the court for visitation in Virginia and Maryland. The courts will usually grant reasonable visitation with grandparents if it is in the best interests of the grandchildren. However, if the parents have a different visitation schedule than the grandparents, the United States Supreme Court has ruled there is a presumption that the parents' schedule is in the best interests of the child. This presumption can be overcome in certain circumstances, such as when the parent is refusing all visitation with the grandparents.

The District of Columbia is the only jurisdiction in the United States where the courts have ruled that visitation is a right that is attached to custody—so grandparents in the District of Columbia, since they do not have custody, do not have automatic visitation rights. They must rely on the agreement of the parents to have visitation with their grandchildren.

MONTGOMERY COUNTY

GUIDELINES FOR EFFECTIVE PARENTING

I. Preamble

Maryland has established the public policy that it is in the child's best interest to maintain contact with the non-residential parent through liberal and meaningful visitation. However, portions of these guidelines may not apply to (1) a child from birth to age three or (2) to a child who, for whatever reason, has been separated from the non-residential parent for a significant period of time.

II. General Rules

1. Each parent (and any subsequent spouse) will refrain from exercising undue influence over the child with regard to the other parent, criticizing the other parent in the presence of the child, inducing the child to challenge the authority of the other parent, or encouraging the child to request a change of custody or to resist visitation. Neither parent will interrogate the child about the other parent.

2. Each parent will refrain from interfering with the custody or visitation rights of the other parent and will take steps to ensure that any parent's subsequent spouse or partner so refrains.

3. Parents will communicate directly with each other concerning the child, and will not require the child to deliver messages (including child support payments) to the other parent. Parents will ensure that their respective subsequent spouses do not interfere with the parents in matters concerning the child.

4. Each parent has the right and responsibility to make decisions concerning the child's daily routine when the child is in that parent's care. Parents with joint legal custody have an equal right and responsibility to make long-range decisions concerning the child, including, without limitation, education, religious training, discipline, medical care, and other matters of major significance concerning the child's life and welfare. The parent without legal custody of the child retains the authority to consent to emergency surgery or other necessary medical care for the child while in his/her care when there is insufficient time to contact the parent with legal custody.

5. Each parent is permitted access to all school and medical records of the child.

(A) The parent with legal custody shall take the necessary action with the authorities of the school in which the child is enrolled to:

(1) List the other parent as a parent of the child;

(2) Authorize the school to release to the other parent any and all information concerning the child;

(3) Ensure that the other parent may receive copies of any notices regarding the child.

(B) The parent with legal custody shall be the parent to authorize participation in school activities, sign permission slips, request excusal from school activities and early departure. The parent without legal custody shall be permitted to authorize the same only when the child is in that parent's care and only with the consent of the parent with legal custody.

(C) If not already furnished by the child's school, the parent with legal custody will promptly transmit to the other parent any information received concerning parent-teacher meetings, school programs, athletic schedules, and any other school and extra-curricular activities in which the child may be engaged or interested. Each parent is permitted and encouraged to attend.

(D) If not already furnished to the other parent by the child's school, the parent with legal custody will promptly, after receipt of the same, furnish to the other parent a photocopy of the child's grades or report, and copies of any other reports concerning the child's status or progress.

(E) The parent with legal custody will notify the other parent of all parent-teacher conferences, which whenever possible shall be arranged at a time when both parents can attend.

(F) The parent with legal custody will authorize medical providers to release to the other parent copies of any and all information concerning medical care provided to the child and will execute any medical release form necessary for the other parent to obtain such information. The parent with legal custody will promptly inform the other parent of any illness or injury of the child which requires medical attention. Emergency surgery necessary for the preservation of the child's life or to prevent a further serious injury or condition may be authorized by either parent provided that the other parent is notified as soon as possible. Elective surgery for the child may be authorized by the parent with legal custody after notification to the other parent.

6. Under Maryland law, a move out of state with the minor children by the parent with legal custody constitutes a change in circumstances that warrants a review of the residential arrangements. Therefore, the parent with legal custody shall notify the other parent at least 45 days in advance of any contemplated move (and sooner if possible), and the parents shall cooperate to work out a new visitation schedule. In the event that a new visitation schedule cannot be agreed upon by the parents, the parents shall promptly submit the issues raised by relocation to mediation.

7. The parent with legal custody will encourage free communications between the child and the other parent and will not do anything to impede or restrict communications by phone or mail between the child and parent. This rule applies equally to the parent without legal custody, most especially when the child is on extended visitation with that parent.

(A) Unless specifically permitted by the Court to withhold such information, each parent will provide the other parent with the following information in advance whenever the child is with him or her: a telephone number and an address where the child may be reached, as well as the name, address, and telephone number of any regular child-care provider.

(B) Unless otherwise ordered by the Court, mail between the child and parent is strictly confidential between the child and that parent, and shall not be opened or read by the other parent or any other person.

(C) One of the following rules shall apply as agreed upon by the parents, or ordered by the Court, considering the circumstances of the parents and child:

(1) Each parent is entitled to reasonable telephone access to the child during those times when the child is with the other parent. Such telephone conversations shall be private, unrecorded, and take place out of the other parent's presence, limited only by the child or the calling parent terminating the telephone call; or

(2) At the request of either parent, telephone communications between parent and child shall be at set times agreed to by the parents, taking into consideration the regular routine of the child and the child's age. Such telephone conversations shall be private, unrecorded, out of the presence of the other parent, and limited only by the child or the calling parent terminating the telephone call.

8. Neither parent shall attempt to modify the religious practice of the child as established prior to the parents' separation without first consulting with the other parent. If after consultation the parties are unable to agree, the decision of the parent with sole legal custody shall prevail. If the parents share joint legal custody, the issue shall be submitted to mediation.

9. A decision to maintain, initiate or terminate therapy for their child should be made after discussion and following an agreement by the parties, but, if they are unable to agree, the parent with sole legal custody shall make the decision, or, if the parents share joint legal custody, the issue shall be submitted to mediation.

10. The parents will schedule weekend and holiday visitation on a regular basis. The following provisions assume that the parent with legal custody is the primary "residential" parent and that the parent without legal custody is the "non-residential" parent.

(A) The non-residential parent will give the residential parent notice of any change to the time of pick up and return of the child for regular weekend and holiday visitation at least 48 hours before a scheduled visit, except in the case of emergency and circumstances beyond the non-residential parent's control, in which case notification of the time of exchange will be made as soon as possible.

(B) The residential parent shall furnish the non-residential parent with any prospective plans for the child's summer camp/activity schedule as soon as it is available to the residential parent. The non-residential parent will notify the residential parent of summer vacation plans with the child as soon as his/her employment schedule permits.

(C) Parents shall not ask the child to communicate with the other parent regarding visitation arrangements.

(D) The residential parent, non-residential parent, and subsequent spouses will be diligent in having the child ready and available at the appointed times for visitation and return from visitation. The transporting parent will be prompt in picking up and delivering the child within the grace periods set out on the applicable visitation schedule.

(E) Holiday visitation commences at the regular hour as set for the commencement of weekend visitation and ends at the regular hour set for the evening of weekend visitation. Holiday visitation will have precedence over the regular visitation schedule, but will not result in weekend visitation more than three (3) weekends in a row.

(F) The residential parent will send with the child on visitation sufficient clothing and outerwear appropriate for the season to last the period of visitation. For example, in the case of an infant, the residential parent will send with the child sufficient bottles, formula, and diapers necessary to last one (1) day of the visitation period. The non-residential parent will provide any additional formula, and diapers necessary. The non-residential parent shall return all such clothing and other reusable items sent with the child. Soiled clothing, including cloth diapers, shall be laundered before return.

(G) Each parent shall provide a car seat as required by law to transport the child.

(H) The residential parent will send with the child sufficient medication for a weekend or holiday visitation period and any prescription for medication necessary for the first week during an extended summer visitation. The non-residential parent will provide any additional medication necessary.

(I) No alcoholic beverage may be consumed by either parent prior to operating a motor vehicle in which the child is riding. No illegal drug may be taken by either parent at any time. As a general practice, visitation does not include picking up the child and leaving the child with a non-family member while the visiting parent pursues personal activities. The children may be picked up by a designated family member or others acceptable to either parent and may spend a portion of the visitation time with members of the respective parent's family, including resident partners not married to that parent. Visitation does not include taking the child to a non-restaurant-type bar.

(J) As much as possible during visitation, the child's customary activities will be continued. The residential parent will make every effort not to schedule activities or appointments during the other parent's visitation period. The non-residential parent shall make every effort to support the child's interests and activities, including, without limitation, sports practice and games, medical appointments, dancing and music lessons and recitals, church, school, and extra-curricular activities, parties and other social gatherings, and scouting and club activities. Both parents are encouraged to attend such activities, whether scheduled during visitation or at other times, but, when such activities occur during visitation, the other parent will be respectful of the visiting parent's time.

(K) When one parent is not available to take care of the children during his or her regularly scheduled time (e.g., business trip, weekend out of town) for more than one day, that parent is encouraged to give the other parent the opportunity to take the children rather than placing the children with a third party. Such an opportunity, however, is not obligatory; nor is it to be used by either party to interfere with the other party's scheduled visitation time.

11. Extended visitation does not terminate or reduce child support for that period except on specific Order of the Court, as the child support formula amount has been calculated to take into account periods of visitation. CHILD SUPPORT AND VISITATION ARE NOT MUTUALLY DEPENDENT UPON THE OTHER. CHILD SUPPORT IS PAYABLE REGARDLESS OF VISITATION. VISITATION IS PERMITTED REGARDLESS OF THE PAYMENT OF CHILD SUPPORT.

12. Repeated violations by either parent of any of the Guidelines for Effective Parenting may constitute a material change in circumstances and may be cause for granting modification of the custody or visitation Order, changing custody, curtailing or expanding visitation, implementing a visitation adjustment policy, or instituting contempt procedures, as the situation may warrant.

III. VISITATION SCHEDULES

Parents are encouraged to establish more convenient visitation schedules by agreement. When the parents do not agree, the parents may be ORDERED by the Court to adhere to one or the other of the following schedules.

VISITATION SCHEDULE A

Schedule A contemplates the parents living one (1) hour or less apart driving door to door, and includes the General Guidelines for Effective Parenting listed earlier. Schedule A provides the minimum visitation, and parents are encouraged to agree on additional visitation.

(A) Visitation by the non-residential parent on alternate weekends from Friday at 7:00 p.m. to Sunday at 7:00 p.m. (the beginning and ending times may be varied to accommodate the work schedule of the parents). Visitation on one evening during one of the weekdays between alternate visitation weekends from _____ p.m. to _____ p.m. (one hour prior to the child's normal bedtime).

(B) Mother's Day the child will be with the mother; Father's Day the child will be with the father. In the event this provision requires the child to be with the residential parent when it is the non-residential parent's normal weekend visitation, the non-residential parent will return the child by 10:00 a.m. on that day. In the event that this provision requires the child to be with the non-residential parent on a day not falling within the non-residential parent's visitation weekend, the non-residential parent may have visitation from 9:00 a.m. to 7:00 p.m.

(C) The parents will alternate having the child with him or her on the child's birthday, and each parent shall be entitled to have the child with him or her on that parent's birthday.

(D) The parents will have the child on holidays as follows: (Holiday visitation will commence and end at the regular hour set for weekend visitation, except as otherwise set forth here.)

EVEN-NUMBERED YEARS

RESIDENTIAL PARENT

Memorial Day:
Friday night through Monday night.

Labor Day:
Friday night through Monday night.

Halloween:
Halloween Day afternoon from after school through the morning after.

Christmas/winter break:
Christmas Eve, 9:00 a.m. through Christmas Day, 2:00 p.m.

NON-RESIDENTIAL PARENT

President's Day:
Sunday night until Monday night.

Easter/spring break:
To coincide with vacation from school; for example, Friday, 7:00 p.m. through week off until Sunday, 7:00 p.m.

Fourth of July:
Night before through morning after, except when the 4th falls on Friday, Saturday, Sunday or Monday, in which case visitation will commence on Friday night and continue to the end of the weekend or end of holiday, whichever is later.

Thanksgiving:
To coincide with vacation from school; for example, Wednesday 7:00 p.m. until Sunday 7:00 p.m.

Christmas/winter break:
Christmas Day, 2:00 p.m. through New Year's Day, 7:00 p.m.

Parents will make appropriate provisions for other holidays and religious observances regularly observed by the parents and child: for example, Hanukkah and Rosh Hashanah.

ODD-NUMBERED YEARS

The above schedule is reversed as to residential parent and non-residential parent unless otherwise indicated.

ADDITIONAL GENERAL GUIDELINES FOR VISITATION SCHEDULE A

1. Each parent shall have a period of two consecutive weeks with the child in the summer. Regular visitation shall be suspended during this period if the parent and child travel out of town. Each party should notify the other of his or her choice of the two-week period as early as possible each spring so that any conflicts can be resolved, if not by agreement of the parties, then by mediation or a Court Order.

2. The transporting parent for visitations may have a grace period of fifteen (15) minutes for pick up and delivery where the parents live within a distance of thirty (30) miles from each other. Where the one-way distance to be traveled is in excess of thirty (30) miles, the grace period is thirty (30) minutes. In the case where the visiting parent suffers an unavoidable breakdown or delay en route, the visiting parent shall promptly notify the other parent by phone of the delay.

VISITATION SCHEDULE B

Schedule B applies presumptively if the parents live more than one (1) hour apart driving door to door, and includes the General Guidelines for Effective Parenting listed earlier. Schedule B provides the minimum visitation and parents are encouraged to agree on additional visitation.

(A) <u>Vacation</u> - The non-residential parent will have an extended visitation each summer to coincide to the extent possible with that parent's vacation from work for seven (7) weeks during the child's summer vacation from school, beginning on the first Sunday after school lets out to the Sunday seven (7) weeks later, subject to the residential parent's right to visit with the child for one (1) weekend during the extended visitation period.

(B) <u>Weekends</u> - The non-residential parent shall have visitation with the child for 48 hours on the first full weekend of the following months (the beginning and ending times of which may be varied to accommodate the work schedule of the parents): February, March (only if the non-residential parent does not have spring vacation), April (only if the non-residential parent does not have spring vacation), May, September, October and November (only if the non-residential parent does not have Thanksgiving visitation). The objective is to enable the non-residential parent to have visitation with the child for 48 hours each month. The residential parent is encouraged to permit the non-residential parent to select three-day weekends, but, in any case, in alternate years, the non-residential parent is entitled to have said visitation on all holiday weekends (example, President's Day in February, Memorial Day in May, Labor Day in September, Columbus Day in October, etc.) and extend the visitation through the holiday.

(C) <u>Other holidays</u> - The non-residential parent may visit with the child on (1) alternating Thanksgiving and spring vacations from school, with spring vacations from school in even years, Thanksgiving vacation from school in odd years; (2) Christmas: residential parent on Christmas Eve, 9:00 a.m. to Christmas Day until 2:00 p.m.; non-residential parent on Christmas Day at 2:00 p.m. until the night of the end of New Year's Day at 7:00 p.m. Parents will make appropriate provisions for other holidays and religious observances regularly observed by the parents and child: for example, Hanukkah or Rosh Hashanah.

(D) <u>Other times</u> - At all other reasonable and seasonable times, as the parents may agree. In addition, if the residential parent of the child is in the state or near the geographical location of the non-residential parent or the non-residential parent is nearby the child, the other parent will be notified and each parent will attempt to arrange visitation if at all possible.

ADDITIONAL GENERAL GUIDELINES FOR VISITATION SCHEDULE B:

(1) The parents are encouraged to share the transportation costs and arrangements. Among the factors to be considered in determining each parent's "share" of these responsibilities are:

> (a) age and any special needs of the children;
>
> (b) work schedules of parents;
>
> (c) distance;
>
> (d) availability of adequate public transportation;
>
> (e) income of parents;
>
> (f) whose decision it was to move; and,
>
> (g) any special circumstances of either party (i.e., disabled, remarried with small children).

(2) Visitation may be exercised outside of the State of Maryland.

(3) The transporting parent for visitations may have a grace period of one (1) hour for pick up and delivery. In the case where the visiting parent suffers an unavoidable breakdown or delay en route, the visiting parent shall promptly notify the other parent by phone of the delay.

Child Support

Maryland, Virginia, and the District of Columbia have enacted child support guidelines. This chapter explains the general concepts of child support, child support guidelines, and the differences in the three jurisdictions.

GENERAL OVERVIEW

In Maryland, Virginia, and the District of Columbia, the child support guidelines are based on the *income shares model*. This model is a formula based on the relative and combined income of the parties, the number of children, and the time spent with the children.

Guidelines   Although the guidelines are based on gross income, a general rule is that you probably will not have to pay more than half of your net income in combined alimony and child support. Net income is total income less taxes and child support payments from any prior cases.

The guidelines provide for an adjustment for health insurance and day care for the children, and assume that the noncustodial parent pays for the children when they are with him or her during normal visitation. If there are any extraordinary expenses (medical, educational, etc.), then the support could be higher than the guidelines. In addition to child support, the court can order you to provide things such as health insurance and can allocate tax exemptions.

Child support will be deducted from your paycheck through a wage withholding order and paid through the registry of the court, unless there is a compelling reason to do otherwise. Child support is not taxable to the recipient or deductible to the payor. The obligation to pay child support cannot be discharged in bankruptcy.

Non-Guideline Cases

Most cases are decided by using the guidelines. However, the guidelines only go up to a certain amount of combined income. The top combined income on the guidelines is $120,000 per year in Maryland and Virginia. In the District of Columbia, the guidelines go up to $75,000 per year for the payor. When the guidelines do not apply or would not result in a fair amount of child support, the court will look at the needs of the children and the financial assets, earnings, and needs of each parent.

Length of Child Support

In Maryland and Virginia, the court can require support of a normal child only until age 18. If the child is still in high school and living at home at age 18, then child support will run until graduation from high school or the 19th birthday, whichever comes first. In the District of Columbia, the court can order child support until age 21. If you have a child with a mental or physical disability, it may be possible to have support continue after this child becomes an adult.

Child Support Modifications

Child support always remains subject to the court's jurisdiction to modify it. The court will modify a prior support order if there has been a *material change in circumstances* and modification is in the child's best interests.

Many things can amount to a material change in circumstances. Some of the more common changes are a child reaching the age at which support ends, a child changing residences from one parent to the other, one parent's income increasing or decreasing substantially, or the custodial parent moving to an area with a substantially higher or lower cost of living.

Try to obtain your spouse's agreement to the modification before filing your request with the court. Even if the modification is agreed to, it should be put in the form of a *consent order* and filed with the court. If the children's needs or the parent's ability to pay support substantially changes, then child support can be raised or lowered.

College Expenses

Maryland, Virginia, and the District of Columbia do not require a parent to put a child through college. You can provide for college, but you must do so by agreement, as the court cannot order it.

MARYLAND GUIDELINES

The **CHILD SUPPORT GUIDELINE WORKSHEETS** provided in Appendix B are used to calculate the proper amount of child support. The guidelines are presumptively correct and must be followed by the master, commissioner, or judge, unless there are some special circumstances that would justify deviation from the guidelines.

Sole Custody Worksheet A

The **SOLE CUSTODY WORKSHEET A** is used when one parent has less than 128 (35%) overnights of visitation during the year. (see form MD–2, p.234.) For purposes of child support calculations only, this is called *sole custody*. It results in higher child support than **SHARED CUSTODY WORKSHEET B**, so there is often a struggle over the 128 overnight visitation. For example, a visitation schedule of three overnights every other weekend, one overnight in alternating weeks, alternating holidays, and several weeks in the summer usually results in more than 128 overnights.

NOTE: *All figures requested in the worksheets are monthly amounts.*

Complete the worksheet by following the line-by-line instructions that are stated on the form. What follows are additional instructions for lines that are fairly complex. You may want to use this information in addition to the instructions with the form.

◈ Complete the top portion of the form with the case caption by filling in the court, the case number, and the names of the parties.

◈ In the next lines, fill your children's names and birth dates.

◈   Complete all lines 1–3 as directed.

◈   At line 4, for the *Basic Child Support Obligation*, go to the child support tables at Appendix B. These tables show what the legislature has determined to be the costs of raising children for people at various income levels. Find the combined income from the first column of the table, then read across the row for the number of minor children of your marriage. Where the row and column intersect will give you the *Basic Child Support Obligation*. Put that amount in the third column of line 4.

◈   At line 4(a), put any day care or other child care expenses that are required by work.

◈   At line 4(c), you may add any additional expenses for the children that you would like the court to consider.

◈   Complete lines 5–7 as directed.

◈   There is a space for comments, calculations, rebuttals, or adjustments for direct payments of extraordinary expenses by the noncustodial parent.

◈   Print your name and date the form.

Shared Custody Worksheet B

The **SHARED CUSTODY WORKSHEET B** is used when the noncustodial parent has more than 128 overnights (35%) of visitation a year. (see form MD–3, p.235.) Complete **WORKSHEET B** as follows.

◈   Complete the top portion of the form with the case caption by filling in the court, the case number, and the names of the parties.

◈   In the next lines, fill in the names and birth dates of your children.

◈   Complete all lines 1–4 as directed on the form.

◈   At line 5, multiply the *Basic Child Support Obligation* on line 4 by one and a half (1.5). This is because the legislature has determined that it costs one and a half times as much to raise children in a shared custody arrangement as it does when one parent has primary custody. The result is called the *Adjusted Basic Child Support Obligation*.

◈ Complete line 6 as directed.

◈ At line 7, determine the percentage of overnights with each parent by dividing line 6 by 365 and multiplying the result by 100. If either column is less than 35%, then you must use **WORKSHEET A** instead.

◈ Complete lines 8–10 as directed.

◈ For certain *Expenses* on line 11(a), (b), and (c), see the instructions for line 4(a), (b), and (c) on **WORKSHEET A**. If you pay these expenses in any other percentage than indicated on line 3 (your percentage share of income), then you will have to adjust them on the third page of **WORKSHEET B**, entitled *Adjustment Worksheet*, before you can go on. There are detailed instructions on the *Adjustment Worksheet* on how to make the adjustment calculations.

◈ Take the result from the *Adjustment Worksheet*, go back to the second page of **WORKSHEET B**, and place it on line 12, entitled *Net Adjustment*.

◈ Complete lines 12–14 as directed on the form.

◈ There is a space for comments, calculations, or rebuttals, including direct payments by the noncustodial parent.

◈ Print your name and date the worksheet.

NOTE: *The court may impute income to a party who voluntarily impoverishes him- or herself (by quitting a job, for example). This rule does not apply in the case of a mother of the child of the parties for two years from the date of the child's birth.*

VIRGINIA GUIDELINES

In Virginia, child support is determined by using the statutory child support guidelines. The guidelines take into account the number of children, the parties' incomes, a child's extraordinary medical or dental expenses, day care and similar expenses incurred to enable a custodial parent to work, and the cost of health care coverage attributable to the children. The parties' incomes are adjusted for spousal support payable between the parties and the expenses associated with other children—children whom a party supports who are not children of both parties.

The starting point for the calculation is finding the amount of basic child support on a schedule based on the combined income of the parties and the number of children. Extrapolate at incomes between those listed on the chart to determine the exact guidelines amount. The schedule lists the amount of basic support for combined monthly gross income of up to $10,000.

For combined monthly gross incomes above $10,000, the basic support amount must be computed by multiplying the income that is over $10,000 by the appropriate percentages and adding that result to the basic support amount for $10,000 of combined monthly gross income. These percentages are as follows.

Combined monthly income between $10,000 and $20,000

One Child	Two Children	Three Children	Four Children	Five Children	Six Children
3.1%	5.1%	6.8%	7.8%	8.8%	9.5%

Combined monthly income between $20,000 and $50,000

One Child	Two Children	Three Children	Four Children	Five Children	Six Children
2.0%	3.5%	5.0%	6.0%	6.9%	27.8%

Combined monthly income over $50,000

One Child	Two Children	Three Children	Four Children	Five Children	Six Children
1.0%	2.0%	3.0%	4.0%	5.0%	6.0%

Example:

There are two children. If Father earns $6,000 a month and Mother earns $9,000 a month, their combined monthly income is $15,000. This is over the $10,000 limit from the basic child support table by $5,000. Find the support required for two children with a combined monthly income of $10,000 in the basic child support table, which is $1,577. (see p.156.) Find the percentage from the table on p.156 to apply to the amount by which they are over $10,000 in combined income. The correct percentage from the table is 5.1%, and 5.1% of $5,000 is $255. Child support is then the basic amount of $1,577 plus the overage of $255, for a total combined child support obligation of $1,832.

Extraordinary medical or dental expenses, work-related child care expenses, and the cost of medical insurance (assuming all these are paid by the custodial parent) are added to the basic child support to arrive at total child support. Responsibility for total child support is allocated between the parents in proportion to their incomes. The custodial parent is presumed to spend his or her share on the children directly, and the noncustodial parent pays his or share to the custodial parent.

The amount determined by application of the guidelines is presumed to be correct. You may be able to overcome this presumption by showing that additional factors in your case cause the guidelines amount to be an unfair amount of child support. The additional factors that Virginia courts have recognized as warranting departure from the guidelines are discussed on the following pages.

Sole Custody Worksheet

Use the CHILD SUPPORT GUIDELINES WORKSHEET to compute child support payable under the guidelines. (see form VA–2, p.276.) Complete the child support guidelines worksheet for sole custody with no spousal support, or spousal support separately computed.

◈ For the caption, enter the names of the plaintiff and the defendant, the case number, and the date.

◈ Complete lines 1–6 using the directions on page 277.

◈ At line 7a, look up the schedule amount of basic child support for the parties' combined gross income and number of children in the child support tables in Appendix F and enter it here.

◈ Complete lines 7b–12d using the directions on page 277.

Deviation from Guidelines

The following are some of the factors listed in Virginia law as reasons for a deviation from child support guidelines in an appropriate case:

✪ a written agreement of the parties for child support;

✪ high debt incurred during the marriage for the benefit of the children;

✪ imputed income to a party who does not work or does not work full-time when family and other circumstances indicate that he or she can;

✪ extraordinary capital gains;

✪ tax consequences of exemption and child care expenses;

✪ disposition of marital property;

✪ age, and physical and mental condition of the children;

✪ independent financial resources of the children; and,

✪ any other factors necessary to do equity.

Shared Custody Worksheet

If the children spend more than ninety days per year with the parent with less custody, the shared custody child support guidelines apply. In addition to the factors that affect child support under the sole custody guidelines, the shared custody child support guidelines take into account the increased cost of maintaining two households with children and the ratio of the time the children spend with each parent.

Complete the **CHILD SUPPORT GUIDELINES WORKSHEET—SHARED CUSTODY** as follows. (see form VA–3, p.278.)

◈ At the top section, enter the names of the plaintiff and the defendant, the case number, and the date.

◈ Complete lines 1–14 by following the directions on page 279.

◈ At line 15, look up the schedule amount of basic child support for the parties' combined gross income and number of children in the child support tables in Appendix F, and enter it here.

◈ Complete lines 16–40 by following the directions on page 279.

Split Custody Worksheet

The term *split custody* refers to the situation in which each parent has custody of one or more children of these parents. Child support is computed for each household using the procedures discussed previously under "Sole Custody," or "Shared Custody" if appropriate, for the children in one or both households. The amount the father owes the mother is netted against the amount the mother owes the father, and the child support order is entered for the difference.

Complete the **SUPPORT GUIDELINES WORKSHEET—SPLIT CUSTODY** as follows. (see form VA–4, p.280.)

◈ At the top, fill in the caption by entering the names of the plaintiff and the defendant, the case number, whose worksheet this is, and the date.

◈ Complete lines 1–7 by following the directions on page 281.

◈ At line 8a, look up the schedule amount for basic child support for the parties' combined gross income, the number of children living with the mother, and the number of children living with the father in the child support tables in Appendix F and enter it here.

◈ Complete lines 8b–12e by following the directions on page 281.

See the discussion on page 158 under the sole custody guidelines for a list of factors that are listed in Virginia law as reasons for a deviation from the guidelines in an appropriate case.

NOTE: *If custody of the children in one or both households is shared, you cannot use the split custody worksheet. Use a sole custody worksheet to compute the support payable by one parent, and a shared custody worksheet to compute the support payable by the other parent, or two shared custody worksheets if appropriate. Then, subtract the smaller support obligation obtained from the larger.*

DISTRICT OF COLUMBIA GUIDELINES

The District of Columbia child support guidelines use a formula that depends on the age of the children, the number of children, the gross income of both parents, and the actual gross earnings of the noncustodial parent. A commissioner may award support that differs from the guidelines by plus or minus 3% for unusual circumstances. For example, a commissioner might add 3% on a finding that the children have moderately more than average needs. Child support may be ordered to be paid through the clerk of the court.

The District of Columbia has recently started using an online CHILD SUPPORT GUIDELINE CALCULATOR. (see form DC–2, p.325.) Go to **www.dccourts.gov/childsupport/servlet/csServlet** and fill out the form as instructed on the page. Note that the District of Columbia uses annual figures. After you submit the page, you will get a new page that will show you the high, low, and guideline recommended amounts, broken down by year, month, every other week, and week. It shows you what percentage of your annual gross income is required, and tells you the basic support required, according to the guidelines.

The CHILD SUPPORT GUIDELINES (Appendix J) break down the guidelines by age of children, number of children, and annual gross income. You can refer to these guidelines to better understand the results of the online support calculation.

Deviation from Guidelines

The guidelines are presumptively correct, and the commissioner cannot deviate more than plus or minus 3%, unless the application of the guidelines would be unjust or inappropriate in the circumstances of a particular case. Then the commissioner must set forth and explain in writing the reason for the deviation.

The following are the eight factors that may be considered to overcome the presumption.

1. The needs of the child are exceptional and require more than average expenditures.

2. The gross income of the noncustodial parent is substantially less than that of the custodial parent.

3. A property settlement provides resources readily available for the support of the child in an amount at least equivalent to the formula amount.

4. The noncustodial parent supports a dependent other than the child for whom the custodial parent receives credit in the formula calculation, and application of the guideline would result in extraordinary hardship.

5. The noncustodial parent needs a temporary period of reduced child support payment to permit the repayment of a debt or rearrangement of his or her financial obligations. A temporary reduction may be included in a child support order if:

    *   the debt or obligation is for a necessary expenditure of reasonable cost in light of the noncustodial parent's family responsibility;

    *   the time of the reduction does not exceed twelve months; and,

    *   the child support order includes the amount that is to be paid at the end of the reduction period and the date that the higher payments are to commence.

6. The custodial parent provides medical insurance coverage for the child at an additional cost to the custodial parent's medical insurance coverage, and the additional cost is significant in relation to the amount of child support prescribed by the guideline.

7. Children of more than one noncustodial parent living in the custodial parent's household receive a child support payment

from the noncustodial parent, and the resulting gross income for the custodial parent and the children in the household causes the standard of living of the children to be greater than that of the noncustodial parent.

8.   Any other exceptional circumstance that would yield an unfair result.

Financial Statements

The courts have their own financial statement forms for reporting your assets and liabilities and income and expenses. These statements are no longer required for any case in the District of Columbia and for uncontested divorces in Maryland and Virginia. In addition, the Maryland court does not require them if alimony or child support is not in dispute. However, even in cases where the forms are not strictly required, they may still be helpful in organizing your financial information for you or your attorney. Once you have a clear picture of your finances, you will also be in a better position to settle or litigate your case.

MARYLAND

The court rules require that you file a **FINANCIAL STATEMENT** on the court's form with your *Complaint for Divorce* if you are seeking alimony or child support. If you fail to do so, your spouse's attorney may file a *Motion to Dismiss* your *Complaint*, and the court will simply throw out your *Complaint* without considering it.

To complete the **Maryland Financial Statement** (long form) (form MD–1, p.225), follow these directions.

❖   Fill in the top part of the form with the name of the court, the names of the parties, and the case number. If you do not have a case number yet, leave it blank.

❖   Put your name in the title of the form.

❖   List the names and ages of all children born or adopted as a result of the marriage.

❖   The next section of the form calls for monthly expenses in various categories. The easiest way to do this is to determine annual expenses in each category from your checkbook, and divide by twelve for an average month. Then allocate expenses between you and your children. If there are two children, many expenses may be allocated one-third to you and two-thirds to the children. However, some expenses, like rent or mortgage, may not lend themselves to this type of allocation, and probably should be allocated more to you. Others, like school expenses, should be allocated all to the children. Total the two columns in the third column and subtotal the three columns in each category of expenses.

❖   On page 6, total the three columns and write the number of dependent children you have.

❖   Page 7 is the Income Statement. Put your gross monthly wages from your pay stub in the first line. If you get paid biweekly (as, for example, do government workers), you will have to multiply by 26 and divide by 12 to get your gross monthly wages.

❖   There are spaces for your monthly deductions, such as federal withholding, state withholding, FICA (Social Security and Medicare), and retirement. Use the above formula if you get paid twice a week.

❖   Subtract total deductions from your gross pay to get net income from wages.

◈ Fill in any other gross income, such as alimony, part-time jobs, rentals, and any deductions you have against this income. Subtract these deductions from other income for your net other income.

◈ Add your net wage income and your net other income to obtain your total monthly income.

◈ Assets and liabilities, sometimes called a *balance sheet*, are set forth on page 8. In the first section, list all of your assets, starting with the fair market value of any real estate owned. Then list the value of your furniture in the marital home, bank accounts, bonds, stocks and other investments, personal property, jewelry, automobiles, boats, and anything else you own. List everything you can think of owned by you or your spouse. If you do not know the value, you can write "unknown" or you can estimate. You can also include footnotes if you need to explain anything to the court. Total your assets.

◈ Liabilities are debts you owe. This includes the principal balance of the mortgage on your house, automobile loans, notes payable to relatives (if someone loans you money for your divorce, be sure to document it with a promissory note and include it here), bank loans, taxes owed, and credit cards. Total the liabilities.

◈ Subtract assets from liabilities for your total net worth.

◈ Subtract total income from total expenses for the excess or deficit.

◈ Sign and date the form. Notice that by signing, you are affirming the form is true under penalties of perjury.

VIRGINIA

While Virginia has no state-approved financial statement form for divorce cases, some counties have their own local forms. A sample **MONTHLY INCOME AND EXPENSES STATEMENT** is given on page 275. This form contains only summary information regarding liquid assets, and no information regarding assets such as real property, vehicles, and business interests.

Complete the **MONTHLY INCOME AND EXPENSE STATEMENT** as follows.

Introductory Information

◈ Enter your name, date of the statement, and case number where indicated.

◈ Enter your employer's name and address, your occupation, pay period, next payday, salary or wage, and number of exemptions where indicated.

◈ List your children's names and ages.

Average Gross Pay Per Month

◈ Calculate your average gross pay per month and enter it where indicated. If you are employed, start with your pay statement. Use your gross income, not income subject to federal tax. Monthly income is 4.33 times weekly income, or biweekly income multiplied by 26, then divided by 12. All income counts, including overtime and part-time jobs. If your pay varies substantially, use the year-to-date figures divided by the number of months to date in the year. If it is early in the year, use last year's figures divided by 12. If you are self-employed, last year's tax return is a good starting point.

◈ Calculate and enter your monthly deduction (or expense, if self-employed) for federal taxes, state taxes, FICA, health insurance, life insurance, and required retirement.

◈ Calculate average monthly net pay by deducting the amount of each of the foregoing expense categories from average gross pay per month, and enter it in the block.

◈ Calculate and enter your average monthly other income. Include any money your spouse pays you and any unearned income, such as interest, dividends, and capital gains.

◈ Calculate monthly net income by adding average monthly net pay and monthly other income, and enter the result in this block.

Expenses

The next section of the form concerns various categories of expenses. Use your check register or print a report from your household financial management software program. If you charge living expenses to a credit card, use the credit card statements in preparing your monthly income and expense statement.

For expenses that vary monthly, it is best to use an average of the most recent twelve months. However, if an expense has changed significantly, you bought or leased a car, or a child started college and you are paying tuition, do not include the months before the change in the average.

Once you have computed your actual expenses, enter that amount. The **MONTHLY INCOME AND EXPENSES STATEMENT** must reflect your actual expenses. If your expenses seem high, it is your adversary's task to bring that up. If your expenses seem low and will hurt your arguments for support, it is up to you to prove that future expenses will be higher and explain why.

Include the full amount of the expenses you incur for yourself or your children in your custody, even if your spouse reimburses you or pays the expense directly. Include your spouse's reimbursement or direct payment under other income.

Household

◈ Enter the monthly average of each of these household expense categories. If there are deferred maintenance and repairs that need to be done, or if you have recently moved and have not furnished your new home, you may want to add a footnote explaining that the expense will increase.

Utilities

◈ Enter the monthly average of each of these utility expense categories. Be sure to use a twelve-month average for electricity and gas or heating oil.

Food

◈   Enter the monthly average of each of these food expense categories. Be careful to include the cost of all the food items you pay for in cash—like your lunches and fast food meals. Check credit card statements for charged meals or groceries.

Automobile

◈   Enter the monthly average of each of these automobile expense categories. Include the cost of public transportation and cab fare under other transportation. If you have no car payment but you have an old car that will need replacing soon, you may enter an appropriate monthly amount under "payment/depreciation."

Children's Expenses

◈   Enter the monthly average of each of these children's expenses categories. Do not be limited by the printed categories. Carefully review your expenditures over the last year to make sure that you calculate and enter all of your children's expenses.

Clothing

◈   Enter the monthly average of each of these clothing expense categories. Be sure to use a twelve-month average for new clothing purchases.

Health Expenses

◈   Enter the monthly average of each of these health expense categories. Include health insurance premiums here unless they are deducted from your paycheck. Again, use a twelve-month average. If you are paying off an existing doctor or dentist bill, include the monthly payment for past services as well as any current expense.

Dues

⟡ Enter the monthly average of each of these dues in the expense categories.

Miscellaneous

⟡ Enter the monthly average of each of these miscellaneous expenses categories. Do not be limited by the printed categories. Carefully review your expenditures over the last year to make sure that you calculate and enter all of your miscellaneous expenses.

Fixed Debts with Payments

⟡ Enter the balance and monthly payment for any fixed debt of yours that is not a mortgage payment or car note, and is not included and claimed in one of the other foregoing expense categories.

Charge Account Debt

⟡ Enter the balance and average monthly payment on each of your charge account debts. Remember that you should include your average monthly charges of expenses in the appropriate categories. List payment of existing balances. Do not list payment of the previous month's charges of your expenses that have already been included. That would be double-counting.

If your charge account payments are comprised of both payment of current charges and payment on existing debt, calculate the amount to enter on monthly debt payment for each as follows.

1. Add all payments on the card during the last twelve months.

2. Add all charges on the card that were claimed as expenses in the expense categories discussed on pages 167–169.

3.　Subtract the result in 2 from the result in 1, divide the remainder by 12, and enter as your monthly payment for the card. If 1 is less than 2, you have no debt payment cash expense, because your debts are increasing. In this case, you can still claim the monthly average of the interest added to your account balance as an expense.

Totals Per Month

If you have a computer software spreadsheet program, you can use it to calculate the totals. Otherwise, a calculator will be useful for the following calculations.

◈　Calculate subtotals for each expense category, and record them in pencil on the form or elsewhere. Add the expense category subtotals and enter the result in the subtotal expenses block.

◈　Calculate subtotals for fixed debts with payments and for charge account debt, and record them in pencil on the form or elsewhere. Add the debt category subtotals and enter the result in the subtotal debt payments block.

◈　Add subtotal expenses and subtotal debts, and enter the result in the total expenses block.

◈　Bring down the entry in monthly net income and enter it again in the total net income block.

◈　Subtract total expenses from total net income.

- If total net income exceeds total expenses, enter the result in the balance (+) block.

- If total expenses exceed total net income, enter the result in the balance (-) block.

Liquid Assets on Hand

◈ Add the current balances of your checking and savings accounts and all currency not in an account, and enter the result in the cash/checking/savings block. You can use your checkbook balance; that is, deduct checks you have written and mailed that have not cleared the bank.

◈ Add the balances or values of all other liquid assets and enter the result in the other liquid assets block. *Liquid assets* are those that are immediately convertible into cash without significant loss of value. The current value of one-hundred shares of IBM stock is a liquid asset. The current value of shares of stock in the corporation through which the family business is owned and operated is not a liquid asset. A treasury note is a liquid asset. The note you had your brother sign to make sure he repays the money you loaned him once he graduates college and finds a job is not a liquid asset (unless he has graduated, found a job, and started repaying you).

Submitted

◈ Print or type your name under the line and sign on the line.

DISTRICT OF COLUMBIA

The court publishes a financial form, but it is no longer required by many of the judges in the new District of Columbia Family Court. However, it is a good idea to complete it, because it helps you and the court focus on the financial issues in dispute.

Complete the District of Columbia **FINANCIAL STATEMENT** (form DC–1, p.323) as follows.

◈ Put the case number and date at the top. If you do not have a case number yet, leave it blank.

◈ Put your name, Social Security number, and occupation in the boxes on the first line.

◈   Fill in the name and address of your current employer and the number of tax exemptions you claim in the boxes on the second line.

◈   Income information is on the left side of the first page. At line 1, state your monthly gross wages. If you get paid every two weeks, multiply your pay stub by 26 and divide by 12 to get monthly figures.

◈   At line 2, fill in deductions from your pay.

◈   At line 3, subtract deductions on line 2 from your gross wages on line 1 to get your monthly net wages.

◈   At line 4, fill in any other income you have.

◈   At line 5, fill in any deductions you have against the income on line 4.

◈   At line 6, subtract other deductions on line 5 from other income on line 4 to get your monthly net income from all other sources.

◈   At line 7, add the net incomes on lines 3 and 6 to get your total monthly net disposable income. Also put this number on line 9 in the summary section at the bottom of the form on the left.

◈   At line 8, add the gross incomes on lines 1 and 4 to get your total monthly gross income.

◈   Now, go to the right-hand section of the first page and itemize your average monthly expenses. If you have children, you will allocate each line of expense between you and the children. Be sure to include credit card payments under periodic payments. If you have a lawyer, do not forget to include legal fees, or loan payments if you have borrowed money for your legal fees.

◈   At the bottom left, total your monthly expenses. Also put this number in line 10 in the summary on the bottom of the form.

◈ At line 11 of the Summary section, subtract expenses on line 10 from income on line 9, and fill in the difference. If you make more than you spend, it will be a positive number. If you have shortfall each month, it will be a negative number.

◈ On page 2 of the form, the first section is for liabilities. For each item that you owe, state the type of debt, to whom it is owed, the date it was incurred, the total amount, the amount you have paid to date, and the balance due. In "type of debt," also indicate whether it is jointly owned or in your name alone. Although there is no space for it, add up the total amount of debt and put the number at the end of the column.

◈ In the second section, the left side is for assets. For everything you own, you will put the value in the column marked "Separate" or "Joint," depending on how it is held. Include cash, automobiles, bank accounts, bonds, notes, real estate, stocks, personal property, and any other items. Add up the total assets in each column.

◈ In the summary on the right side, you will fill in total assets from the assets side. Then, divide the total amount of debt into debt in your name and joint debt, and use those numbers for total liabilities in the summary section. Subtract total liabilities from total assets in each column to get your net worth.

◈ Sign the form in front of a notary public and attach a copy of your most recent pay stub.

Alimony

Alimony is *spousal support* paid by one spouse to the other. This chapter first discusses different alimony issues common to all three jurisdictions. Then, the differences between the jurisdictions concerning *rehabilitative* and *permanent* alimony are discussed. Finally, the similar but different factors for determining alimony in each jurisdiction are set forth.

GENERAL INFORMATION

In Maryland, Virginia, and the District of Columbia, alimony is based upon the relative needs and resources of the parties. If you do not get alimony at the time of the divorce, you cannot get alimony later on. It is possible for either spouse to receive alimony.

Taxes and Bankruptcy

There are certain important things to know about alimony. Alimony can be deducted from your paycheck by an *Earnings Withholding Order* directed to your employer. Also, alimony is taxable to the person receiving and deductible to the person paying, unless otherwise agreed. Finally, alimony is not a debt that can be discharged in bankruptcy.

Rehabilitative or Indefinite

Alimony can be *rehabilitative* or *indefinite* in Maryland, Virginia, and the District of Columbia.

Rehabilitative alimony. Rehabilitate means to restore a party to an economically functioning level, such as earning a reasonable living. The public policy is to assist the former spouse to be self-supporting. Rehabilitative alimony is temporary, so it is set for a specific time period.

Indefinite alimony. If rehabilitative alimony cannot bring about rehabilitation (for example, when a spouse has a disability), then the court can, in proper circumstances, order alimony on a long-term or indefinite basis. In Maryland and Virginia, indefinite alimony may also be granted when one spouse is disabled or the incomes of the spouses are *unconscionably disparate* (meaning one spouse makes far more than the other).

Indefinite alimony is granted less often these days, except in the District of Columbia, where that is the only type of alimony available. Indefinite alimony can be raised or lowered over time if there is a change of circumstances. Indefinite usually means until you die, your spouse dies, or your spouse remarries (although alimony can continue even past remarriage in some cases).

Pendente Lite

You can also ask the court for *pendente lite* alimony, meaning temporary spousal support during the litigation. The test for pendente lite alimony is more strict than permanent alimony in Maryland and Virginia. It is based on the needs of the party seeking alimony and the ability of the other party to pay. *Needs* are defined as necessities and suit moneys in Maryland. In Virginia, it is sums necessary for maintenance and support, and to enable a spouse to carry on the suit. In the District of Columbia, it is genuine need, but the court uses the same criteria as it does for permanent alimony.

Termination

Living with someone after the divorce, regardless of whether you have sex or not, may cause indefinite alimony to be lowered or stopped. Death of one of the persons paying or receiving alimony, or marriage of the person receiving alimony, will terminate alimony unless the *Separation Agreement* provides otherwise.

ALIMONY FACTORS

The legislature has set out specific criteria for the court to consider in alimony awards in all three jurisdictions. Because they are similar, but with subtle differences, all are set forth in detail.

NOTE: *The factors for rehabilitative and indefinite alimony are differ-ent from the standards for pendente lite alimony.*

Maryland   In Maryland, the court must consider the following factors in awarding alimony:

- income from salaries, investments, etc.;

- pension, profit-sharing, and retirement plans;

- education and ability of the parties, as well as opportunities for additional education;

- length of the marriage;

- age, physical condition, and mental condition of the two parties;

- children;

- whether one of the parties should stay at home with the children of the parties instead of working;

- separate property a person has;

- marital property a person has;

- standard of living the parties enjoyed during the marriage;

- tangible and intangible contributions of a homemaker;

- the tangible and intangible contributions of one party to the education or increased earning power of the other party;

- fault of one of the parties (if the court desires);

- ✪ tax consequences; and,

- ✪ other factors that the court considers appropriate. (Maryland Code, Family Law Article, Sec. 11-016(b).)

Virginia   In Virginia, the alimony factors include:

- ✪ need for support and ability to pay;

- ✪ standard of living during the marriage;

- ✪ length of marriage;

- ✪ parties' age and health;

- ✪ effect of the children's ages and health on a party's ability to work outside the home;

- ✪ contributions to the family during the marriage;

- ✪ property of the parties;

- ✪ division of marital property;

- ✪ education and training, and prospects for future earnings;

- ✪ time and expense involved in a party's appropriate additional training or education;

- ✪ effect of the parties' decisions regarding their education, employment, and parenting on the parties' current and future earning potential;

- ✪ extent to which one party has contributed to the other's education and career; and,

- ✪ other factors, including tax consequences, necessary to make an equitable alimony decision. (Virginia Code, Sec. 20-107.1(E).)

In Virginia, unlike Maryland and the District of Columbia, alimony may *not* be awarded to a spouse who commits adultery when that is grounds for divorce, unless *manifest injustice* would result. The judge determines what manifest injustice may be, based on the facts and circumstances of each case.

District of Columbia

In the District of Columbia, the alimony factors are:

✪ ability of the party seeking alimony to be wholly or partly self-supporting;

✪ time necessary for the party seeking alimony to gain sufficient education or training to enable that party to secure suitable employment;

✪ standard of living that the parties established during their marriage (but giving consideration to the fact that there will be two households to maintain);

✪ duration of the marriage;

✪ circumstances that contributed to the estrangement of the parties;

✪ age of each party;

✪ ability of the party from whom alimony is sought to meet his or her needs while meeting the needs of the other party;

✪ financial needs and financial resources of each party, including:

• income;

• income from assets, both marital and nonmarital;

• potential income which may be imputed to non-income-producing assets of a party;

- any previous award of child support in this case;

- the financial obligations of each party;

- the right of a party to receive retirement benefits; and,

- the taxability or non-taxability of income.

Property

The legislatures in all three jurisdictions of Maryland, Virginia, and the District of Columbia have set out a process for property division by the divorce court called *equitable distribution*. *Equitable* means fair, which does not necessarily mean equal. This chapter explains how property is equitably distributed between the spouses by the court, noting the differences in distribution among the three jurisdictions. The similar factors in each jurisdiction the court must consider in distributing property are detailed.

EQUITABLE DISTRIBUTION

Property in all three jurisdictions includes assets and liabilities, real estate, and personal property—both tangible and intangible. Property can include houses, pensions, businesses, coin collections—almost anything.

This is how the courts of Maryland, Virginia, and the District of Columbia distribute property. First, the court finds and values the property (equity in the house, value of pensions, value of antique furniture). Next, the court determines whether the particular piece of property is separate or nonmarital property, and remains with the person who owned it. Then, the court distributes the marital property.

If you and your spouse can agree on how things will be divided, and if your agreement is reasonable, it will be approved by the court, even if it does not follow this process. If you cannot agree, the court will divide the property, provided you can prove grounds to divorce.

Nonmarital Property

Nonmarital, or *separate*, property is usually acquired before the marriage or outside the marriage (such as by gift or inheritance), or is excluded by a valid agreement. A gift from a spouse, however, is marital property. Nonmarital property can be converted into marital property, for example, by mingling marital and nonmarital accounts, or by changing the title on premarital accounts from sole to joint.

Marital Property

Marital property is usually acquired during the marriage, no matter whose name is on the title. This comes as a surprise to many. They believe that because they have worked hard or their name is on a business, stock account, or pension, that it belongs to them. All the work efforts of each party, all the income earned, and all the assets acquired during the marriage are marital property. Since one spouse may work while the other stays home, the court can look at monetary and nonmonetary contributions when dividing property.

Date of Valuation

In Maryland, Virginia, and the District of Columbia, the court determines the value of property on the date of the divorce. However, in Virginia, pensions are valued at the date of separation. Also in Virginia, you may try to convince the court that another valuation date is more appropriate than the trial date, if you have good cause to do so.

Debt

Despite an agreement for one spouse to pay a debt that is in both parties' names, if the party responsible for the debt does not pay the debt, the other party can still be sued for the debt.

Example:

Mary gets the house and her husband, George, agrees to pay the mortgage. George files for bankruptcy. Mary may or may not be able to sue George. In any case, the mortgage company can foreclose on the house if the payments go unpaid, and can sue Mary for any unpaid balance after foreclosure. The best way to protect Mary in this case would be for George to refinance the property and remove Mary from the debt if possible. Sometimes this is financially impossible for large debts such as houses, but can still be done with smaller debts, such as second mortgages and charge accounts.

The court can distribute *marital debt*. Marital debt is that which is used to acquire a marital asset, like a mortgage or a car loan. The court can also order one party or the other to pay a certain debt, or consider debt in making a marital award. In practice, however, the court will usually leave credit card debt, school loans, and loans from family and friends alone, and may not even mention the debt in the final order.

Hiding Property

Do not hide assets. These assets are usually found, and when they are, you look like a crook to the court. The judge will have trouble believing what you say about anything after that, and he or she will not have too much trouble assessing attorney's fees against you for your behavior.

Use and Possession

If you jointly own your house, you cannot force your spouse to leave. If you change the locks, your spouse can hire a locksmith and change them again, or call the police, who will probably force you to let your spouse back in. There are two exceptions to this rule. The court can order a spouse to leave for domestic violence, and the court can give exclusive use and possession of a house, furniture, and automobile, to a parent with primary custody of the children.

The Maryland courts can order use and possession for up to three years after the divorce. The Virginia courts can only order pendente lite (temporary) use and possession in cases of domestic violence. The District of Columbia does not have a use and possession statute.

Pets

Some people think of their pets as children. They get into custody and visitation fights over them. However, the courts tend to view pets as personal property, like a table or a lamp. You have no custody or visitation rights in a table or a lamp. If you want to make sure there are no disputes over your pet, you can put a provision in your *Separation Agreement*.

EQUITABLE DISTRIBUTION FACTORS

In all three jurisdictions, to determine who gets what marital property, the court will consider certain factors as set forth in the following sections.

Maryland   In Maryland, the court will consider:

- ✪ length of the marriage;

- ✪ age, health, skills, and abilities of the parties;

- ✪ amount of separate property owned by each spouse;

- ✪ relative ability of the parties to acquire property in the future;

- ✪ financial needs and liabilities of the parties;

- ✪ contribution by one spouse to the education or to the earning power of the other spouse;

- ✪ contribution to the value of the marital property or the separate property;

- ✪ premarital property and postmarital property;

- ✪ financial conditions of each party;

- ✪ tax consequences;

- ✪ use and possession—allowing the custodial parent and children to continue to live in the home permanently or for a period of time (the Maryland statute permits up to three years following divorce); and,

- ✪ other factors that the court considers appropriate. (Maryland Code, Family Law Article, Sec. 8-205(b).)

The court must divide joint accounts equally. The court cannot change title to property (except pensions). Therefore, jointly owned items, such as the house and furniture, or even a jointly owned home if there is no use and possession order, are ordered sold by a trustee and the proceeds divided equally. After calculating what marital property will be in the hands of each party, the court can then make a marital award to adjust the amounts divided equitably. A marital award is usually reduced to a *judgment*. A judgment, however, is not the same as getting cash. You may then have to *enforce* the judgment to obtain payment, which means additional legal proceedings after your divorce.

The court can distribute *marital debt* in Maryland, which is debt used to acquire marital property.

Virginia In Virginia, the factors considered are:

- contributions to family unit;

- monetary and nonmonetary contributions to acquisition and maintenance of property;

- length of marriage;

- parties' age and health;

- circumstances contributing to dissolution (i.e., fault);

- how and when property was acquired;

- the parties' debts, what was received for the debt, and property securing the debt, if any;

- character of property (whether it is liquid or illiquid);

- tax consequences; and,

- other relevant factors that the court considers appropriate. (Virginia Code, Sec. 20-107.3.)

Unlike Maryland, the Virginia court can transfer title to property if it is jointly owned.

District of Columbia   In the District of Columbia, the factors are:

- duration of the marriage;

- age;

- health;

- occupation;

- amount and sources of income;

- vocational skills;

- employability;

- assets (including nonmarital property);

- debts;

- needs of each party;

- custody;

- alimony;

- obligations from a prior marriage or for other children;

- future income and asset opportunity;

- contribution to the education of the other party;

- change in income as a result of the marriage or duties of home-making and child care;

- taxation of assets;

- whether the debt or asset was acquired before or after the parties' separation;

- circumstances contributing to the estrangement;

- contribution to assets; and,

- contribution as a homemaker or otherwise to the family. (District of Columbia Code, Sec. 16-910(b).)

The court can transfer title to property and distribute debt in the District of Columbia.

PENSIONS

Pensions can be divided by the court by entry of a *Qualified Domestic Relations Order* (QDRO). Having a QDRO drafted, approved by the pension administer, and entered by the court is not an easy task. The stakes are usually high. If your spouse has a substantial pension earned during the marriage, you probably should hire a lawyer.

After the Divorce

Most people think it is over when the judge grants your divorce. However, there are many possible postdivorce issues, including reconciliation, records, changes, bankruptcy, and a postdivorce checklist, that apply to all three jurisdictions.

FINANCES

After the divorce, you and your ex-spouse will have two separate households. You will have to maintain those two homes on the money with which you maintained one earlier. Two cannot live as cheaply as one.

DIFFICULT FORMER SPOUSE

If your spouse has been a difficult person all of his or her life, it is very unlikely that going through a divorce will make him or her a less difficult person. After the divorce, you may be separated, but still connected by visitation, child support, alimony, or debt payments. In that case, you will still have to deal with the problems together.

If your spouse is difficult, then no matter how hard you try or how well you succeed, your spouse will probably still be difficult.

APPEALS

You may be able to appeal a decision in your case if you are not satisfied with the outcome. If the trial judge made an error in finding the facts or applying the law that affected the outcome, your appeal may be successful. If not, appealing to a higher (appellate) court probably will not do you any good.

The appellate courts do not rehear all the evidence. They decide, based on the record of the trial court hearing, whether the trial judge made one or more mistakes, and if so, whether they were important enough to warrant changing the decision or sending the case back to the trial judge.

Maryland   There are slight differences in appeal procedures between Maryland, Virginia, and the District of Columbia and the appeals process is described here for each jurisdiction. In Maryland, if your case is heard by a master, the master will provide *Findings and Recommendations*. You then have ten days to file *exceptions* with the clerk. Exceptions must be in writing and state the errors you assert with particularity. You also need to order a transcript of the hearing before the master from the clerk and file it with the court.

If you request a hearing, the court will hold one within sixty days of filing your exceptions. The hearing is before a judge who will listen to your argument and make an independent decision on your case.

You then have thirty days from the date of the judge's order to file a *Notice of Appeal*. If you did not take exceptions, then you have waived your appeal rights. Once you file your *Notice of Appeal*, you must transmit the record of your case to the appeals court. You will then receive a briefing schedule from the appeals court. If there is no appeal, your divorce will be final thirty days after the judge signs the final decree.

Virginia   In Virginia, if your case is heard by a commissioner and you are not satisfied with the commissioner's report, you have ten days to file exceptions to the report. If a party files exceptions, the court will schedule a hearing before a judge. File the exceptions with the clerk of court, mail a copy to the opposing party, and file a *Certificate of Mailing*.

If you want to appeal the decision of the trial court judge in your divorce case to the court of appeals, you must first file a *Notice of Appeal* in the circuit court. Then, mail a copy to the opposing party, and file a certificate listing the names, addresses, and telephone numbers of the parties and lawyers, stating that a copy of the *Notice of Appeal* has been sent to the opposing party or lawyer, and stating that a transcript of the hearing has been ordered, if one will be filed. You must also file copies of the *Notice* and *Certificate* in the court of appeals, and pay a $25 fee. There are detailed rules about filing the trial court record, the form and content of appeal briefs, and the schedule for filing briefs. There may or may not be oral argument before the court of appeals.

If you want to petition the Supreme Court to review your case, you must file a *Notice of Appeal* within thirty days of the date of the trial court or court of appeals judgment. You must obtain and file a transcript of the trial court hearing. There is no automatic right to Supreme Court review. You must file a *Petition for Appeal* in the Supreme Court within three months of the date of the circuit court judgment or thirty days from the date of the court of appeals judgment.

Your petition should be about why your case is important and ought to be heard, not just about why you should win. The opposing party can file a brief in opposition and you can file a reply brief. The Supreme Court will decide, based on the briefs and maybe oral argument, whether it will hear your appeal. If the Supreme Court decides to hear your appeal, the process continues under detailed rules of procedure similar to the rules for the court of appeals.

District of Columbia   In the District of Columbia, you have ten days to request a review of the commissioner's decision by a judge. The ten days starts counting from the entry of your *Divorce Decree* on the court docket by the court clerk. A judge can extend the time by another twenty days for good cause. A judge may also review any decision on his or her own within thirty days of docketing. After the judge has reviewed the commissioner's decision and issued a decision of his or her own, you may appeal to the Court of Appeals of the District of Columbia. If there is no appeal, your divorce is effective thirty days from entry on the court record.

CHANGES

If you and your spouse or ex-spouse agree to change the terms of a court order (such as *Temporary Support Order* or *Final Decree*), you must change it with another order. If your ex-spouse says, "You do not have to pay alimony for the next year if you will take the children to Disneyland this summer," you must get it in writing and entered in court for it to be binding on your ex-spouse and to protect you from contempt.

If you need to change child support or certain types of alimony, you can petition the court for a change. If you show a change of circumstances, then the court may modify those provisions. The change of circumstances that most impresses the court are those changes that are unexpected, such as, "I lost my job because the company went bankrupt." The courts are less sympathetic to, "I just don't want to work as hard as I used to work."

Sometimes changes that everybody knew were coming are not a change of circumstances, such as, "When my children became teenagers, they were so much more expensive." This should have been anticipated.

RECORDS

It is very important that you keep records of payments you make or receive for alimony and child support. If you are paying, pay by check and keep all canceled checks. If you cannot prove you paid it, you might as well not have paid it. If you are receiving payments, keep a running account in a permanent place. If you cannot prove what you did get, the court might not believe you when you testify about what you did not get. It is easier for both parties, and sometimes required by law, to have payments deducted from the paycheck of the person who is paying.

BANKRUPTCY

Bankruptcy is federal law that gives overburdened debtors certain relief from payment of their debts. Divorce and bankruptcy go together like love and marriage. In our credit-driven society, family budgets are often based on two incomes supporting one household. When the one household becomes two, income can become insufficient resulting in eventual bankruptcy. The Bankruptcy Abuse Prevention and Consumer Protection Act of 2005 made important changes to bankruptcy law that can affect your divorce.

Chapter 7 Bankruptcy

Briefly, the person who files bankruptcy is called the *debtor*. The persons or businesses owed money are called *creditors*. In a Chapter 7 bankruptcy (liquidation), the debtor gives up his or her nonexempt property and receives a discharge of the obligation to pay his or her dischargeable debts. In theory, creditors are paid from the debtor's nonexempt assets, but in consumer cases, nonexempt assets almost never exist.

Discharge

Discharge means that the debtor does not have to pay the debt and the creditor cannot take action to collect it. Generally, if the debtor is not ineligible and has completed all of the debtor's duties, he or she will be granted a discharge in the bankruptcy case. The 2005 Act created a new requirement, that debtors complete a financial management course before they receive a Chapter 7 or 13 discharge.

Debts owed to a spouse or former spouse for support, property division, or debts based on allocation of marital debt are not dischargeable in a Chapter 7 bankruptcy. This means that the debtor former spouse must pay the obligation despite the bankruptcy and that the creditor former spouse can take legal action to collect. The creditor spouse does not need to take any action in the bankruptcy case to preserve the right to collect the debt.

Automatic Stay

The filing of a bankruptcy case operates as an *automatic stay* of all other litigation involving the debtor, including divorce. Judgments, decrees, and orders entered in violation of the stay are generally void, but most court actions that happen in a divorce case are exceptions to the automatic stay. Examples of actions that are exceptions to the bankruptcy stay are actions to establish paternity, determine or modify child support, determine child custody and visitation, obtain relief in domestic violence cases, or to obtain a divorce. Examples of actions that are subject to the stay are division of marital property, earnings withholding orders to collect support, and interception of an income tax refund. If there is any doubt, the only safe courses are to go into bankruptcy court to have the stay lifted to allow your divorce court action to proceed, or to wait until the conclusion of the bankruptcy case.

Chapter 13 Bankruptcy

In a Chapter 13 bankruptcy, the debtor files a plan that provides for payment of the debts, usually from future income. Chapter 13 plans are subject to various rules regarding the treatment of creditors. One such rule is that the plan must provide for full payment of *priority* claims. Domestic support obligations are first priority claims. Also, a Chapter 13 plan cannot be confirmed if the debtor is not current with all post petition domestic support obligations.

The Chapter 13 discharge is broader that the discharge under Chapter 7. The one exception to the rule that divorce obligations are not dischargeable is that divorce obligations that are not *domestic support obligations* can be discharged in a Chapter 13 case under certain circumstances if the debtor makes all payments required under the plan.

Joint Bankruptcy

In those cases where it appears that bankruptcy is inevitable for both spouses, the possibility of a joint bankruptcy should not be overlooked. The spouses must still be husband and wife to be eligible to file a joint bankruptcy case, so the bankruptcy petition would have to be filed before entry of the divorce decree.

If Your Former Spouse Files Bankruptcy

If you are the creditor spouse, your legal position is secure in Chapter 7 and secure with respect to support obligations in a Chapter 13. Nevertheless, you should carefully review all pleadings and notices and consult counsel early in the process if the stakes are high and there is any doubt about what you must do to preserve your rights. If your former spouse files a Chapter 13, owes you obligations that are not for support, and provided for less than full payment of that debt in the Chapter 13 plan, you should act promptly to minimize the chance that the unpaid balance of the debt will be discharged at the conclusion of the Chapter 13 bankruptcy case. Unless the stakes do not justify it, it is best to consult an experienced bankruptcy lawyer in these circumstances.

If You are Considering Bankruptcy

If you are the debtor spouse, you may find that your postdivorce or mid-divorce circumstances require you to seek bankruptcy relief. Your former spouse is holding a lot of cards—especially if support debts are involved. Your interests and your spouse's interests are not necessarily directly adverse in the bankruptcy case. This is not the divorce where every dollar one of you gets, the other one has to give up. Your former spouse's and your children's economic interests are protected in bankruptcy in a way that other creditors' interests are not. If most of your debt is owed to persons other than your former spouse, and most of your debt is not joint with him or her, your bankruptcy is probably not a bad thing for your former spouse. In these circumstances, it may be wise to give him or her advance notice, explain what you are doing and why, and persuade your former spouse that it is in his or her economic interest not to interfere with your obtaining bankruptcy relief.

Former Law

As far as divorce goes, the most important change made in the 2005 bankruptcy reform legislation was the almost complete elimination of the distinction that formerly existed between support obligations and other divorce-related debt. Former law applies to bankruptcy cases filed prior to October 17, 2005. Under former law, as currently, support obligations were not dischargeable and the creditor spouse did not need to take any action in bankruptcy court to preserve the debt. However, nonsupport marital debts were not automatically excepted from the debtor spouse's Chapter 7 discharge. Examples are property settlements payments and indemnification agreements. In *indemnification agreements*, your spouse agrees with you that he or she will pay a debt you both owe, then he or she files bankruptcy and receives a discharge of his or her obligation to the joint creditor. These marital debts were not automatically excepted from the debtor spouse's Chapter 7 discharge. The creditor spouse had to file a timely complaint in the bankruptcy case. The bankruptcy court may or may not decide that the marital debt should be excepted from the debtor's discharge. It depends on the relative financial circumstances of the two spouses.

Conclusion

In general, bankruptcy does not afford any relief from divorce-related debt. However, divorce law and bankruptcy law are both complicated. The overlap of these two bodies of law, though simplified by the 2005 bankruptcy legislation, can still be tricky for both debtor and creditor spouses.

POSTDIVORCE CHECKLIST

Your work does not end with the divorce. Check the following list of action items to be sure you have handled the applicable issues.

❑ Complete pension fund transfers and arrange rollovers.

❑ Prepare and record deed for real estate transfer, or sell property.

❑ Transfer automobile titles.

❑ Transfer bank accounts and close joint accounts.

❑ Transfer stock and close joint accounts.

❑ Transfer household items.

❑ Cancel joint credit cards or remove ex-spouse's name.

❑ Send letters to creditors and reporting agencies if your spouse has agreed to pay debt.

❑ Notify the IRS and state tax authority if you have changed address. (IRS Form 8822)

❑ Change beneficiaries on insurance policies and pension plans.

❑ Convert health insurance under COBRA by the deadline.

❑ Notify school of addresses of both parents for mailing records.

❑ Revise will.

Glossary

A

abandonment. A spouse's unjustified departure from the marital home.

absolute divorce. A completed divorce that dissolves the bonds of matrimony and permits the parties to marry again. (Contrast with *limited divorce* and *divorce from bed and board*.)

adultery. Sexual intercourse by a married person with a person other than his or her spouse. This is immediate grounds for divorce in Maryland and Virginia.

alimony. Financial support paid by one spouse or former spouse to the other. Also called spousal support.

alimony factors. The factors a court considers in setting the amount of alimony. They are set by statute in Maryland and Virginia, and by case law in the District of Columbia.

annulment. A legal proceeding whereby a court declares a marriage never existed because some impediment prevented a valid marriage. Thus, the marriage is nullified.

alternative dispute resolution (ADR). Any process by which legal adversaries reach a decision other than bringing the matter to trial for a judge's decision; in divorce cases, it usually refers to mediation.

appeal. Procedure by which a trial court decision is brought before a higher court for review.

C

child support. The payment the noncustodial parent pays to the custodial parent for support of the parties' children.

child support guidelines. The charts used to determine the amount of child support to be paid. The guidelines take account of objective economic factors, which generally include the custodial parent's income, the noncustodial parent's income, alimony payable between the parties, the cost of health insurance, the cost of day care, and, usually in some fashion, either parent's obligations with respect to other children who are not children of both parties.

circuit court. The trial court for divorce case in Maryland and Virginia. There is one in each county in Maryland. There is one in most counties and cities in Virginia, but some circuit courts cover more than one county.

collaborative family law. A settlement process in which the lawyers contract to withdraw if one of the parties decides to litigate the divorce.

commissioners. *See masters.*

conclusions of law. The basis for a court's decision in a case. The result of the judge's application of the law to his or her findings of fact in the case.

constructive desertion. A spouse's withdrawal from spousal duties and the marital relationship without leaving the marital home. Generally, this is grounds for limited divorce immediately and for absolute divorce after a waiting period.

contested divorce. A divorce in which the parties do not agree on one or more issues, and bring the case to court for a contested divorce hearing.

contested divorce hearing. The hearing or trial in a divorce case in which the parties do not agree on one or more issues.

corroboration. Additional proof. The laws of Maryland and Virginia require corroboration of a party's testimony to the facts entitling him or her to a divorce.

court clerk. There are different clerks for different paperwork tasks at the court house. The first clerk you see will be the one that processes your complaint, starts a court file, and assigns your case a number. There is also a file clerk who keeps track of all the files. The judge may also have a courtroom clerk at the hearing, and a law clerk to help research the law. (Clerks are not permitted to give you legal advice, but they can be helpful in moving your case along.)

cruelty. One spouse's mistreatment of the other that is so serious that it is grounds for divorce. Usually, cruelty includes physical violence. It is generally grounds for limited divorce immediately and for absolute divorce after a waiting period.

custody. The legal right to act as parent to the children, have the children live with you, and make decisions about their welfare and upbringing. In a divorce case, unless the parties reach an agreement, the court decides which parent will have custody of the children.

custody evaluator or assessor. Most courts hire therapists to make an investigation and report to the court on issues of custody. The evaluator will interview you, your spouse, the children, and sometimes third parties, like teachers and neighbors. The assessor usually only interviews the children and the parties. The court places great weight on the recommendations of the evaluator or assessor as to custody.

custody mediator. The court has several therapists on staff to try to resolve custody disputes. For example, you may be ordered to have two, two-hour sessions with the custody mediator.

custodial parent. The parent who has custody of the children.

D

deposition. A discovery procedure. A party to litigation can compel the other party or other witnesses to submit to oral questions under oath before a court reporter.

decree of divorce. The court's decision concluding a divorce case.

desertion. Abandonment. A spouse's unjustified departure from the marital home. It is generally grounds for limited divorce immediately and for absolute divorce after a waiting period.

direct examination. A party's (or his or her attorney's) questioning of a witness that the party has called as part of his or her case in trial or hearing.

discovery. A variety of pretrial procedures that can be used to discover facts from the other party. The most common methods are depositions, interrogatories, request for production of documents, and requests for admission.

divorce. Judicial dissolution of the bonds of matrimony between married persons.

divorce from bed and board. Virginia term for limited divorce. Judicial recognition of the separate status of the parties and a divorce for tax and many other purposes, but it does not permit the parties to marry again.

divorce hearing. In an uncontested case, the hearing at which the spouse who filed a complaint for divorce presents evidence of the facts constituting grounds for divorce and of facts relevant to any other issue, such as the parties' separation and property settlement agreement, or the amount of child support to be paid.

domestic violence. Violence against a spouse or a person in some other family or romantic relationship. The laws of Maryland, Virginia, and the District of Columbia provide special expedited procedures to meet the security and financial needs of victims of domestic violence.

E

equitable distribution. The process of identifying, valuing, and equitably dividing marital property, or ordering compensatory payment from one spouse to the other.

evidence. The proofs presented at trial. A witness's answer under oath or documents or other tangible things presented by a party and accepted as evidence by the court.

exceptions. Procedure by which a master or commissioner's findings and recommendations are brought before the judge for review.

expert witness. A witness who can give the court an expert opinion (unlike a regular witness, who can generally only report facts). For example, a therapist can testify about custody and visitation, or a real estate appraiser can give values for real estate.

F

family court. The District of Columbia court that hears divorce and other family matters; part of the Superior Court.

family division. In some counties in Maryland, there are special divisions of the circuit court that hear divorce and other family law matters.

family home. In Maryland, if there are minor children, the spouse with custody can be awarded exclusive use and possession of the family home, furniture, and automobile. There is no similar process in Virginia or the District of Columbia.

findings of fact. The judge's (or other judicial officer's) decision about what he or she finds the facts to be after a trial or hearing. The findings of fact state what the judge believed, and sometimes, what he or she did not believe.

Findings and Recommendations. The title of the master's report after the hearing in Maryland. In Virginia, the commissioner's report is titled a report. In the District of Columbia, a commissioner's report is called Findings of Fact and Conclusions of Law.

G

grounds for divorce. The legal basis for granting a divorce.

guardian ad litem. The court may appoint a lawyer for the children if custody is in dispute. This lawyer can consult with the evaluator or assessor, and may also recommend which parent should have custody. In Maryland, the court sometimes appoints a *Nagle v. Hooks attorney*, which is an attorney who can waive the child-therapist privilege. (You will probably have to pay for a portion of this lawyer's fees and usually payment is required in advance.)

I

incorporated but not merged. The term used to mean that the parties' agreement is part of the court's decree, in that failure to perform will be a violation of a court order punishable by contempt. The agreement also remains a private contract that can be enforced by suit for breach of contract. Incorporation does merge the agreement with the decree in the District of Columbia by operation of law, even if the parties agree otherwise.

indefinite alimony. Alimony that is payable until the death of either party, remarriage of the payee, or further order of court. The court can modify or terminate indefinite alimony if a party shows that there has been a material change in circumstances since entry of the decree setting alimony, and that the change warrants modifying or terminating alimony.

interrogatories. A discovery procedure. A party's written questions to the other party that have to be answered in writing and under oath.

J

judge. The judge will hear your case and decide your divorce.

jurisdiction. The power of a court to hear and decide the matter that is before it and bind the parties by its decision.

L

lawyers. One or both of you may hire a lawyer to represent you. In litigation, the lawyer will be called *attorney for the plaintiff* or *attorney for the defendant*. Lawyers are also sometimes referred to as *counsel* or *counsel of record*.

legal custody. The right to make long-term parenting decisions about the child's upbringing, health, education, religion, and so on.

limited divorce. Judicial recognition of the separate status of the parties, and a divorce for tax and many other purposes, but it does not permit the parties to marry again.

M

marital property. Marital property is the property that the court will equitably divide between the parties in a divorce, or that it will consider in ordering any compensating payment (monetary award) from one party to the other. Generally, this is property acquired by one or both spouses during the marriage.

masters. Masters are not quite judges, but they are appointed as special assistants to the court to hear uncontested divorces and some contested divorces in order to make recommendations to the judge. The recommendations are usually adopted by the judge.

mediation. A process by which the parties meet to discuss the disputed issues with a skilled neutral person who guides the process and helps the parties reach agreements on the issues in the case.

monetary award. The compensatory payment the court may order one spouse to pay another as an adjustment of their respective equity in marital property.

N

Nagle v. Hooks attorney. In Maryland, the court sometimes appoints an attorney who can waive the child-therapist privilege so that the therapist can testify if that is in the best interests of the child. (*Nagle v. Hooks* is the name of the case in which the court explained this requirement.)

noncustodial parent. The parent who does not have custody of the children, or if custody is shared, the parent with whom the children do not live on a full-time basis.

nonmarital property. Property that was owned by a spouse prior to the marriage; acquired by gift from a third person; or, inherited. Also, property that is excluded from marital property by a valid agreement.

P

parenting classes. Court-sponsored classes on the negative impact of divorce on children and how to minimize it. The court may order parties to attend in contested custody cases. Maryland, Virginia, and the District of Columbia all have a parenting class program.

party. You and your spouse are the parties to the divorce. In the litigation, the person who files first is called the *Plaintiff* and the other spouse is then the *Defendant*. (In a *Separation Agreement*, you may be referred to as *Husband* and *Wife*.)

pendente lite. During the litigation; temporary, until the trial.

pendente lite alimony. Alimony ordered to be paid until the final hearing; pendente lite alimony is usually only an amount sufficient to pay for necessities.

pendente lite facilitator. Family lawyers with mediation training are available in some courts at the scheduling conference to try to help you settle temporary support and related issues.

pendente lite relief. Court orders regarding support or other matters entered during the litigation to allow the parties to maintain the status quo until the final hearing.

personal jurisdiction. The power of a court to bind a person to its decision. Acquired by proper service of process on the person or his or her voluntary appearance in the case.

physical custody. Refers to the home in which the children primarily reside. The parent who lives in that home has physical custody of the children.

pleadings. Papers filed with the court such as the complaint, answer, and counterclaim.

pretrial conference. Final conference with the court before trial. At or before the conference, the parties have to file a joint statement of marital property and a pretrial statement regarding such things as identification of witnesses, documents, and pending motions.

prayer for relief. The last section of a pleading where the party tells the court what the party wants the court to do.

process servers. Your complaint can be served by mail, but if your spouse does not sign or does not accept the mail, you can have it hand delivered by someone other than yourself.

property settlement agreement. An agreement under which the spouses divide marital property.

R

rehabilitative alimony. Alimony for a stated term to permit a party to become self-supporting.

requests for production of documents. A discovery procedure. A party's written request to the other party to produce documents for inspection and copying.

S

scheduling conference. First court appearance at which the court schedules various hearings depending on the issues in the case, and may schedule mediation or order the parties to attend parenting classes.

separate maintenance. Spousal support paid by one spouse or former spouse to the other.

separate property. Property that is not marital property, generally because it was owned by a spouse prior to the marriage. It may have been acquired by gift from a third party or inheritance, or it was excluded from marital property by a valid agreement.

shared custody. The noncustodial parent has custody a significant amount of time.

separation agreement. Spouses' agreement regarding the terms of their separation. In addition to the agreement that the spouse shall live separately, it will often cover matters such as child custody and support, alimony, division of property, allocation of responsibility for debt, and allocation of tax benefits.

split custody. Each parent has physical custody of one or more of the party's children.

stealth contract. The *authors'* term, referring to the body of law contained in statutes, rules, and cases that governs marriage and divorce in the absence of a prenuptial agreement. Although you usually have no knowledge of this contract when you get married, you are deemed to have understood and agreed to it when you get divorced.

suit money. Litigation costs the court can order one spouse to pay to another; comprised of attorney's fees, court costs, and other litigation charges, such as expert witness fees.

superior court. Trial court in the District of Columbia. A similar court in Virginia and Maryland is the circuit court.

T

time-sharing. *See visitation.*

trial. The hearing at which the parties to litigation present witnesses, documents, and other evidence about the facts bearing on the contested issues in a case.

U

uncontested divorce hearing. The hearing at which the spouse who filed a Complaint for Divorce presents evidence of the facts constituting grounds for divorce and of facts relevant to any other issue, such as the parties' Separation and Property Settlement Agreement or the amount of child support to be paid.

use and possession. In Maryland, a spouse with custody of the minor child or children of the parties can be granted exclusive use and possession of the family home, furniture, and automobile.

V

visitation. The noncustodial parent's time with the children. Sometimes referred to in an agreement and orders as *time-sharing*.

W

witness. One who sees, knows, or vouches for something. Also, one who gives testimony under oath.

Summary of Maryland Divorce Laws

This appendix summarizes the most important laws concerning divorce in Maryland. You can use this summary to find a quick answer to a question or as a starting point for further research.

SUMMARY OF MARYLAND DIVORCE LAWS

1. FILING.

(a) the Complaint is filed in the "Circuit Court of _____ County, Maryland";

(b) it is titled a "Complaint for Divorce" or "Complaint for Limited Divorce";

(c) it is filed by the "Plaintiff";

(d) the other spouse is the "Defendant";

(e) it is filed in a county where either spouse resides; and

(f) the final papers are called the "Judgment of Absolute Divorce". *Maryland Rules.*

2. RESIDENCY.
One of the parties has lived in Maryland for at least one year immediately prior to filing for divorce, or the grounds for divorce occurred in Maryland. If insanity is the grounds for divorce, residency is increased to two years. *Maryland Code; Family Law Article, Title 7, Section 7-103.*

3. GROUNDS FOR ABSOLUTE DIVORCE.

(a) the parties have voluntarily lived under separate roof for one year without interruption or cohabitation and there is no reasonable expectation of reconciliation;

(b) the parties have lived separate and apart without interruption for two years;

(c) adultery;

(d) deliberate desertion for twelve months with no chance for reconciliation;

(e) confinement for incurable insanity of at least three years;

(f) conviction of a felony or a misdemeanor with at least a three-year sentence and after one year having been served; and,

(g) cruelty and excessively vicious conduct with no reasonable expectation of reconciliation. *Maryland Code; Family Law Article, Title 7, Section 7-103.*

4. GROUNDS FOR LIMITED DIVORCE.

(a) willful desertion;

(b) cruel and excessively vicious conduct;

(b) voluntary separation and living separate and apart without cohabitation. *Maryland Code; Family Law Article, Title 7, Section 7-102.*

5. MEDIATION AND PARENTING CLASSES.
Maryland specifically declares that it is in the best interests of children that there be mediated resolutions of parental disputes regarding custody. In cases where the custody of a child is in dispute, the court may order the parents to attempt to mediate that issue, unless there is a history of physical or sexual abuse of the child. Some courts require the parents to attend parenting classes. Cases may be referred to Alternative Dispute Resolution on the financial issues as well. *Maryland Rules.*

6. UNCONTESTED DIVORCE.
Marital settlement agreements are specifically authorized by statute and may be used for full corroboration of a plaintiff's testimony that a separation was voluntary if:

(a) the agreement states that the spouses voluntarily agreed to separate and

(b) the agreement was signed under oath before the application for divorce was filed.

For alimony or child support cases, each party must file a Financial Statement Affidavit and a Child Support Guideline

Worksheet is required. *Maryland Code; Courts and Judicial Procedure Article, Title 3, Section 3-409; and Title 8, Section 8-104.*

7. CHILD CUSTODY. Joint or sole custody may be awarded to either or both parents, based on the best interests of the child. Custody may be denied if the child has been abused by the parent seeking custody. The factors for consideration are established in Maryland case law, not the statute. The court shall attempt to allow the child to live in the environment and community that are familiar to the child and may allow the use and possession of the family home by the person with custody of the children for up to three years from the date of divorce. *Maryland Code; Family Law Article, Title 7, Sections 5-203, 8-208, and 9-101.*

8. CHILD SUPPORT. The court can award child support based on the child support guidelines in the statute. There is a presumption that the amount shown for support in the guidelines is correct. However, the amount may be adjusted up or down if it is shown to be inappropriate or unjust under the circumstances of the case. In determining whether the amount would be unjust, the court may consider:

(a) the terms of any marital settlement agreement between the parents, including any provisions for payments of marital debts, mortgages, college education expenses, the right to occupy the family home, and any other financial terms and

(b) the presence in the household of either parent of other children that the parent has a duty to support. *Maryland Code; Family Law Article, Title 7, Sections 12-101, 12-201, 12-202, 12-203, 12-204 and 8-206.*

9. ALIMONY. The court may award rehabilitative or indefinite alimony based on the following factors:

(a) the time necessary to acquire sufficient education and training to enable the spouse to find appropriate employment, and that spouse's future earning capacity;

(b) the standard of living established during the marriage;

(c) the duration of the marriage;

(d) the ability of the spouse from whom support is sought to meet his or her needs while meeting those of the spouse seeking support;

(e) the financial resources of the spouse seeking alimony, including marital property apportioned to such spouse and such spouse's ability to meet his or her needs independently;

(f) the comparative financial resources of the spouses, including their comparative earning abilities in the labor market;

(g) the contribution of each spouse to the marriage, including services rendered in homemaking, child care, education, and career building of the other spouse;

(h) the age of the spouses;

(i) the physical and emotional conditions of the spouses;

(j) any mutual agreement between the spouses concerning financial or service contributions by one spouse with the expectation of future reciprocation or compensation by the other;

(k) the ability of the spouse seeking alimony to become self-supporting;

(l) the circumstances which lead to the breakdown of the marriage; and,

(m) any other factor the court deems just and equitable.

Indefinite alimony may only be awarded if:

(a) the payee spouse cannot become self-supporting or

(b) after the payee spouse has made all expected progress toward self-sufficiency, there will still be an unconscionable disparity between the spouse's living standards. *Maryland Code; Family Law Article, Title 11, Section 11-106.*

10. EQUITABLE DISTRIBUTION OF PROPERTY. The parties keep their separate property, including:

(a) any gifts from third parties and inheritances;

(b) property acquired prior to the marriage (except real property held as tenants by the entireties); and,

(c) property which is directly traceable to property listed in (a) or (b).

Marital property, including retirement benefits and military pensions, is then divided on an equitable basis. The court may order a division of jointly owned property, a sale of the property and a division of the proceeds, or a monetary award as an adjustment of the values. The court considers the following factors:

(a) the monetary and non-monetary contributions of each spouse to the acquisition of the marital property, including contribution as a homemaker;

(b) the value of each spouse's property;

(c) the economic circumstances of each spouse at the time the division of property is to become effective;

(d) the length of the marriage;

(e) whether the property award is in stead of or in addition to alimony;

(f) how and by whom the property was acquired, including any retirement, profit-sharing, or deferred compensation plans;

(g) the circumstances that contributed to the estrangement of the spouses;

(h) the age, physical and mental condition of the spouses; and

(i) any other factor necessary to do equity and justice between the spouses. A Joint Statement of Marital and Non-Marital Property is required for trial. *Maryland Code; Family Law Article, Title 8, Sections 8-202, 8-203, and 8-205; and Maryland Rules.*

11. NAME CHANGE. A spouse's former or birth name may be restored if it is not for any illegal, fraudulent, or immoral purpose. *Maryland Code; Family Law Article, Title 7, Section 7-105.*

12. PREMARITAL AGREEMENTS. The courts will enforce premarital agreements, but Maryland does not have any specific statutes concerning premarital agreements.

Child Support Guidelines in Maryland

The **CHILD SUPPORT GUIDELINES WORKSHEET** is used to calculate the proper amount of child support. The guidelines are presumptively correct and must be followed by the master or judge, unless there are some special circumstances that would justify deviation from the guidelines.

Find your monthly income in the left column, then the number of children you have in the next few columns, and use the resulting figure as the basic amount of child support required by the state.

MARYLAND CHILD SUPPORT GUIDELINES

Combined Adjusted Actual Income	number of children					6 or more
	1	2	3	4	5	
0-850	$20–$150 Per Month, Based On Resources and Living Expenses of Obligor and Number of Children Due Support					
900	184	273	276	279	282	285
950	191	296	304	307	311	314
1000	198	307	332	336	340	343
1050	205	318	360	364	368	372
1100	212	329	389	393	397	401
1150	219	339	416	421	425	430
1200	226	350	438	449	454	458
1250	233	360	451	477	482	487
1300	239	371	465	504	510	515
1350	246	382	478	532	538	544
1400	253	392	491	554	566	572
1450	260	403	504	569	594	601
1500	267	413	517	584	623	629
1550	274	424	531	599	651	658
1600	282	436	546	616	672	691
1650	288	447	559	631	688	725
1700	295	457	572	645	704	753
1750	302	467	585	660	720	770
1800	308	477	598	674	735	787
1850	315	488	611	689	751	804
1900	321	498	624	703	767	821
1950	327	506	634	715	780	835
2000	332	515	645	727	793	848
2050	338	523	655	739	806	862
2100	343	531	666	751	819	876
2150	349	540	677	763	832	890
2200	354	548	687	774	845	904
2250	359	557	698	786	858	918
2300	365	565	708	798	871	931
2350	370	573	719	810	884	945
2400	376	582	729	822	897	959
2450	381	590	740	833	909	973
2500	386	598	750	845	922	987
2550	392	607	761	857	935	1000
2600	397	615	771	869	948	1014
2650	403	624	782	881	961	1028
2700	408	632	793	893	974	1042
2750	413	640	803	904	987	1056

2800	419	649	814	916	1000	1070
2850	424	657	824	928	1013	1083
2900	429	666	835	940	1026	1097
2950	435	675	846	953	1039	1112
3000	441	684	857	965	1053	1126
3050	446	693	868	978	1067	1141
3100	452	702	879	990	1080	1156
3150	458	710	890	1003	1094	1170
3200	463	719	901	1015	1108	1185
3250	469	728	912	1028	1121	1199
3300	475	737	923	1040	1135	1214
3350	480	746	934	1053	1148	1228
3400	486	755	945	1065	1162	1243
3450	491	764	957	1078	1176	1258
3500	497	773	968	1090	1189	1272
3550	503	782	979	1103	1203	1287
3600	508	790	990	1115	1216	1301
3650	514	799	1001	1128	1230	1316
3700	520	808	1012	1140	1244	1330
3750	525	817	1023	1152	1257	1345
3800	532	827	1035	1166	1273	1361
3850	538	837	1048	1181	1288	1378
3900	544	847	1060	1195	1303	1394
3950	551	857	1073	1209	1319	1411
4000	557	867	1085	1223	1334	1427
4050	563	877	1097	1236	1349	1442
4100	569	886	1109	1249	1363	1458
4150	575	895	1120	1262	1377	1473
4200	581	905	1132	1275	1391	1488
4250	587	914	1143	1288	1405	1503
4300	593	923	1155	1301	1420	1518
4350	598	932	1166	1314	1434	1534
4400	604	942	1178	1327	1448	1549
4450	610	951	1189	1340	1462	1564
4500	616	960	1201	1353	1477	1579
4550	622	970	1212	1366	1491	1594
4600	628	979	1224	1379	1505	1610
4650	634	987	1234	1391	1518	1624
4700	639	995	1244	1403	1530	1637
4750	644	1003	1254	1414	1543	1650
4800	649	1011	1264	1425	1555	1663
4850	655	1019	1274	1437	1567	1676
4900	660	1027	1284	1448	1580	1689
4950	665	1035	1294	1459	1592	1703
5000	670	1043	1304	1470	1604	1716
5050	676	1051	1314	1482	1617	1729
5100	681	1059	1324	1493	1629	1742
5150	686	1067	1334	1504	1641	1755
5200	691	1075	1344	1515	1654	1768
5250	696	1083	1354	1527	1666	1781

5300	702	1091	1364	1538	1678	1794
5350	707	1099	1374	1549	1691	1807
5400	712	1107	1384	1561	1703	1821
5450	717	1115	1394	1572	1715	1834
5500	722	1123	1404	1583	1728	1847
5550	728	1131	1414	1594	1740	1860
5600	733	1139	1424	1606	1752	1873
5650	738	1147	1434	1617	1765	1886
5700	743	1155	1444	1628	1777	1899
5750	748	1163	1454	1639	1789	1912
5800	754	1171	1464	1651	1801	1926
5850	759	1179	1474	1662	1814	1939
5900	764	1187	1484	1673	1826	1952
5950	769	1195	1494	1685	1838	1965
6000	774	1203	1504	1696	1851	1978
6050	780	1211	1513	1707	1863	1991
6100	785	1219	1523	1718	1875	2004
6150	790	1227	1533	1730	1888	2017
6200	795	1235	1543	1741	1900	2030
6250	800	1243	1553	1752	1912	2044
6300	806	1251	1563	1763	1925	2057
6350	811	1259	1573	1775	1937	2070
6400	815	1266	1582	1785	1947	2081
6450	819	1271	1589	1793	1956	2091
6500	823	1277	1597	1801	1965	2100
6550	827	1283	1604	1809	1974	2110
6600	831	1289	1611	1817	1983	2119
6650	834	1294	1618	1826	1992	2129
6700	838	1300	1626	1834	2001	2138
6750	842	1306	1633	1842	2010	2148
6800	846	1311	1640	1850	2019	2157
6850	850	1317	1647	1858	2028	2167
6900	854	1323	1654	1866	2037	2176
6950	857	1329	1662	1874	2045	2186
7000	861	1334	1669	1882	2054	2195
7050	865	1340	1676	1891	2063	2205
7100	869	1346	1683	1899	2072	2214
7150	873	1351	1691	1907	2081	2224
7200	876	1357	1698	1915	2090	2233
7250	880	1363	1705	1923	2099	2243
7300	884	1369	1712	1931	2108	2253
7350	888	1374	1720	1939	2117	2262
7400	892	1380	1727	1947	2126	2272
7450	895	1386	1734	1956	2135	2281
7500	899	1391	1741	1964	2144	2291
7550	903	1397	1748	1972	2153	2300
7600	906	1402	1755	1979	2161	2309
7650	909	1407	1761	1986	2168	2317
7700	912	1412	1768	1993	2175	2325
7750	915	1417	1774	1999	2182	2333

7800	918	1422	1780	2006	2190	2340
7850	921	1427	1786	2012	2197	2348
7900	923	1431	1792	2019	2204	2356
7950	926	1436	1798	2026	2211	2364
8000	929	1441	1804	2032	2219	2372
8050	932	1446	1810	2039	2226	2380
8100	935	1451	1817	2045	2233	2388
8150	938	1456	1823	2052	2240	2396
8200	941	1461	1829	2059	2248	2404
8250	944	1465	1835	2065	2255	2412
8300	947	1470	1841	2072	2262	2420
8350	949	1475	1847	2078	2270	2428
8400	952	1480	1853	2085	2277	2436
8450	955	1485	1860	2092	2284	2444
8500	958	1490	1866	2098	2291	2452
8550	961	1494	1872	2105	2299	2460
8600	964	1499	1878	2111	2306	2468
8650	967	1504	1884	2118	2313	2476
8700	970	1509	1890	2125	2320	2484
8750	973	1514	1896	2131	2328	2492
8800	975	1518	1901	2137	2334	2498
8850	978	1521	1906	2142	2340	2504
8900	980	1525	1910	2147	2345	2510
8950	982	1528	1915	2152	2351	2516
9000	989	1539	1928	2168	2367	2534
9050	992	1543	1933	2173	2373	2540
9100	994	1547	1938	2179	2379	2546
9150	997	1551	1943	2184	2385	2552
9200	999	1554	1948	2190	2391	2559
9250	1002	1558	1953	2195	2397	2565
9300	1004	1562	1958	2201	2403	2571
9350	1007	1566	1963	2206	2409	2578
9400	1009	1570	1967	2212	2415	2584
9450	1012	1574	1972	2217	2421	2590
9500	1014	1577	1977	2223	2427	2596
9550	1017	1581	1982	2228	2433	2603
9600	1020	1585	1987	2234	2439	2609
9650	1022	1589	1992	2239	2445	2615
9700	1025	1593	1997	2245	2451	2622
9750	1027	1597	2001	2250	2457	2628
9800	1030	1601	2006	2256	2463	2634
9850	1032	1604	2011	2261	2469	2640
9900	1035	1608	2016	2267	2475	2647
9950	1037	1612	2021	2272	2481	2653
10000	1040	1616	2026	2278	2487	2659

Maryland Resources

The following information provides some additional resources for Maryland legal clinics, domestic shelters, and family law websites.

LEGAL CLINICS
STATEWIDE PROGRAMS

Family Law Hotline
800-845-8550

House of Ruth Domestic Violence Legal Clinic
2201 Argonne Drive
Baltimore, MD 21218
410-554-8463

Legal Aid Bureau
500 East Lexington Street
Baltimore, MD 21202
410-951-7777

Maryland Legal Services Corporation
15 Charles Plaza
Suite 102
Baltimore, MD 21201
410-576-9494
Toll-Free: 800-492-1340

Maryland Volunteer Lawyers Service
1 North Charles Street
Suite 222
Baltimore, MD 21202
410-547-6537 or 800-510-0050 (clients)
410-539-6800 (administration)

Public Justice Center
500 East Lexington Street
Baltimore, MD 21202
410-625-9409

Women's Law Center
305 West Chesapeake Avenue
Suite 201
Towson, MD 21204
410-321-8761

LOCAL PROGRAMS

ALLEGANY COUNTY

Allegany Law, Pro Bono Provider
City: Cumberland
301-722-3390

ANNE ARUNDEL COUNTY

Anne Arundel County Bar Foundation
City: Annapolis
410-280-6950

BALTIMORE CITY

Advocates for Children & Youth
City: Baltimore
410-547-9200

Baltimore Bar Pro Bono Project
City: Baltimore
410-539-5418

Community Law Center, Inc.
City: Baltimore
410-366-0922

St. Ambrose Legal Services
City: Baltimore
410-366-8537

MONTGOMERY COUNTY

**Montgomery County, MD,
Bar Foundation, Inc.
Pro Bono Program**
City: Rockville
301-424-7651

PRINCE GEORGE'S COUNTY

**Law Foundation of Prince George's
County
Pro Bono Project**
City: Hyattsville
301-864-8354
301-864-8353

SAINT MARY'S COUNTY

Saint Mary's Women's Center
City: Lexington Park
301-862-3636

DOMESTIC VIOLENCE SHELTERS

ALLEGANY COUNTY

**Allegany County Family Crisis
Resource Center**
146 Bedford Street
Cumberland, MD 21539
301-759-9246
HOTLINE: 301-759-9244

ANNE ARUNDEL COUNTY

Family and Children's Services
1001 North Crane Highway
110 B
Glen Burnie, MD 21061
410-263-5743

Sexual Assault and Crisis Center
Suite 100
1419 Forest Drive
Annapolis, MD 21403
410-267-8741
HOTLINE: 410-222-7273

**YWCA Woman's Center
YWCA of Annapolis & Anne Arundel
County**
1517 Ritchie Highway
Suite 101
Arnold, MD 21012
24-Hour Domestic Violence
HOTLINE: 410-222-6800
Domestic Violence and Counseling:
410-626-7800 (Anne Arundel County)

BALTIMORE COUNTY

ACTS, Inc.
40 East Burke Avenue
Towson, MD 21286
HOTLINE: 410-825-8773

**CHANA (Counseling Helpline and Aid
Network for Abused Women)
The Associated Jewish Community
Federation of Baltimore**
101 West Mt. Royal Avenue
Baltimore, MD 21202
410-234-0030
HOTLINE: 410-234-0023

Family and Children's Services
3104 Lord Baltimore Drive
Suite 206
Baltimore, MD 21244
410-281-1334
HOTLINE: 410-828-6390

**Family Crisis Center of Baltimore
County**
P.O. Box 3909
Baltimore, MD 21222
410-285-4357
HOTLINE: 410-828-6390
Shelter: 410-285-7496

House of Ruth
Victim Advocate Office and Protective
  Order Advocacy Representation Project
501 East Fayette Street
Room #105
Baltimore, MD 21202
410-554-8463

Turnaround, Inc.
330 North Charles Street
Baltimore, MD 21201
410-837-7000
HOTLINE: 410-828-6390

Women's Law Center Office for Domestic
  Violence Assistance POARP
  (Protective Order and
  Representation Project)
Circuit Court for Baltimore County
401 Bosley Avenue
Room 101
Towson, MD 21204
410-887-3162

CALVERT COUNTY

Abused Persons Program
Calvert County Health Department
P.O. Box 980
Prince Frederick, MD 20678
HOTLINE: 410-535-1121
Baltimore Line: 410-269-1051
Health Department: 410-535-5400

CARROLL COUNTY

Family and Children's Services
Domestic Violence Program
22 North Court Street
Westminster, MD 21157
410-876-1233
HOTLINE: 410-857-0077

Rape Crisis Intervention Service of
  Carroll County
Mailing Address:
P.O. Box 1563
Westminster, MD 21158
Walk-In Address:
224 North Center Street
Room 102
Westminster, MD 21157
410-857-0900
HOTLINE: 410-857-7322

CAROLINE AND TALBOT COUNTIES

For All Seasons, Inc.
300 Talbot Street
Easton, MD 21601
410-822-1018
HOTLINE: 800-310-7273

Life Crisis Center, Inc.
P.O. Box 387
Salisbury, MD 21803
410-479-0774
410-749-4357
HOTLINE: 410-749-4363
              800-422-0009

Mid-Shore Council on Family Violence
P.O. Box 5
Denton, MD 1629
410-479-1149
HOTLINE: 800-927-4673

CECIL COUNTY

Cecil County Department of Social
  Services Domestic Violence/Rape
  Crisis Center
P.O. Box 2137
Elkton, MD 21922
24-Hour Hotline, Information, and Services:
  410-996-0333

CHARLES COUNTY

Center for Abused Persons/Community
  Crisis and Referral Center, Inc.
2670 Crain Highway
Suite 303
Waldorf, MD 20601
301-645-8994
HOTLINE: 301-645-9387
Teen Hotline: 301-645-9387
Metro Line: 301-843-1110

St. Mary's Women's Center, Inc.
(Main Office)
20945 Great Mills Road
Suite N
Lexington Park, MD 20653
301-862-3636

DORCHESTER COUNTY

For All Seasons, Inc.
300 Talbot Street
Easton, MD 21601
410-822-1018
HOTLINE: 800-310-7273

Mid-Shore Council on Family Violence
P.O. Box 5
Denton, MD 21629
410-479-1149
HOTLINE: 800-927-4673

Mid-Shore Counseling & Outreach
208 Cedar Street
Cambridge, MD 21613
410-479-1149
HOTLINE: 800-927-4673

FREDERICK COUNTY

Heartly House
P.O. 857 Box
Frederick, MD 21705-0857
HOTLINE: 301-662-8800
24-Hour TTY: 301-662-1565

GARRETT COUNTY

Dove Center
Domestic Violence/Sexual Assault
  Center, Inc.
12978 Garrett Highway
Suite 201
Oakland, MD 21550
301-334-6255
HOTLINE: 301-334-9000
            800-656-4673

HARFORD COUNTY

CHANA (Counseling Helpline and Aid
  Network for Abused Women)
The Associated Jewish Community
  Federation of Baltimore
101 West Mt. Royal Avenue
Baltimore, MD 21201
410-234-0030
HOTLINE: 410-234-0023

Helpline and Aid Network for
  Abused Women
Community Federation of Baltimore
410-234-0030
Phone leads to CHANA

Sexual Assault/Spouse Abuse Resource
  Center
21 West Courtland Street
Bel Air, MD 21014
HOTLINE: 410-836-8430
Baltimore Line: 410-879-3486

HOWARD COUNTY

Domestic Violence Center of Howard
  County
8950 Route 108
Parkridge Plaza Building
Suite 116
Columbia, MD 21045
HOTLINE: 410-997-2272
Toll-free: 800-752-0191
            410-997-0304

KENT AND QUEEN ANNE'S COUNTIES

For All Seasons, Inc.
300 Talbot Street
Easton, MD 21601
HOTLINE: 800-310-7273
            410-820-5600

Life Crisis Center, Inc.
P.O. Box 387
Salisbury, MD 21803
410-479-0774
HOTLINE: 410-749-4537
            800-422-0009

Mid-Shore Council on Family Violence
Families First—Family Support Center
(Kent County)
400 South Cross Street
Suite 2
Chestertown, MD 21620
410-778-4316
(Queen Anne's County)
5441 Main Street
Grasonville, MD 21639

MONTGOMERY COUNTY

Abused Person Program
1301 Piccard Drive
Rockville, MD 20850
240-777-4210
HOTLINE: 240-777-4673

House of Ruth (POARP)
Connected with Women's Law Center
Domestic Violence Assistance Project
Montgomery County Judicial Center
50 Maryland Avenue
Rockville, MD 20850
240-777-9077

Victim Assistance & Sexual Assault Program
1301 Piccard Drive
Rockville, MD 20850
HOTLINE: 301-315-HELP
Phone: 240-777-1355

Women's Law Center
Office for Domestic Violence Assistance
Montgomery County (POARP)
Circuit Court for Montgomery County
50 Maryland Avenue
2nd Floor
Family Division—DVA
Rockville, MD 20850
240-777-9078

PRINCE GEORGE'S COUNTY

Family Crisis Center of Prince George's County
3601 Taylor Street
Brentwood, MD 20722
301-779-2100
HOTLINE: 301-731-1203

House of Ruth (POARP)
Court House Location:
   (Hyattsville)
4990 Rhode Island Avenue
Hyattsville, MD 20781
Mailing Address:
P.O. Box 376
Hyattsville, MD 20781
301-699-7790

House of Ruth (POARP)
Court House Location:
   (Upper Marlboro)
Room 155 Courthouse
14735 Main Street
Upper Marlboro, MD 20772
Mailing Address:
P.O. Box 376
Hyattsville, MD 20781
301-952-4303

Sexual Assault Center— Prince George's Hospital
3001 Hospital Drive
Cheverly, MD 20785
HOTLINE: Sexual Assault Center:
   301-618-3154
Emergency Psychiatric: 301-618-3162

SOMERSET, WICOMICO, AND WORCESTER COUNTIES

Life Crisis Center, Inc.
410-749-4357
HOTLINE: 410-749-4363

ST. MARY'S COUNTY

St. Mary's Women's Center, Inc.
(Main Office)
21027 Great Mills Road
Suite 100
Lexington Park, MD 20653
301-862-3636

Walden-Sierra, Inc.
26845 Point Lookout Road
Leonardtown, MD 20650
HOTLINE: 301-863-6661
24-Hour TTY: 301-863-6664
Walk-In Office: 8am–8 pm 301-863-6677
   301-997-1300

WASHINGTON COUNTY

CASA (Citizens Assisting & Sheltering the Abused)
116 West Baltimore Street
Hagerstown, MD 21740
301-739-4990
HOTLINE: 301-739-8975

FAMILY LAW WEBSITES

About Divorce in Maryland
www.divorcesupport.about.com/cs/maryland

All Law Maryland Page
www.alllaw.com/state_resources/maryland

Children's Rights Council of Maryland
www.members.tripod.com/~mdcrc

Divorce Law Info
www.divorcelawinfo.com/MD/fk.htm

Divorcenet Family Law Advisor
www.divorcenet.com/states/maryland

Family Mediation Services
www.familymediator.com/lawlinks.html

Maryland Child Support Enforcement
www.dhr.state.md.us/csea

Maryland Judicial System
www.courts.state.md.us

Maryland Legal Aid
www.mdlab.org

Maryland Legal Links
www.lawlib.state.md.us

Maryland Manual Online
www.mdarchives.state.md.us/msa/
mdmanual/html/mmtoc.html

Montgomery County Circuit Court
www.montgomerycountymd.gov/mc/judicial

Mediation Matters
www.mediationmatters.com

People's Law Library
www.peoples-law.org

The Divorce Resource Network
www.divorceresourcenetwork.com

**Thyden, Gross, and Callahan
(the authors' homepage)**
www.mddivorcelawyers.com

**The Women's Law Center of
Maryland, Inc.**
www.wlcmd.org

Maryland Blank Forms

This section contains the forms you will use to file your divorce case, obtain service of process on your spouse; obtain an order of default, if applicable; calculate child support, if applicable; and, conclude your case with a divorce hearing. Make copies of these forms and amend them to fit your specific situation.

TABLE OF FORMS

Circuit Court for_____ **Case No.**_____

City or County

Name_____		Name_____

Street Address _____ Apt. # ____   VS.   Street Address _____ Apt. # ____

( )

City   State   Zip Code   Area   Telephone   City   State   Zip Code   Area   Telephone
                          Code   Code

Plaintiff   *Defendant*

FINANCIAL STATEMENT OF _____
(Name)
(Long)
(DOM REL 31)

Children	Age

MONTHLY EXPENSES

ITEM	SELF	CHILDREN	TOTAL
A. PRIMARY RESIDENCE			
Mortgage			
Insurance (homeowners)			
Rent/Ground Rent			
Taxes			
Gas & Electric			
Electric Only			
Heat (Oil)			
Telephone			
Trash Removal			
Water Bill			

Cell Phone/Pager			
Repairs			
Lawn & Yard Care (snow removal)			
Replacement Furnishings/Appliances			
Condo Fee (not included elsewhere)			
Painting/Wallpapering			
Carpet Cleaning			
Domestic Assistance/Housekeeper			
Pool			
Other:			
SUB TOTAL			
B. SECONDARY RESIDENCE (i.e. Summer Home/Rental)			
Mortgage			
Insurance (homeowners)			
Rent/Ground Rent			
Gas & Electric			
Electric Only			
Heat (Oil)			
Telephone			
Trash Removal			
Water Bill			
Cell Phone/Pager			
Repairs			
Lawn & Yard Care (snow removal)			
Replacement Furnishings/Appliances			

Condo Fee (not included elsewhere)			
Painting/Wallpapering			
Carpet Cleaning			
Domestic Assistance/Housekeeper			
Pool			
Other:			
SUB TOTAL			
C. OTHER HOUSEHOLD NECESSITIES			
Food			
Drug Store Items			
Household Supplies			
Other:			
SUB TOTAL			
D. MEDICAL/DENTAL			
Health Insurance			
Therapist/Counselor			
Extraordinary Medical			
Dental/Orthodontia			
Ophthalmologist/Glasses			
Other:			
SUB TOTAL			
E. SCHOOL EXPENSES			
Tuition/Books			
School Lunch			

Extracurricular Activities			
Clothing/Uniforms			
Room & Board			
Daycare/Nursery School			
Other:			
SUB TOTAL			
F. RECREATION & ENTERTAINMENT			
Vacations			
Videos/Theater			
Dining Out			
Cable TV/Internet			
Allowance			
Camp			
Memberships			
Dance/Music Lessons etc.			
Horseback Riding			
Other:			
SUB TOTAL			
G. TRANSPORTATION EXPENSE			
Automobile Payment			
Automobile Repairs			
Maintenance/Tags/Tires/etc.			
Oil/Gas			
Automobile Insurance			
Parking Fees			
Bus/Taxi			

Other:			
SUB TOTAL			
H. GIFTS			
Holiday Gifts			
Birthdays			
Gifts to Others			
Charities			
SUB TOTAL			
J. CLOTHING			
Purchasing			
Laundry			
Alterations/Dry Cleaning			
Other:			
SUB TOTAL			
K. INCIDENTALS			
Books & Magazines			
Newspapers			
Stamps/Stationary			
Banking Expense			
Other:			
SUB TOTAL			
L. MISCELLANEOUS/OTHER			
Alimony/Child Support (from a previous Order)			
Religious Contributions			

Hairdresser/Haircuts			
Manicure/Pedicure			
Pets/Boarding			
Life Insurance			
Other:			
SUB TOTAL			
TOTAL MONTHLY EXPENSES:			

Number of Dependent Children _____

INCOME STATEMENT

GROSS MONTHLY WAGES:		$
Deductions:		
Federal	$	
State	$	
Medicare	$	
F.I.C.A.	$	
Retirement	$	
Total Deductions:	$	
NET INCOME FROM WAGES:		
OTHER GROSS INCOME:(alimony, part-time job, rentals, etc.)		$
Deductions:		
a.	$	
b.	$	
c.	$	
Total deductions from Other income:	$	
NET OTHER INCOME:		
TOTAL MONTHLY INCOME:		

     DR 31 - 17 September 2001

ASSETS & LIABILITIES

ASSETS:		
Real Estate	$	
Furniture (in the marital home)	$	
Bank Accounts/Savings	$	
U.S. Bonds	$	
Stocks/Investments	$	
Personal Property	$	
Jewelry	$	
Automobiles	$	
Boats	$	
Other:	$	
TOTAL ASSETS:		$
LIABILITIES:		
Mortgage	$	
Automobiles	$	
Notes Payable to Relatives	$	
Bank Loans	$	
Accrued Taxes	$	
Balance of Credit Card Accounts	$	
a.		
b.		

c.		
Other:		
TOTAL LIABILITIES:		$
TOTAL NET WORTH:		$
SUMMARY:		
TOTAL INCOME:		$
TOTAL EXPENSES:		$
EXCESS OR DEFICIT:		$

I solemnly affirm under the penalties of perjury that the contents of the foregoing Financial Statement, Monthly Expense List and Assets and Liabilities Statement are true to the best of my knowledge, information, and belief.

_____   _____
Date   Signature

DR 31 - 17 September 2001

Circuit Court for_____ Case No._____

City or County

Name_____		Name_____
Street Address_____ Apt. #	VS.	Street Address_____ Apt. #
City____ State Zip Code Area Telephone Code		City____ State Zip Code Area Telephone Code

CHILD SUPPORT GUIDELINES WORKSHEET A
(Primary Physical Custody to One Parent)
(DOM REL 34)

Name of Child	Date of Birth	Name of Child	Date of Birth
Name of Child	Date of Birth	Name of Child	Date of Birth
Name of Child	Date of Birth	Name of Child	Date of Birth

	Mother	Father	Combined
1. MONTHLY ACTUAL INCOME (Before taxes)	$	$	
a. Minus pre-existing child support payment actually paid	-	-	
b. Minus health insurance premium (if child included)	-	-	
c. Minus alimony actually paid	-	-	
d. Plus / minus alimony awarded in this case	+/-	+/-	
2. MONTHLY ADJUSTED ACTUAL INCOME	$	$	$
3. PERCENTAGE SHARE OF INCOME (Divide each parent's income on Line 2 by the combined income on Line 2).	%	%	
4. BASIC CHILD SUPPORT OBLIGATION (Apply Line 2 Combined Income to Child Support Schedule)			$
a. Work-Related Child Care Expenses (Code, FL § 12-204(h))			+
b. Extraordinary Medical Expenses (Code, FL § 12-204(g))			+
c. Additional Expenses (Code, FL § 12-204(i))			+
5. TOTAL CHILD SUPPORT OBLIGATION (Add lines 4, 4a, 4b, and 4c).			$
6. EACH PARENT'S CHILD SUPPORT OBLIGATION (Multiply Line 3 times Line 5 for each parent).	$	$	
7. RECOMMENDED CHILD SUPPORT ORDER (Bring down amount from Line 6 for the non-custodial parent only. Leave custodial parent column blank).	$	$	$

Deduct from the recommended child support order amount (Line 7) any third party benefits paid to or for a child (e.g. SSADisability, retirement or other third party dependency benefit).
Comments, calculations, or rebuttals to schedule or adjustments if non-custodial parent directly pays extraordinary expenses:

PREPARED BY: Date:

Circuit Court for _____ Case No. _____

City or County

Name _____

Street Address _____ Apt. #

City _____ State Zip Code Area Telephone
                                Code

VS.

Name _____

Street Address _____ Apt. #

City _____ State Zip Code Area Telephone
                                Code

CHILD SUPPORT GUIDELINES WORKSHEET B
(Shared Physical Custody)
(DOM REL 35)

Name of Child	Date of Birth	Name of Child	Date of Birth
Name of Child	Date of Birth	Name of Child	Date of Birth
Name of Child	Date of Birth	Name of Child	Date of Birth

	Mother	Father	Combined
1. **MONTHLY ACTUAL INCOME** (Before taxes)	$	$	
a. Minus pre-existing child support payment actually paid	-	-	
b. Minus health insurance premium (if child included)	-	-	
c. Minus alimony actually paid	-	-	
d. Plus / minus alimony awarded in this case	+/-	+/-	
2. **MONTHLY ADJUSTED ACTUAL INCOME**	$	$	$
3. **PERCENTAGE SHARE OF INCOME** (Divide each parent's income on Line 2 by the combined income on Line 2).	%	%	
4. **BASIC CHILD SUPPORT OBLIGATION** (Apply Line 2 Combined Income to the Child Support Schedule)			$
5. **ADJUSTED BASIC CHILD SUPPORT OBLIGATION** (Line 4 times 1.5)			$
6. **OVERNIGHTS** with each parent (must total 365)			365
7. **PERCENTAGE WITH EACH PARENT** (Line 6 divided by 365)	A %	B %	
STOP HERE IF Line 7 is less than 35% for either parent. Shared physical custody does not apply. Use DOM. REL. 34 instead.			

DR 35 - Revised 19 Sept. 2005

	Mother	Father	Combined
8. EACH PARENT'S THEORETICAL CHILD SUPPORT OBLIGATION (Multiply Line 3 times Line 5 for each parent)	A$	B$	
9. BASIC CHILD SUPPORT OBLIGATION FOR TIME WITH OTHER PARENT (Multiply Line 7A times Line 8B and put answer on Line 9B. Multiply Line 7B times Line 8A and put answer on Line 9A).	A$	B$	
10. NET BASIC CHILD SUPPORT OBLIGATION (Subtract lesser amount from greater amount in Line 9 and place answer here under column with greater amount in Line 9).			
11. EXPENSES			
a. Work-Related Child Care Expenses (Code, FL § 12-204(g))			+
b. Extraordinary Medical Expenses (Code, FL § 12-204(h))			+
c. Additional Expenses (Code, FL § 12-204(i))			+
12. NET ADJUSTMENT from ADJUSTMENT WORKSHEET, below, if applicable. If not, continue to Line 13.	$	$	
13. NET BASIC CHILD SUPPORT OBLIGATION (From Line 10 of this worksheet, above.)	$	$	
14. RECOMMENDED CHILD SUPPORT ORDER (If the same parent owes money under Lines 12 and Line 13, add these two figures to obtain amount owed by that parent. If one parent owes money under Line 12 and the other owes money under Line 13, subtract the lesser amount from the greater to obtain the difference. The parent owing the greater of the two amounts on Lines 12 and 13 will owe that difference as the child support obligation. <u>NOTE</u>: The amount owed in a shared custody arrangement may not exceed the amount that would be owed if the obligor parent were a non-custodial parent. See DOM. REL. __34__).	$	$	

Comments, calculations, or rebuttals including in-kind responsibility because of sharing or special adjustments because of direct payments:

Deduct from the recommended child support order amount (Line 7) any third party benefits paid to or for a child (e.g. SSA Disability, retirement or other third party dependency benefit).

PREPARED BY: Date:

ADJUSTMENT WORKSHEET
(For Calculating Line 12 of Shared Physical Custody Worksheet, above)

INSTRUCTIONS FOR ADJUSTMENT WORKSHEET: *Use this Worksheet ONLY if any of the Expenses listed in Lines 11a, 11b, or 11c, is directly paid out or received by the parents in a different proportion than the percentage share of income entered on Line 3 of the Shared Physical Custody Worksheet, above. Example: If the mother pays all of the daycare, or parents split education/medical costs 50/50 and Line 3 is other than 50/50. If there is more than one 11c expenses, the calculations on Lines e and f below must be made for each expense.*

		Mother	Father
a.	Total amount of direct payments made for Line 11a expenses times each parent's percentage of income (Line 3, Shared Physical Custody Worksheet) (Proportionate share)	$	$
b.	The excess amount of direct payments made by the parent who pays more than the amount calculated in Line a, above. (The difference between amount paid and proportionate share).	$	$
c.	Total amount of direct payments made for Line 11b expenses times each parent's percentage of income (Line 3, Shared Physical Custody Worksheet).	$	$
d.	The excess amount of direct payments made by the parent who pays more than the amount calculated on Line c, above.	$	$
e.	Total amount of direct payments made for Line 11c expenses times each parent's percentage of income (Line 3, Shared Physical Custody Worksheet).	$	$
f.	The excess amount of direct payments made by the parent who pays more than the amount calculated in Line e, above.	$	$
g.	For each parent, add lines b, d and f.	$	$
h.	Subtract lesser amount from greater amount in Line g, above. Place the answer on this line under the lesser amount in Line g. Also enter this answer on Line 12 of the Shared Physical Custody Worksheet, in the same parent's column.	$	$

DR 35 - Revised 19 Sept. 2005

Circuit Court for _____ Case No. _____
                        City or County

Name _____   Name _____

Street Address _____ Apt. #   Street Address _____ Apt. #

City ___ State ___ Zip Code ___ Area ___ Telephone   City ___ State ___ Zip Code ___ Area ___ Telephone
                              Code   Code

                Plaintiff   *Defendant*

COMPLAINT FOR ABSOLUTE DIVORCE
(DOM REL 20)

I, _____ , representing myself, state that:
        Your Name

1. The Defendant and I were married on_____
                                        Month   Day   Year

   in_____ in a ☐ civil ☐ religious ceremony.
      City/County/State where Married   (Check One)

2. *Check all that apply:*

   ☐ I have lived in Maryland since:_____
                                        Month/Year

   ☐ My spouse has lived in Maryland since: _____
                                                Month/Year

   ☐ The grounds for divorce occurred in the State of Maryland.

3. *Check one:*

   ☐ We have no children together (skip paragraphs 5 and 6) or

   ☐ My spouse and I are the parents of the following child(ren:)

Name	Date of Birth	Name	Date of Birth
Name	Date of Birth	Name	Date of Birth
Name	Date of Birth	Name	Date of Birth

4. I know of the following related cases concerning the child(ren) or parties (such as domestic violence, paternity, divorce, custody, visitation, termination of parental rights, adoption or other cases):

Court	Case No.	Kind of Case	Year Filed	Results or Status (if known)

5. I have been a party, witness, or otherwise involved in the following cases about custody or visitation of the child(ren) :

State	Court	Case No.	Date of Child Custody Determination

Attach the most recent court order for the above-referenced court cases.

DR 20 (Rev. 9/2005)   Page 1 of 3

6. I know of the following people, not parties to this case, who have physical custody of, or claim rights of legal custody or physical custody of, or visitation with the child(ren) :

_____   _____
              Name   Current Address

_____   _____
              Name   Current Address

_____   _____
              Name   Current Address

7. The child(ren) are currently living with:_____
                                                         Name

8. The child(ren) have lived in the following places, with the persons indicated during the last five years:

   Time Period   Place   Name(s)/Current Address of Person(s) with whom Child Lived

   _____   _____   _____

   _____   _____   _____

9. It is in the best interests of the child(ren) that I have (*check all that apply*):

   ☐ joint ☐ sole physical custody of _____
   (Check One)   Name of Children

   ☐ joint ☐ sole legal custody of _____
   (Check One)   Name of Children

   ☐ visitation with_____
                               Name of Children

10. I ☐ am ☐ am not seeking alimony because_____
    (Check One)

11. (You do not have to complete paragraph 11 if you are not asking the court to make decisions about your property.) My spouse and/or I have the following property (*check all that apply*)

   ☐ House(s)   ☐ Furniture

   ☐ Pensions   ☐ Bank account(s) and investment(s)

   ☐ Motor Vehicle(s)   ☐ Other_____

   ☐ Debts (attach list)

12. My grounds for absolute divorce are: (*check all that apply*)

   ☐ Two-Year Separation - From on or about_____, my spouse and I have lived
                                             Month/Day/Year
   separate and apart from each other in separate residences, without interruptions, without sexual
   intercourse, for more than two years and there is no reasonable expectation that we will reconcile.

   ☐ Voluntary Separation - From on or about_____, my spouse and I by mutual and
                                                Month/Day/Year
   voluntary agreement have lived separate and apart from one another in separate residences,
   without interruption, without sexual intercourse, for more than 12 months with the express
   purpose and intent of ending our marriage, and there is no reasonable expectation that we will
   reconcile.

   ☐ Adultery - My spouse committed adultery.

   ☐ Actual Desertion - On or about_____, my spouse, without just cause or reason,
                                      Month/Day/Year
   abandoned and deserted me, with the intention of ending our marriage. This abandonment has
   continued without interruption for more than 12 months and there is no reasonable expectation
   that we will reconcile.

DR 20 (Rev. 9/2005)   Page 2 of 3

☐ Constructive Desertion - I left my spouse because his/her cruel and vicious conduct made the continuation of our marriage impossible, if I were to preserve my health, safety, and self-respect. This conduct was the final and deliberate act of my spouse and our separation has continued without interruption for more than 12 months and there is no reasonable expectation that we will reconcile.

☐ Criminal Conviction of a Felony or Misdemeanor - On or about_____, my
Month/Day/Year
spouse was sentenced to serve at least three years or an indeterminate sentence in a penal institution and has served 12 or more months of the sentence.

☐ Cruelty/Excessively Vicious Conduct Against Me or my minor child - My spouse has persistently treated me or my minor child cruelly and has engaged in excessively vicious conduct rendering continuation of the marital relationship impossible if I am to preserve my health, safety, and self-respect, and there is no reasonable expectation that we will reconcile.

☐ Insanity - On or about_____, my spouse was confined to a mental institution,
Month/Day/Year
hospital, or other similar institution and has been confined for 3 more years. Two doctors competent in psychiatry will testify that the insanity is incurable and there is no hope of recovery. My spouse or I have been a resident of Maryland for at least two years before the filing of this complaint.

FOR THESE REASONS, I request (*check all that apply*):

☒ An Absolute Divorce

☐ A change back to my former name:_____
Full Former Name

☐   ☐ Sole ☐ Joint physical custody of the minor child(ren).
(Check One)

☐   ☐ Sole ☐ Joint legal custody of the minor child(ren).
(Check One)

☐ Visitation with the minor child(ren).

☐ Use and possession of the family home for up to three years from the date of the divorce.

☐ Use and possession of the family use personal property for up to three years from the date of the divorce.

☐ Child support (Attach Form DOM REL 30 or DOM REL 31).

☐ Health insurance for the child(ren).

☐ Health insurance for me.

☐ My share of the property or its value.

☐ Transfer of family use personal property.

☐ A monetary award (money) based on marital property.

☐ Alimony (Attach Form DOM. REL 31).

☒ Any other appropriate relief.

I, _____ , solemnly affirm under the penalties of
Your Name
perjury, that the contents of this document are true to the best of my knowledge, information and belief.

_____   _____
Date   Signature

DR 20 (Rev. 9/2005)

Circuit Court for _____
City or County

CIVIL–DOMESTIC CASE INFORMATION REPORT

Directions:

    Plaintiff: *This Information Report must be completed and attached to the complaint filed with the Clerk of Court unless your case is exempted from the requirement by the Chief Judge of the Court of Appeals pursuant to Rule 2-111.* **A copy must be included for each defendant to be served.**

    Defendant: *You must file an Information Report as required by Rule 2-323(h).*

    THIS INFORMATION REPORT CANNOT BE ACCEPTED AS AN ANSWER OR RESPONSE.

FORM FILED BY: ☐ PLAINTIFF ☐ DEFENDANT   CASE NUMBER:_____
(Clerk to insert)

CASE NAME: _____ v _____
Plaintiff   Defendant

PARTY'S NAME:_____ PHONE: (___)_____
(Daytime phone)

ADDRESS: _____

PARTY'S ATTORNEY'S NAME: _____ PHONE: (___)_____

ATTORNEY'S ADDRESS:_____

    ☐ I am not represented by an attorney

RELATED CASE PENDING? ☐ Yes   ☐ No   If yes, Court and Case #(s), if known:_____

Special Requirements? ☐ Interpreter/communication impairment   Which language_____

(Attach Form 1-332 if Accommodation or Interpreter Needed)   Which dialect_____

    ☐ ADA accommodation:_____

ALTERNATIVE DISPUTE RESOLUTION INFORMATION

Is this case appropriate for referral to an ADR process under Md. Rule 17-101? (Check all that apply)

    A. Mediation ☐ Yes ☐ No   C. Settlement Conference ☐ Yes ☐ No

    B. Arbitration ☐ Yes ☐ No   D. Neutral Evaluation ☐ Yes ☐ No

IS THIS CASE CONTESTED?   ☐ Yes ☐ No   If yes, which issues appear to be contested?

    ☐ Ground for divorce

    ☐ Child Custody   ☐ Visitation

    ☐ Child Support

    ☐ Alimony   ☐ Permanent   ☐ Rehabilitative

    ☐ Use and possession of family home and property

    ☐ Marital property issues involving:

        ☐ Valuation of business ☐ Pensions ☐ Bank accounts/IRA's   ☐ Real Property

        ☐ Other: _____

    ☐ Paternity

    ☐ Adoption/termination of parental rights

    ☐ Other: _____

Request is made for: ☐ Initial order ☐ Modification ☐ Contempt ☐ Absolute Divorce ☐ Limited Divorce

For non-custody/visitation issues, do you intend to request:

    ☐ Court-appointed expert (name field)_____   ☐ Mediation by a Court-sponsored settlement program

    ☐ Initial conference with the Court   ☐ Other: _____

For custody/visitation issues, do you intend to request:

    ☐ Mediation by a private mediator   ☐ Appointment of counsel to represent child (not just to

    ☐ Evaluation by mental health professional   waive psychiatric privilege)

    ☐ Other Evaluation _____   ☐ A conference with the Court

Is there an allegation of physical or sexual abuse of party or child?   ☐ Yes ☐ No

CASE NAME: _____ V _____ CASE NUMBER: _____
                      Plaintiff   Defendant   (Clerk to insert)

TIME ESTIMATE FOR A MERITS HEARING: _____ hours _____ days

TIME ESTIMATE FOR HEARING OTHER THAN A MERITS HEARING: _____ hours _____ days

_____   _____
           Signature of Counsel/Party   Date

_____
           Print Name

_____
           Street Address

_____
           City/State/ZIP

Circuit Court for_____ **Case No.**_____

City or County

Name _____   Name _____

_____   **VS.**   _____

Street Address   Apt. #   Street Address   Apt. #

                              ( )   ( )

_____   _____

City   State   Zip Code   Area   Telephone   City   State   Zip Code   Area   Telephone
                                 Code   Code

Plaintiff   *Defendant*

AFFIDAVIT OF SERVICE
(Certified Mail)
(DOM REL 56)

I certify that I served a copy of the _____

Name of ALL pleadings/documents served

(which were previously filed with this Court) upon _____

Name of person served

on _____ , _____ , at _____

Date   Street Address   City   State   Zip Code

by certified mail, restricted delivery, return receipt requested. The **original** return receipt signed

by _____ is attached. Also attached is a copy of any

Name of person served

summons ("process") issued by the Court, the original of which I included in the certified mail

service upon the person served. I certify that I am over eighteen (18) years of age and I am not

the Plaintiff or the Defendant.

I SOLEMNLY AFFIRM under the penalties of perjury that the contents of the foregoing paper
are true to the best of my knowledge, information, and belief.

_____   _____

Date   Name of person certifying service (signature)

                                        _____

                                        Name of person certifying service (printed or typed)

                                        _____

                                        Street Address   City   State   Zip Code
                                        of person certifying service

                                        ( )

                                        Area Code   Telephone Number of person certifying service

DR 56 - Revised 8 Nov 2000

Circuit Court for_____ **Case No.**_____

City or County

Name_____   Name_____

_____ **VS.** _____
Street Address   Apt. #   Street Address   Apt. #

( )   ( )
City   State   Zip Code   Area   Telephone   City   State   Zip Code   Area   Telephone
                          Code   Code

Plaintiff   Defendant

AFFIDAVIT OF SERVICE
(Private Process)
(DOM REL 55)

I certify that I served _____ at _____ a.m. p.m.
Name of person served   Time   Check One

on _____ , _____ , at _____ ,
Date   Street Address   City   State   Zip Code

a copy of the _____
Name of ALL pleadings/documents served

which were previously filed with this Court. Attached is a copy of any summons ("process")

issued by the Court, the original of which I served upon the person served. I certify that I am over

eighteen (18) years of age and I am not the Plaintiff or the Defendant.

I SOLEMNLY AFFIRM under the penalties of perjury that the contents of the foregoing paper are true to the best of my knowledge, information, and belief.

_____   _____
Date   Name of Server (signature)

                                          _____
                                          Name of Server (printed or typed)

                                          _____
                                          Street Address   City   State   Zip
                                          of Server   Code

                                          ( )
                                          _____
                                          Area Code   Telephone Number of Server

DR 55 - Revised 8 Nov 2000

Circuit Court for_____ **Case No.**_____
                                   City or County

Name_____   Name_____

_____ **VS.**   _____
Street Address   Apt. #   Street Address   Apt. #
                              ( )   ( )
City   State Zip Code Area Telephone City   State Zip Code Area Telephone
                           Code   Code

            Plaintiff   *Defendant*

MOTION FOR ALTERNATE SERVICE
(DOM REL 70)

I,_____ , representing myself state that:
        My name

1. I filed the following document(s): _____
                                          Name of Document(s)
    with the Circuit Court for _____ on _____ ,_____ .
                              County or City   Date document(s) filed

2. Since that time I have made reasonable efforts to locate the Defendant to effect service of

    process, but have been unable to do so as more fully set forth in the Affidavit below.

    FOR THESE REASONS, I request that the Court order service by posting, or in the

    alternative by publication, or any other means of notice that the court may deem appropriate,

    pursuant to Maryland Rule 2-121 or 2-122.

_____   _____
          Date   Signature

AFFIDAVIT IN COMPLIANCE WITH
MARYLAND RULE 2-121 OR 2-122

STATE OF MARYLAND, COUNTY OF _____ :

    I HEREBY CERTIFY that before me, the subscriber, a Notary Public in and for the State
and County aforesaid, personally appeared _____ , Plaintiff,
                                                          My Name
in the above-entitled case, and made oath, in due form of law as follows:

1. I filed the following document(s): _____
                                          Name of Document(s)
    with the Circuit Court for _____ on _____ ,_____ .
                              County or City   Date document(s) filed

DR 70 - Revised 9 March 2001

2. Since that time I have attempted to serve the opposing party with that document and any related court summons in the following manner *(Check all that apply and attach appropriate documents.)*:

❐ I have attempted to serve the opposing party at _____

Address

but the opposing party has avoided service by _____ .

❐ I have tried to serve the opposing party by **certified mail** at their last known address ____ times, as shown by the attached Affidavit(s) of Service.

❐ I have tried to get the opposing party's current address by **sending letter(s) to the following relative(s) or friend(s),** as indicated by the attached copies of letters, mail return receipts, Affidavit(s) of Service and responses, if received:

Name of Person to Whom Letter Was Sent	Date Sent	Indicate whether you received a reply.
Name of Person to Whom Letter Was Sent	Date Sent	Indicate whether you received a reply.
Name of Person to Whom Letter Was Sent	Date Sent	Indicate whether you received a reply.

❐ I have tried to get the opposing party's current address by sending a letter to his/her last known employer, _____ , as shown by the attached copy of my letter, mail return receipts, Affidavit(s) of Service and response, if received:

Name of Employer	Date Sent	Indicate whether you received a reply.

❐ I have hired a private investigator or attorney who was unable to locate the opposing party as shown on the attached affidavit.

❐ I looked in the telephone directory and/or called directory assistance in the following areas:

_____ .

❐ I have contacted the Motor Vehicle Administration of Maryland and have learned the following: _____ .

❐ I have contacted the Military Worldwide Locator for Defendant's branch of the armed services and have learned the following: _____ .

❐ I asked the following former neighbors of the opposing party at his/her last known address, as indicated on the attached affidavits signed by those neighbors:

Name of Neighbor	Their Address	Date You Spoke With Them
Name of Neighbor	Their Address	Date You Spoke With Them
Name of Neighbor	Their Address	Date You Spoke With Them

DR 70 - Revised 9 March 2001

❒ I tried to get the opposing party's current address by contacting the local child support enforcement agency. They reported that they have been unable to locate the opposing party.

❒ I have tried the following additional means to obtain the opposing party's current address:

3. I have not seen the opposing party since _____ , _____ and (*Check all that apply below and attach Financial Statement if required*):

        ❒ I do not know his/her current address.
        ❒ I do not know where he/she is working.
        ❒ I have no current address for any close relatives.
        ❒ I have no money to hire a private investigator or attorney to find him/her, as indicated in the attached Financial Statement.
        ❒ I have no money to do service by publication, as indicated in the attached Financial Statement.

I have made reasonable efforts to locate the Defendant, but have been unable to do so. I am over eighteen years old and am competent to testify.

_____
Signature

SUBSCRIBED AND SWORN to before me, this _____ day of _____ , _____ .

_____
Notary Public
MY COMMISSION EXPIRES: _____

DR 70 - Revised 9 March 2001

MILITARY SERVICE LOCATORS

To contact the Military Services, you will need the following information about the defendant: Name, Social Security Number, assigned base (if relevant). If you do not have any of the above information, include whatever you do have.

United States Army:	Commander U.S. Army Enlisted Records & Evaluation Center ATTN: Locator Fort Benjamin Harrison, IN 46249-5301
United States Navy:	Navy World Wide Locator Navy Personnel Command PERS 312F Integrity Drive Millington, TN 38055-3120 877-414-5359
United States Marine Corps:	Commandant of the Marine Corps Headquarters, USMC Code MMSB-10 Quantico, VA 22134-5030 703-640-3942/43
United States Air Force:	HQ AFMPC/RMIQL 550 C Street, West Suite 50 Randolph AFB, TX 78150-4752 210-652-5774 210-652-5775

Circuit Court for_____ Case No._____

City or County

Name _____   Name _____

                                    VS.

Street Address _____ Apt. #   Street Address _____ Apt. #
                              ( )   ( )
City   State   Zip Code   Area   Telephone   City   State   Zip Code   Area   Telephone
                             Code   Code

              Plaintiff   *Defendant*

REQUEST FOR ORDER OF DEFAULT

I, _____ , representing myself, request an Order of Default against

My name

_____ for failure to file a responsive pleading to:

Opposing Party

_____

Indicate the name of the petition, complaint or motion you originally filed.

as provided by the Maryland Rules. The last known address of the opposing party is

_____

_____

_____   _____
        Date   Signature

NON-MILITARY AFFIDAVIT

_____ :

Opposing Party

1.   is not in the military service of the United States;
2.   is not in the military service of any nation allied with the United States;
3.   has not been ordered to report for induction under the Selective Training and Service Act; and
4.   is not a member of the Enlisted Reserve Corps who has been ordered to report for military service.

I solemnly affirm under the penalties of perjury that the contents of the foregoing paper are true to the best of my knowledge, information, and belief.

_____   _____
        Date   Signature

DR 54 - Revised 25 Aug 2003

250

Circuit Court for_____ **Case No.**_____

City or County

_____   _____

Name of Plaintiff   Name of Defendant

ORDER OF DEFAULT

(Order to be Completed by Court)

This court enters an Order of Default against _____ for

Opposing Party

failure to file a responsive pleading to: _____,

Name of Complaint/Petition/Motion

and orders that testimony to support the allegations of the Complaint be taken before

☐ one of the Judges or ☐ a Standing Examiner/Master of this Court.

_____

Judge

_____

Date

IMPORTANT: Person obtaining Order of Default must contact the Clerk's Office at

_____ for further instructions to schedule a hearing.

Telephone Number

DR 54 - Revised 25 Aug 2003

Circuit Court for_____ Case No._____

City or County

Name_____   Name_____

                                VS.

Street Address_____ Apt. #   Street Address_____ Apt. #

                ( )   ( )

City   State Zip Code Area Telephone   City   State Zip Code Area Telephone
                          Code   Code

Plaintiff   Defendant

JOINT REQUEST TO SCHEDULE AN UNCONTESTED DIVORCE HEARING

The parties agree that this matter is uncontested as to all issues and request that this matter be scheduled for a ten-minute divorce hearing. They further agree that they have read the statements below and have checked all appropriate lines that apply to their case.

Grounds for divorce_____ **Separation date (if appropriate)**_____
(Grounds and separation date (if appropriate) must be entered or request will have no effect.)

1a._____   There are no minor children of the marriage who are subject to this Court's jurisdiction.

OR

1b._____   Custody and visitation have been agreed to or have been previously determined by the Court.

2._____   Child support has been established in compliance with the Child Support Guidelines. <u>IF THIS LINE IS CHECKED, THIS JOINT REQUEST MAY NOT BE FILED UNLESS A COMPLETED CHILD SUPPORT GUIDELINES WORKSHEET IS ATTACHED</u>.

3._____   All parties/witnesses speak and understand English, and there is no need for a translator. The court will provide an interpreter only in cases where a party/witness is hearing impaired. **NOTE: You must provide your own language interpreter.**

4._____   There are no pension rights <u>or</u> any pension rights have been waived <u>or</u> pension rights shall be addressed by a consent qualified domestic relations order to be submitted at the divorce hearing.

5._____   There are no support or property rights to be adjudicated by the Court and/or there is a written agreement disposing of all such rights.

_____   _____
Plaintiff or Plaintiff's   Defendant or Defendant's
Attorney (signature)   Attorney (signature)

_____   _____

_____   _____
Address   Address

_____   _____
Daytime Telephone   Daytime Telephone

THIS JOINT REQUEST IS NOT AN ANSWER AND SHOULD NOT BE FILED **UNTIL** AN **ANSWER** HAS BEEN FILED.

MARYLAND STATE DEPARTMENT OF HEALTH AND MENTAL HYGIENE
Division of Vital Records   4201 Patterson Avenue, Baltimore, MD 21215-2290
REPORT OF ABSOLUTE DIVORCE OR ANNULMENT OF MARRIAGE

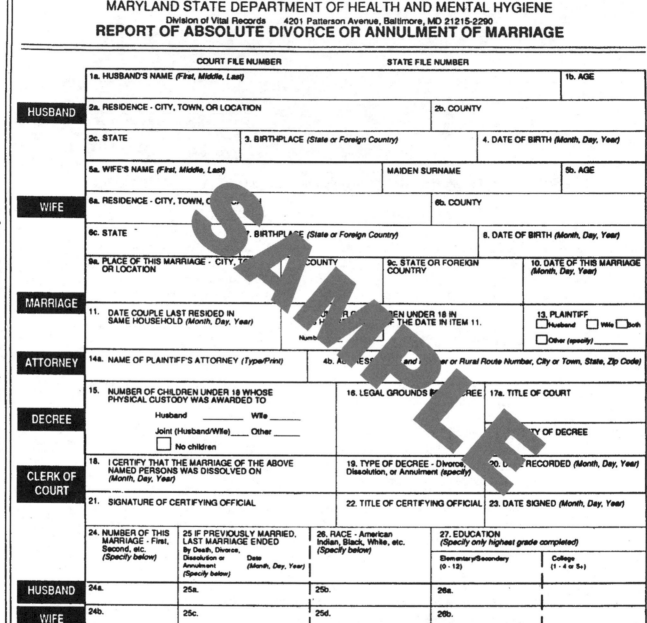

Authority for This Report is Article Health-General, Title 4, Subtitle 2, Section 4-206, Annotated Code of Maryland

	COURT FILE NUMBER	STATE FILE NUMBER	

HUSBAND

1a. HUSBAND'S NAME *(First, Middle, Last)* — 1b. AGE

2a. RESIDENCE - CITY, TOWN, OR LOCATION — 2b. COUNTY

2c. STATE — 3. BIRTHPLACE *(State or Foreign Country)* — 4. DATE OF BIRTH *(Month, Day, Year)*

WIFE

5a. WIFE'S NAME *(First, Middle, Last)* — MAIDEN SURNAME — 5b. AGE

6a. RESIDENCE - CITY, TOWN, OR LOCATION — 6b. COUNTY

6c. STATE — 7. BIRTHPLACE *(State or Foreign Country)* — 8. DATE OF BIRTH *(Month, Day, Year)*

MARRIAGE

9a. PLACE OF THIS MARRIAGE - CITY, TOWN, COUNTY OR LOCATION — 9c. STATE OR FOREIGN COUNTRY — 10. DATE OF THIS MARRIAGE *(Month, Day, Year)*

11. DATE COUPLE LAST RESIDED IN SAME HOUSEHOLD *(Month, Day, Year)* — 12. NUMBER OF CHILDREN UNDER 18 IN THIS HOUSEHOLD OF THE DATE IN ITEM 11. Number — 13. PLAINTIFF ☐ Husband ☐ Wife ☐ Both ☐ Other *(specify)* ____

ATTORNEY

14a. NAME OF PLAINTIFF'S ATTORNEY *(Type/Print)* — 14b. ADDRESS *(Street and Number or Rural Route Number, City or Town, State, Zip Code)*

DECREE

15. NUMBER OF CHILDREN UNDER 18 WHOSE PHYSICAL CUSTODY WAS AWARDED TO

Husband ____ Wife ____

Joint (Husband/Wife) ____ Other ____

☐ No children

16. LEGAL GROUNDS FOR DECREE — 17a. TITLE OF COURT — 17b. COUNTY OF DECREE

CLERK OF COURT

18. I CERTIFY THAT THE MARRIAGE OF THE ABOVE NAMED PERSONS WAS DISSOLVED ON *(Month, Day, Year)* — 19. TYPE OF DECREE - Divorce, Dissolution, or Annulment *(specify)* — 20. DATE RECORDED *(Month, Day, Year)*

21. SIGNATURE OF CERTIFYING OFFICIAL — 22. TITLE OF CERTIFYING OFFICIAL — 23. DATE SIGNED *(Month, Day, Year)*

	24. NUMBER OF THIS MARRIAGE - First, Second, etc. *(Specify below)*	25 IF PREVIOUSLY MARRIED, LAST MARRIAGE ENDED — By Death, Divorce, Dissolution or Annulment *(Specify below)* — Date *(Month, Day, Year)*	26. RACE - American Indian, Black, White, etc. *(Specify below)*	27. EDUCATION *(Specify only highest grade completed)* Elementary/Secondary (0 - 12)	College (1 - 4 or 5+)
HUSBAND	24a.	25a.	25b.	26a.	
WIFE	24b.	25c.	25d.	26b.	

CLERK OF THE COURT: When a petition for absolute divorce or annulment is filed, please give a copy of this form to the attorney for completion of Items 1-20 and 24-27b. When the decree is signed, check completeness of these items, execute the bottom section, and mail it to the Maryland Department of Health and Mental Hygiene, Division of Vital Records, 4201 Patterson Avenue, Baltimore, Maryland 21215-2299 on or before the 10th of the month succeeding the divorce.

ATTORNEY: Please complete items 1-20 and 24-27b of this form and ask your client to verify the information. RETURN THIS FORM TO THE CLERK OF THE COURT FOR CERTIFICATION.

Entries should be typewritten or printed in indelible black ink.

VR A24   3/94

(An original of this document must be obtained directly from the court.)

Circuit Court for_____ Case No._____

City or County

Name _____

Street Address _____ Apt. #

( )

City   State Zip Code Area   Telephone
Code

Plaintiff

VS.

Name _____

Street Address _____ Apt. #

( )

City   State Zip Code Area   Telephone
Code

Defendant

SUBMISSION FOR JUDGMENT OF DIVORCE

TO THE HONORABLE, THE JUDGES OF SAID COURT:

The above case is respectfully submitted for judgment and Rule S74Ad is hereby waived.

_____
Plaintiff

_____
Defendant

M2 950920

Circuit Court for_____ Case No._____

City or County

Name_____

Street Address_____ Apt. #_____

( )

City   State   Zip Code Area   Telephone
                              Code

Plaintiff

VS.

Name_____

Street Address_____ Apt. #_____

( )

City   State   Zip Code Area   Telephone
                              Code

Defendant

JOINT STATEMENT OF PARTIES CONCERNING MARITAL AND NON-MARITAL PROPERTY

(DOM REL 33)

1.   The parties agree that the following property is "**marital property**" as defined by MD. FAM. LAW CODE ANN. § 8-201(1999):

Description of Property	How Titled		Fair Market Value		Liens, Encumbrances or Debt Directly Attributable	
	Husband's Assertion	Wife's Assertion	Husband's Assertion	Wife's Assertion	Husband's Assertion	Wife's Assertion

DR 33 - Revised 21 Nov 2000

2. The parties agree that the following property is **not marital property** because the property (a) was acquired by one party before marriage, (b) was acquired by one party by inheritance or gift from a third person, (c) has been excluded by valid agreement, or (d) is directly traceable to any of these sources:

Description of Property	Reason Why Non-Marital	How Titled		Fair Market Value		Liens/Debts	
		Husband's Assertion	Wife's Assertion	Husband's Assertion	Wife's Assertion	Husband's Assertion	Wife's Assertion

3. The parties are **not in agreement** as to whether the following property is marital or non-marital:

Description of Property	Marital ?		How Titled		Fair Market Value		Liens/Debts	
	Husband's Assertion	Wife's Assertion	Husband's Assertion	Wife's Assertion	Husband's Assertion	Wife's Assertion	Husband's Assertion	Wife's Assertion

_____
Date

_____
Signature of Plaintiff or Attorney

_____
Date

_____
Signature of Defendant or Attorney

DR 33 - Revised 21 Nov 2000

Summary of Virginia Divorce Laws

This appendix summarizes the most important laws concerning divorce in Virginia. You can use this summary to find a quick answer to a question or as a starting point for further research.

1. FILING.
(a) the Complaint is filed in "Virginia: In the Circuit Court of _____";
(b) it is titled a "Complaint for Divorce" or "Complaint for Limited Divorce";
(c) it is filed by the "Plaintiff";
(d) the other spouse is the "Defendant";
(e) The divorce may be filed for in:
(i) the county or city in which the spouses last lived together; or at the option of the plaintiff;
(ii) the county or city where the defendant resides, if the defendant is a resident of Virginia; or
(iii) if the defendant is a non-resident of Virginia, the county or city where the plaintiff resides; and
(f) the final papers are called the "Final Decree of Divorce". *Code of Virginia; Title 20, Sections 20-96 and 20-97.*

2. RESIDENCY. One of the spouses must have been a resident of Virginia for at least six months prior to filing for divorce. *Code of Virginia; Title 20, Section 20-97.*

3. GROUNDS FOR ABSOLUTE DIVORCE.
(a) living separate and apart without cohabitation for one year;
(b) living separate and apart without cohabitation for six months if there are no minor children and the spouses have entered into a separation agreement;
(c) adultery (including homosexual acts);
(d) conviction of a felony and imprisonment for one year;
(e) cruelty, one year after the act complained of; and

(f) willful desertion or abandonment continuing for one year. *Code of Virginia; Title 20, Section 20-91.*

4. GROUNDS FOR LIMITED DIVORCE.
(a) cruelty;
(b) willful desertion or abandonment; and
(c) reasonable apprehension of bodily injury. *Code of Virginia; Title 20, Section 20-95.*

5. MEDIATION AND PARENTING CLASSES. The courts can order mediation of child custody disputes and parenting classes. *Code of Virginia; Title 20, Section 20-124.4.*

6. UNCONTESTED DIVORCE. Written separation agreements are specifically authorized by statute. A party may waive service of process, but the waiver of service of process form must be signed in front of the clerk of the court or a notary. The testimony of either spouse must be corroborated by a witness. *Code of Virginia; Title 20, Sections 20-99(1), 20-99.1:1, and 20-109.1.*

7. CHILD CUSTODY. Joint or sole child custody will be awarded based on the best interests of the child, taking into account the following factors:
(a) the age and physical and mental condition of the child;
(b) the age and physical and mental condition of the parents;
(c) the relationship between the child and each parent;
(d) the needs of the child;
(e) the role each parent has played in the upbringing and care of the child;
(f) the propensity of each parent to support contact of the child with the other parent;

(g) the willingness of the parents to maintain a relationship with the child and cooperate in parenting;

(h) the preference of the child;

(i) any history of family abuse; and,

(j) any other factors the court deems necessary and proper. No preference is to be given to either parent. *Code of Virginia; Title 20, Sections 20-124.2 and 20-124.3.*

8. CHILD SUPPORT. Child support is determined based on guidelines are provided in the statute, which are presumed to be correct unless there is a showing that the amount would be unjust or inappropriate and the following:

(a) support provided for other children or family members;

(b) custody arrangements;

(c) voluntary unemployment or under-employment, unless it is the custodial parent and the child is not in school and child care services are not available and the cost of child care services are not included in the computations for child support;

(d) debts incurred during the marriage for the benefit of the child;

(e) debts incurred for the purpose of producing income;

(f) direct court-ordered payments for health insurance or educational expenses of the child; and,

(g) any extraordinary capital gains, such as gains from the sale of the marital home. *Code of Virginia; Title 20, Sections 20-107.2, 20-108.1, and 20-108.2.*

9. ALIMONY. Either spouse may be awarded maintenance, to be paid in either a lump sum, periodic payments, or both. The factors for consideration are:

(a) the obligations, needs, and financial resources of the parties;

(b) the standard of living established during the marriage;

(c) the age and physical and mental condition of the parties and any special circumstances of the family;

(d) the duration of the marriage;

(e) circumstances involving a child that make it appropriate that a parent not work outside the home;

(f) the contributions, monetary and nonmonetary, to the well-being of the family;

(g) property of the parties;

(h) provisions made regarding marital property;

(i) earning capacity of each party;

(j) the ability and time necessary to acquire sufficient education and training to enable the spouse to find appropriate employment, and that spouse's future earning capacity;

(k) decisions about employment made during the marriage;

(l) contributions by either party to the education or career of the other spouse; and,

(m) any other factor, including tax consequences, that the court deems necessary and equitable. However, permanent maintenance will not be awarded to a spouse who was at fault in a divorce granted on the grounds of adultery, unless such a denial of support would be unjust. *Code of Virginia; Title 20, Sections 20-95, 20-107.1 and 20-108.1.*

10. EQUITABLE DISTRIBUTION OF PROPERTY. Each party will keep his or her separate property consisting of property:

(a) acquired prior to the marriage;

(b) any gifts from third parties and inheritances;

(c) any increase in the value of separate property, unless marital property or significant personal efforts contributed to such increases; and,

(d) any property acquired in exchange for separate property.

The court will equitably divide marital property, consisting of:

(a) all property acquired during the marriage that is not separate property;

(b) all property titled in the names of both spouses, whether as joint tenants or tenants-by-the-entireties;

(c) income from or increase in value of separate property during the marriage if the income or increase arose from significant personal efforts; and,

(d) any separate property which is commingled with marital property and can not be clearly traced. The court may also order a payment from one spouse's retirement benefits, profit-sharing benefits, personal injury award, or worker's compensation award, to the other spouse. The court may order the division or transfer of jointly owned marital property or permit one party to purchase the other's interest. The court may also grant a monetary award payable by one spouse to the other.

In distributing property or granting a monetary award, the court considers the following factors:

(a) the contribution of each spouse to the acquisition, care, and maintenance of the marital property;

(b) the liquid or non-liquid character of the property;

(c) the length of the marriage;

(d) the age and health of the spouses;

(e) the tax consequences;

(f) any debts and liabilities of the spouses, the basis for such debts and liabilities, and the property which serves as security for such debts and liabilities;

(g) how and when the property was acquired;

(h) the circumstances that contributed to the divorce;

(i) the contributions, monetary and non-monetary of each spouse to the well-being of the family; and,

(j) any other factor necessary to do equity and justice between the spouses. *Code of Virginia; Title 20, Section 20-107.3.*

11. NAME CHANGE. Upon request, a spouse may have his or her former name restored. *Code of Virginia; Title 20, Section 20-121.4.*

12. PREMARITAL AGREEMENTS. The agreement shall be in writing and signed by both parties and is enforceable without consideration. The agreement is not enforceable if it is proven that:

(1) the agreement was not executed voluntarily or

(2) the agreement was unconscionable when executed and before execution the party was not provided a fair and reasonable disclosure of the property or financial obligations of the other party and did not waive the right to the disclosure of this information.

If the marriage is determined to be void, the agreement is enforceable only to the extent necessary to avoid an inequitable result. *Code of Virginia; Title 20, Sections 20-149 and 20-151.*

Child Support Guidelines in Virginia

The **CHILD SUPPORT GUIDELINES WORKSHEET** is used to calculate the proper amount of child support. The guidelines are presumptively correct and must be followed by the master, commissioner, or judge, unless there are some special circumstances that would justify deviation from the guidelines.

Find your monthly income in the left column, then the number of children you have in the next few columns, and use the resulting figure as the basic amount of child support required by the state.

MONTHLY BASIC CHILD SUPPORT OBLIGATIONS

SCHEDULE OF
MONTHLY BASIC CHILD SUPPORT OBLIGATIONS

COMBINED MONTHLY GROSS INCOME	ONE CHILD	TWO CHILDREN	THREE CHILDREN	FOUR CHILDREN	FIVE CHILDREN	SIX CHILDREN
0-599	65	65	65	65	65	65
600	110	111	113	114	115	116
650	138	140	142	143	145	146
700	153	169	170	172	174	176
750	160	197	199	202	204	206
800	168	226	228	231	233	236
850	175	254	257	260	263	266
900	182	281	286	289	292	295
950	189	292	315	318	322	325
1000	196	304	344	348	351	355
1050	203	315	373	377	381	385
1100	210	326	402	406	410	415
1150	217	337	422	435	440	445
1200	225	348	436	465	470	475
1250	232	360	451	497	502	507
1300	241	373	467	526	536	542
1350	249	386	483	545	570	576
1400	257	398	499	563	605	611
1450	265	411	515	581	633	645
1500	274	426	533	602	656	680
1550	282	436	547	617	672	714
1600	289	447	560	632	689	737
1650	295	458	573	647	705	754
1700	302	468	587	662	721	772
1750	309	479	600	676	738	789
1800	315	488	612	690	752	805
1850	321	497	623	702	766	819
1900	326	506	634	714	779	834
1950	332	514	645	727	793	848
2000	338	523	655	739	806	862
2050	343	532	666	751	819	877
2100	349	540	677	763	833	891
2150	355	549	688	776	846	905
2200	360	558	699	788	860	920
2250	366	567	710	800	873	934
2300	371	575	721	812	886	948
2350	377	584	732	825	900	963
2400	383	593	743	837	913	977
2450	388	601	754	849	927	991
2500	394	610	765	862	940	1006
2550	399	619	776	874	954	1020
2600	405	627	787	886	967	1034
2650	410	635	797	897	979	1048
2700	415	643	806	908	991	1060
2750	420	651	816	919	1003	1073
2800	425	658	826	930	1015	1085
2850	430	667	836	941	1027	1098
2900	435	675	846	953	1039	1112

COMBINED MONTHLY GROSS INCOME	ONE CHILD	TWO CHILDREN	THREE CHILDREN	FOUR CHILDREN	FIVE CHILDREN	SIX CHILDREN
2950	440	683	856	964	1052	1125
3000	445	691	866	975	1064	1138
3050	450	699	876	987	1076	1152
3100	456	707	886	998	1089	1165
3150	461	715	896	1010	1101	1178
3200	466	723	906	1021	1114	1191
3250	471	732	917	1032	1126	1205
3300	476	740	927	1044	1139	1218
3350	481	748	937	1055	1151	1231
3400	486	756	947	1067	1164	1245
3450	492	764	957	1078	1176	1258
3500	497	772	967	1089	1189	1271
3550	502	780	977	1101	1201	1285
3600	507	788	987	1112	1213	1298
3650	512	797	997	1124	1226	1311
3700	518	806	1009	1137	1240	1326
3750	524	815	1020	1150	1254	1342
3800	530	824	1032	1163	1268	1357
3850	536	834	1043	1176	1283	1372
3900	542	843	1055	1189	1297	1387
3950	547	852	1066	1202	1311	1402
4000	553	861	1078	1214	1325	1417
4050	559	871	1089	1227	1339	1432
4100	565	880	1101	1240	1353	1448
4150	571	889	1112	1253	1367	1463
4200	577	898	1124	1266	1382	1478
4250	583	907	1135	1279	1396	1493
4300	589	917	1147	1292	1410	1508
4350	594	926	1158	1305	1424	1523
4400	600	935	1170	1318	1438	1538
4450	606	944	1181	1331	1452	1553
4500	612	954	1193	1344	1467	1569
4550	618	963	1204	1357	1481	1584
4600	624	972	1216	1370	1495	1599
4650	630	981	1227	1383	1509	1614
4700	635	989	1237	1395	1522	1627
4750	641	997	1247	1406	1534	1641
4800	646	1005	1257	1417	1546	1654
4850	651	1013	1267	1428	1558	1667
4900	656	1021	1277	1439	1570	1679
4950	661	1028	1286	1450	1582	1692
5000	666	1036	1295	1460	1593	1704
5050	671	1043	1305	1471	1605	1716
5100	675	1051	1314	1481	1616	1728
5150	680	1058	1323	1492	1628	1741
5200	685	1066	1333	1502	1640	1753
5250	690	1073	1342	1513	1651	1765
5300	695	1081	1351	1524	1663	1778
5350	700	1088	1361	1534	1674	1790
5400	705	1096	1370	1545	1686	1802
5450	710	1103	1379	1555	1697	1815
5500	714	1111	1389	1566	1709	1827
5550	719	1118	1398	1576	1720	1839
5600	724	1126	1407	1587	1732	1851
5650	729	1133	1417	1598	1743	1864
5700	734	1141	1426	1608	1755	1876
5750	739	1148	1435	1619	1766	1888
5800	744	1156	1445	1629	1778	1901

COMBINED MONTHLY GROSS INCOME	ONE CHILD	TWO CHILDREN	THREE CHILDREN	FOUR CHILDREN	FIVE CHILDREN	SIX CHILDREN
5850	749	1163	1454	1640	1790	1913
5900	753	1171	1463	1650	1801	1925
5950	758	1178	1473	1661	1813	1937
6000	763	1186	1482	1672	1824	1950
6050	768	1193	1491	1682	1836	1962
6100	773	1201	1501	1693	1847	1974
6150	778	1208	1510	1703	1859	1987
6200	783	1216	1519	1714	1870	1999
6250	788	1223	1529	1724	1882	2011
6300	792	1231	1538	1735	1893	2023
6350	797	1238	1547	1745	1905	2036
6400	802	1246	1557	1756	1916	2048
6450	807	1253	1566	1767	1928	2060
6500	812	1261	1575	1777	1940	2073
6550	816	1267	1583	1786	1949	2083
6600	820	1272	1590	1794	1957	2092
6650	823	1277	1597	1801	1965	2100
6700	827	1283	1604	1809	1974	2109
6750	830	1288	1610	1817	1982	2118
6800	834	1293	1617	1824	1990	2127
6850	837	1299	1624	1832	1999	2136
6900	841	1304	1631	1839	2007	2145
6950	845	1309	1637	1847	2016	2154
7000	848	1315	1644	1855	2024	2163
7050	852	1320	1651	1862	2032	2172
7100	855	1325	1658	1870	2041	2181
7150	859	1331	1665	1878	2049	2190
7200	862	1336	1671	1885	2057	2199
7250	866	1341	1678	1893	2066	2207
7300	870	1347	1685	1900	2074	2216
7350	873	1352	1692	1908	2082	2225
7400	877	1358	1698	1916	2091	2234
7450	880	1363	1705	1923	2099	2243
7500	884	1368	1712	1931	2108	2252
7550	887	1374	1719	1938	2116	2261
7600	891	1379	1725	1946	2124	2270
7650	895	1384	1732	1954	2133	2279
7700	898	1390	1739	1961	2141	2288
7750	902	1395	1746	1969	2149	2297
7800	905	1400	1753	1977	2158	2305
7850	908	1405	1758	1983	2164	2313
7900	910	1409	1764	1989	2171	2320
7950	913	1414	1770	1995	2178	2328
8000	916	1418	1776	2001	2185	2335
8050	918	1423	1781	2007	2192	2343
8100	921	1428	1787	2014	2198	2350
8150	924	1432	1793	2020	2205	2357
8200	927	1437	1799	2026	2212	2365
8250	929	1441	1804	2032	2219	2372
8300	932	1446	1810	2038	2226	2380
8350	935	1450	1816	2045	2232	2387
8400	937	1455	1822	2051	2239	2395
8450	940	1459	1827	2057	2246	2402
8500	943	1464	1833	2063	2253	2410
8550	945	1468	1839	2069	2260	2417
8600	948	1473	1845	2076	2266	2425
8650	951	1478	1850	2082	2273	2432
8700	954	1482	1856	2088	2280	2440

COMBINED MONTHLY GROSS INCOME	ONE CHILD	TWO CHILDREN	THREE CHILDREN	FOUR CHILDREN	FIVE CHILDREN	SIX CHILDREN
8750	956	1487	1862	2094	2287	2447
8800	959	1491	1868	2100	2294	2455
8850	962	1496	1873	2107	2300	2462
8900	964	1500	1879	2113	2307	2470
8950	967	1505	1885	2119	2314	2477
9000	970	1509	1891	2125	2321	2484
9050	973	1514	1896	2131	2328	2492
9100	975	1517	1901	2137	2334	2498
9150	977	1521	1905	2141	2339	2503
9200	979	1524	1909	2146	2344	2509
9250	982	1527	1914	2151	2349	2514
9300	984	1531	1918	2156	2354	2520
9350	986	1534	1922	2160	2359	2525
9400	988	1537	1926	2165	2365	2531
9450	990	1541	1930	2170	2370	2536
9500	993	1544	1935	2175	2375	2541
9550	995	1547	1939	2179	2380	2547
9600	997	1551	1943	2184	2385	2552
9650	999	1554	1947	2189	2390	2558
9700	1001	1557	1951	2194	2396	2563
9750	1003	1561	1956	2198	2401	2569
9800	1006	1564	1960	2203	2406	2574
9850	1008	1567	1964	2208	2411	2580
9900	1010	1571	1968	2213	2416	2585
9950	1012	1574	1972	2218	2421	2590
10000	1014	1577	1977	2222	2427	2596

Virginia Resources

The following information provides some additional resources for Virginia legal clinics, domestic shelters, and family law websites.

LEGAL CLINICS

**Blue Ridge Legal Services—
Harrisonburg Office**
P.O. Box 551
204 North High Street
Harrisonburg, VA 22803
540-433-1830
www.brls.org

**Blue Ridge Legal Services—
Lexington Office**
203 North Main Street
Lexington, VA 24450
540-463-7334
www.brls.org

**Blue Ridge Legal Services—
Roanoke Office**
132 Campbell Avenue, SW
Suite 300
Roanoke, VA 24011
540-344-2080
www.brls.org

**Blue Ridge Legal Services—
Winchester Office**
P.O. Box 436
119 South Kent Street
Winchester, VA 22604
540-662-5021
www.brls.org

Blue Ridge Legal Services, Inc.
P.O. Box 551
204 N. High Street
Harrisonburg, VA 22803
540-433-1830
www.brls.org

**Central Virginia Legal Aid Society—
Piedmont Branch Office**
1000 Preston Avenue
Suite B
Charlottesville, VA 22903
434-296-8851
www.cvlas.org

**Central Virginia Legal Aid Society—
    Southside Branch Office**
10 Bollingbrook Street
Petersburg, VA 23803
804-862-1110
www.cvlas.org

**Central Virginia Legal Aid Society—
    Richmond Branch Office**
101 West Broad Street
Suite 101
Richmond, VA 23220
804-648-1012
www.cvlas.org

Community Tax Law Project
P.O. Box 11322
Richmond, VA 23230
804-358-5855
www.ctlp.org

JustChildren Program
1000 Preston Avenue
Suite A
Charlottesville, VA 22903
434-977-0553
www.justice4all.org

**Legal Aid Justice Center—
    Main/Charlottesville Office**
1000 Preston Avenue
Suite A
Charlottesville, VA 22903
434-977-0553
www.justice4all.org

**Legal Aid Justice Center—
    Petersburg Office**
8 Bollingbrook Street
Petersburg, VA 23803
804-862-2205
www.justice4all.org

**Legal Aid Justice Center—
    Richmond Office**
101 West Broad Street
Suite 111
Richmond, VA 23220
804-643-1086
www.justice4all.org

Legal Aid Society of Eastern Virginia
125 St. Paul's Boulevard
Suite 400
Norfolk, VA 23510
757-627-5423

Legal Aid Society of Roanoke Valley
132 Campbell Avenue SW
Suite 200
Roanoke, VA 24011
540-344-2088

Legal Services Corporation of Virginia
700 East Main Street
S-1504
Richmond, VA 23219

Legal Services of Eastern Virginia
2017 Cunningham Drive
Suite 300
Hampton, VA 23666

Legal Services of Northern Virginia
6400 Arlington Boulevard
Suite 630
Falls Church, VA 22042
703-534-4343
www.lsnv.org

Potomac Legal Aid Society, Inc.
6400 Arlington Boulevard
Suite 600
Falls Church, VA 22042
703-538-3975
http://potomaclegalaid.info

Rappahannock Legal Services, Inc.
910 Princess Anne Street
2nd Floor
Fredericksburg, VA 22401
540-371-1105
www.erols.com/rlsfred

**Rappahannock Legal Services, Inc.—
    Culpeper Office**
314 North West Street
Culpeper, VA 22701
540-825-3131
www.erols.com/rlsfred

**Rappahannock Legal Services, Inc.—
    Tappahannock Office**
P.O. Box 1662
Tappahannock, VA 22560
540-371-1105
www.erols.com/tapp

Southwest Virginia Legal Aid Society
227 West Cherry Street
Marion, VA 24354
276-783-8300 or 800-277-6754
www.svlas.org

**Southwest Virginia Legal Aid Society—
    Christiansburg Field Office**
155 Arrowhead Trail
Christiansburg, VA 24073
540-382-6157 or 800-468-1366
www.svlas.org

**Southwest Virginia Legal Aid Society—
    Castlewood Field Office**
16932 West Hills Drive
P.O. Box 670
Castlewood, VA 24224
276-762-9354 or 888-201-2772
www.svlas.org

**Virginia Justice Center for Farm and
Immigrant Workers—
    Charlottesville Office**
1000 Preston Avenue
Suite A
Charlottesville, VA 22903
434-977-0553
www.justice4all.org

**Virginia Justice Center for Farm and
Immigrant Workers—
    Northern Virginia Office**
6400 Arlington Boulevard
Suite 630
Falls Church, VA 22042
703-538-3953
www.justice4all.org

**Virginia Legal Aid Society—
    Danville Branch Office**
Masonic Temple Building
Suite 400
Danville, VA 24541
866-534-5243
www.vlas.org

Virginia Legal Aid Society—Emporia
Branch Office
412 South Main Street
Emporia, VA 24847
866-534-5243
www.vlas.org

Virginia Legal Aid Society—Farmville
Branch Office
104 High Street
Farmville, VA 23901
866-534-5243
www.vlas.org

**Virginia Legal Aid Society—
    Lynchburg Branch Office**
513 Church Street
Lynchburg, VA 24504
866-534-5243
www.vlas.org

**Virginia Legal Aid Society—
    Suffolk Branch Office**
112 West Washington
Suite 300
Suffolk, VA 23434
866-534-5243
www.vlas.org

Virginia Legal Aid Society, Inc.
513 Church Street
Lynchburg, VA 24503
866-534-5243
www.vlas.org

Virginia Poverty Law Center
201 West Broad Street
S-302
Richmond, VA 23220
804-782-9430
www.vplc.org

**Virginia State Bar
    Lawyer Referral Service**
801 East Main Street
Richmond, VA 23219
804-775-0808
www.vsb.org

DOMESTIC VIOLENCE
SHELTERS

Abuse Alternatives, Inc.
2022 Euclid Avenue
Bristol, VA 24201
703-645-9499
HOTLINE: 615-764-2287

ACTS: Turning Points
Box 74
Dumfries, VA 22026
703-221-4951
HOTLINE: 703-221-4951

Alexandria Domestic Violence Program
421 King Street
Suite 400
Alexandria, VA 22314
703-838-4911
HOTLINE: 703-838-4911
Toll-free: 800-838-VADV

Alternatives for Abused Adults
P.O. Box 1414
Staunton, VA 24402
703-886-4001
HOTLINE: 703-886-6800
Toll-free: 800-56-HAVEN

Amherst County Commission Against Domestic Violence
P.O. Box 1157
Amherst, VA 24521
804-946-7446

Arlington Community Temporary Shelter, Inc.
P.O. Box 1258
Arlington, VA 22210
703-522-8858
HOTLINE: 703-237-0881

AVALON
P.O. Box 1079
Williamsburg, VA 23187
804-258-5022
HOTLINE: 804-258-5051

Bethany House of Northern Virginia
5901 Leesburg Pike
Falls Church, VA 22041
804-998-8811
HOTLINE: 804-256-3526

CARES, Inc. (Crisis Assistance Response Emergency Services)
P.O. Box 1142
Petersburg, VA 23804
804-861-0849
HOTLINE: 804-861-0849

Chesterfield City Victim/Witness Assistance Program
101000 Iron Bridge Road
P.O. Box 554
Chesterfield, VA 23832
804-796-7087

CHOICES–Council on Domestic Violence for Page County, Inc.
15 South Court Street
Luray, VA 22835
540-743-4414
HOTLINE: 540-743-4414

Citizens Against Family Violence, Inc.
P.O. Box 210
Martinsville, VA 24114
703-632-8701
HOTLINE: 703-632-8701

Domestic Violence Intervention Project c/o Richmond
501 North 9th Street
Richmond, VA 23219
804-780-6900
HOTLINE: 804-780-6924

DOVES, Inc.
P.O. Box 2381
Danville, VA 24541
804-799-3683
HOTLINE: 804-791-1400

Eastern Shore Coalition Against Domestic Violence
P.O. Box 3
Onancock, VA 23417
804-787-1329
HOTLINE: 804-787-1329

Fairfax County Women's Shelter
P.O. Box 1174
Vienna, VA 22183
703-435-4940
HOTLINE: 703-435-4940

Fairfax Victim Assistance Network
8119 Holland Road
Alexandria, VA 22306
703-3606910
HOTLINE: 703-360-7273

Family Advocacy Network Services (FANS)
2nd Judicial Court Service Unit
Juvenile Court Building Municipal Center
Virginia Beach, VA 23456
804-427-4426

Family Crisis Services
P.O. Box 487
Tazewell, VA 24651
703-988-5583

Family Resource Center, Inc.
P.O. Box 612
Wytheville, VA 24382
703-228-8431
HOTLINE: 703-228-7141
Toll-free: 800-838-VADV

Family Violence Prevention Program
420 South Main Street
Emporia, VA 23847
804-348-0100
HOTLINE: 804-348-0100

**Family Violence Prevention Program—
    Child and Family**
1805 Arlington Boulevard
Portsmouth, VA 23707
804-397-2121
Hotline: 804-399-6393

**Family Violence Prevention Program—
    Family Service of Roanoke**
P.O. Box 6600
3208 Hershberger Road, NW
Roanoke, VA 24017
703-563-5316

**First Step: A Response to Domestic
    Violence, Inc.**
P.O. Box 621
Harrisonburg, VA 22801
703-434-0295
HOTLINE: 703 434 0295

Franklin County Family Resource Center
P.O. Box 4
Rocky Mount, VA 24151
703-483-5088
HOTLINE: 703-483-1234
Toll-free: 800-838-8238

The Genieve Shelter
123 Bank Street
Suffolk, VA 23424
804-925-4365
Toll-free: 800-969-HOPE

**Halifax County Community Action—
    Domestic Violence Program**
P.O. Box 799
South Boston, VA 24592
804-575-7916
HOTLINE: 804-275-1000

The Haven
P.O. Box 713
Warsaw, VA 22572
804-333-5370
HOTLINE: 804-333-5433
Toll-free: 800-22-HAVEN

Help and Emergency Response (H.E.R.)
P.O. Box 1515
Portsmouth, VA 23705
804-393-7833
HOTLINE: 804-393-9449

**Henrico City Area Mental Health
    Center Domestic Violence Treatment**
10299 Woodman Road
Glen Allen, VA 23060
804-261-8500
HOTLINE: 804-261-8484

HOPE House
P.O. Box 447
Norton, VA 24273
703-679-7240
Toll-free: 800-572-2278

Loudoun Abused Women's Shelter
1 Loudoun, SE
Leesburg, VA 22075
703-777-6552
HOTLINE: 703-777-6552
Toll-free: 703-771-7845

**Middle Peninsula—
    Northern Neck COPE**
P.O. Box 427
Gloucester, VA 23061
804-693-7959
HOTLINE: 804-693-COPE
Toll-free: 800-542-COPE

Northern Virginia Family Service
5249 Duke Street
Suite 308
Alexandria, VA 22304
703-370-3223

Project Horizon
P.O. Box 529
Lexington, VA 24450
703-463-7861
HOTLINE: 703-463-2594

Rappahannock Council on Domestic Violence
P.O. Box 5923
Fredericksburg, VA 22403
703-373-9373
HOTLINE: 703-373-9373

Response, Inc.
P.O. Box 287
Woodstock, VA 22664
703-436-3136
HOTLINE: 703-459-5161

Route One Corridor Housing, Inc.
P.O. Box 6465
Alexandria, VA 22306
703-768-3400

Safehomes Systems
115 West Main Street
Covington, VA 24426
703-965-4490
HOTLINE: 703-965-3727

Samaritan House
2697 International Parkway
Parkway II
Suite 107
Virginia Beach, VA 23451
804-430-2642
HOTLINE: 804-430-2120
Toll-free: 800-838-VADV

Services to Abused Families, Inc.
P.O. Box 402
Culpeper, VA 22701
703-825-8876
Hotline: 703-825-8876

The Shelter for Abused Women
P.O. Box 14
Winchester, VA 22604
703-667-6466
HOTLINE: 703-667-6466

Shelter for Help in Emergency (SHE)
P.O. Box 3013
Charlottesville, VA 22903
804-293-6155
HOTLINE: 804-293-8509

Total Action Against Poverty—Women's Resources Center
145 Campbell Avenue, SW
P.O. Box 2868
Roanoke, VA 24001
703-345-6781

The Turning Point—The Salvation Army
815 Salem Avenue, SW
Roanoke, VA 24016
703-345-0400
HOTLINE: 703-345-0400

Victims of Violence
1725 North George Mason Drive
Arlington, VA 22205
703-358-5150
HOTLINE: 703-358-4848

Victims Witness Office of Loudoun County
20 East Market Street
Leesburg, VA 22075
703-777-0417

Virginia Beach Department of Social Services
3432 Virginia Beach Boulevard
Virginia Beach, VA 23452
804-431-3373
HOTLINE: 804-463-2000

Virginia Peninsula Council on Domestic Violence
P.O. Box 561
Hampton, VA 23669
804-722-2261
HOTLINE: 804-723-7774

Virginians Against Domestic Violence
2850 Sandy Bay Road
#101
Williamsburg, VA 23185
804-221-0990
800-838-8238

Warren County Council on Domestic Violence
P.O. Box 1831
Front Royal, VA 22630
703-635-9062
HOTLINE: 703-635-9062

Women's Resource Center of the New River Valley
P.O. Box 306
Radford, VA 24141
703-639-9592
HOTLINE: 703-639-1123
Toll-free: 800-788-1123

**YWCA Family Violence Prevention
  Program**
600 Monroe Street
Lynchburg, VA 24504
804-528-1041
HOTLINE: 804-528-1041

YWCA Women in Crisis Program
253 West Freemason Street
Norfolk, VA 23510
804-625-4248
HOTLINE: 804-625-5570

YWCA Women's Advocacy Program
6 North 5th Street
Richmond, VA 23219
804-643-6761
HOTLINE: 804-643-0888
Toll-free: 804-796-3066

FAMILY LAW WEBSITES

About Virginia Divorce
http://divorcesupport.about.com/cs/virginia

DivorceInfo.Com
www.divorceinfo.com/vahelps.htm

Divorce Law Info
www.divorcelawinfo.com/VA/flc.htm

Fairfax County Divorce
www.co.fairfax.va.us/courts/circuit/
  divorce.htm

Virginia Child Support Calculator
www.alllaw.com/calculators/childsupport/
  virginia

**Virginia Child Support Guidelines
Statute**
http://leg1.state.va.us

Virginia Courts and Cases
www.courts.state.va.us/opine.htm

Virginia Divorce Laws
www.divorcenet.com/states/virginia/va.diva

Virginia Family Law Forms at Findlaw
http://forms.lp.findlaw.com/states/vaf_1.html

Virginia Judicial System
www.courts.state.va.us

Virginia Blank Forms

This section contains the forms you will use to file your divorce case, obtain service of process on your spouse; obtain an order of default, if applicable; calculate child support, if applicable; and, conclude your case with a divorce hearing. Make copies of these forms and amend them to fit your specific situation.

TABLE OF FORMS

Monthly Income and Expenses of _____   Date: _____

Chancery No. _____

Employed By	
City & State	
Occupation	
Pay Period	
Next Payday	
Salary/Wage	
# Exemptions	

Children in Household

Name	Age

Average Gross Pay per Month	
LESS: Federal Taxes	
State Taxes	
FICA	
Health Insurance	
Life Insurance	
Required Retirement	
Average Monthly Net Pay	
Other Income	
MONTHLY NET INCOME	

Household
Mortgage (PITI) or Rent	
Real Estate Property Taxes	
Homeowner's Insurance	
Repairs/Maintenance	
Furniture/Furnishings	

Utilities
Electricity	
Gas/Heating Oil	
Water/Sewer	
Telephone	
Trash	
Cable TV	

Food
Groceries	
Lunches	

Automobile
Payment/Depreciation	
Gasoline	
Repair/Tags/Inspection, etc.	
Auto Insurance	
Parking/Other Transportation	
Personal Property Tax	

Children's Expenses
Child Care	
School Tuition	
Lunch Money	
School Supplies	
Lessons, Sports	
New Clothing	
_____	
_____	

Clothing
New (Excluding Children)	
Cleaning/Laundry	
Uniforms	

Health Expenses
Doctor	
Dentist	
Therapist	
Eyeglases	
Hospital	
Medicines	
Other	

Dues
Professional Associations	
Social Associations	
Homeowner's Association	

Miscellaneous
Gifts (Xmas, Birthday)	
Church/Charity	
Entertainment	
Vacations	
Hobbies	
Personal Grooming	
Newspaper/Magazines	
Disability Insurance	
Life Insurance	
Legal Expenses	

Totals Per Month
Subtotal Expenses	
Subtotal Debt Payments	
TOTAL EXPENSES	
TOTAL NET INCOME	
BALANCE (+)	
BALANCE (-)	

Fixed Debts with Payments

	Balance	Mo. Pmt.
_____		
_____		
_____		
_____		

Charge Account Debt

_____		
_____		
_____		
_____		
_____		

Liquid Assets on Hand
Cash/Checking/Savings	
Other Liquid Assets	
TOTAL LIQUID ASSETS	

Submitted By: _____

CHILD SUPPORT GUIDELINES WORKSHEET

Commonwealth of Virginia   Va. Code § 20-108.2

Case No.: _____

_____ v. _____   _____

DATE

	MOTHER	FATHER
1. Monthly Gross Income (see instructions on reverse)	$	$
2. Adjustments for spousal support payments (see instructions on reverse)	$	$
3. Adjustments for support of child(ren) (see instructions on reverse)	$	$
4. Deductions from Monthly Gross Income allowable by law (see instructions on reverse)	-$	-$
5. a. Available monthly income	$	$

5. b. Combined monthly available income

(combine both available monthly income figures from line 5.a.) $ _____

6. Number of children in the present case for whom support is sought: _____

7. a. Monthly basic child support obligation
(from schedule — see instructions on reverse)   a. $_____

b. Monthly amount allowable for health care coverage
(see instructions on reverse)   b. $_____

c. Monthly amount allowable for employment-related child care expenses
(see instructions on reverse)   c. $_____

8. Total monthly child support obligation (add lines 7.a., 7.b., and 7.c.) $ _____

	MOTHER	FATHER
9. Percent obligation of each party (divide "available monthly income" on line 5.a. by line 5.b.)	____ %	____ %
10. Monthly child support obligation of each party (multiply line 8 by line 9)	$	$
11. Deduction by non-custodial parent for health care coverage when paid directly by non-custodial parent (from line 7.b.)	$	$

	MOTHER	FATHER
12. Adjustments (if any) to Child Support Guidelines Calculation (see instructions on reverse)		
a. Credit for benefits received by or for the child derived from the parent's entitlement to disability insurance benefits to the extent that such derivative benefits are included in a parent's gross income	-$	-$
b. _____	$	$
c. _____	$	$
13. Each party's adjusted share	$	$

CHILD SUPPORT GUIDELINES WORKSHEET INSTRUCTIONS

General — Use monthly financial information rounded to the nearest dollar in making these calculations. To convert data to monthly figures,
- multiply weekly financial data by 4.33
- multiply bi-weekly financial data by 2.167
- multiply semi-monthly financial data by 2
- divide annual financial data by 12

Amounts of $.50 or more should be rounded up to the nearest dollar; amounts less than $.50 should be rounded down to the nearest dollar.

Line 1 — Gross income is defined by Virginia Code § 20-108.2(C).

a. Gross income "shall mean all income from all sources, and shall include, but not be limited to, income from salaries, wages, commissions, royalties, bonuses, dividends, severance pay, pensions, interest, trust income, annuities, capital gains, social security benefits, worker's compensation benefits, disability insurance benefits, veterans' benefits, spousal support, rental income, gifts, prizes or awards. If a parent's gross income includes disability insurance benefits, it shall also include any amounts paid to or for the child who is the subject of the order and derived by the child from the parent's entitlement to disability insurance benefits."

b. Gross income "shall not include benefits from public assistance programs as defined in Virginia Code § 63.2-100 [Temporary Assistance to Needy Families, auxiliary grants to the aged, blind and disabled, medical assistance, energy assistance, food stamps, employment services, child care, general relief] federal Supplemental Security benefits, child support received, or income received by the payor from secondary employment income not previously included in "gross income," where the payor obtained the income to discharge a child support arrearage established by a court or administrative order and the payor is paying the arrearage pursuant to the order."

Line 2 — If spousal support is being paid by a party pursuant to an existing court or administrative order or written agreement, regardless of whether it is being paid to the other party or to a person not a party to this proceeding, subtract that amount under the payee's column. If spousal support is being received by a party pursuant to an existing court or administrative order or written agreement, regardless of whether it is being paid by the other party to this proceeding, add the amount under the payee's column. Use plus and minus signs appropriately. If a party is not paying or receiving spousal support, insert "none" in the appropriate column(s).

Line 3 — When a party is paying child support payments pursuant to an existing court or administrative order or written agreement for a child or children who are not the subject of the proceeding, subtract this amount from gross income. When a party has a child or children who are not the subject of the proceeding in their household or primary physical custody, subtract the amount as shown on the schedule of Monthly Basic Child Support Obligations that represents that party's support obligation for that child or children based solely on the party's income as the total income available. If these provisions are inapplicable, insert "none" in the appropriate column(s). There is only a presumption that these amounts will be deducted from gross income.

Line 4 (Virginia Code § 20-108.2(C)) — If either parent has income from self-employment, a partnership or a closely-held business, subtract reasonable business expenses under the column of the party with such income. Include one-half of any self-employment tax paid, if applicable. If none, insert "none."

Line 5.a. — As applicable, add to and subtract from line 1 the figures in lines 2, 3 and 4 and enter the total for each column.

NOTE: Any adjustments to gross income shall not create or reduce a support obligation to an amount which seriously impairs the custodial parent's ability to maintain minimal adequate housing and provide other basic necessities for the child.

Line 7.a. — Using § 20-108.2(B) SCHEDULE OF MONTHLY BASIC CHILD SUPPORT OBLIGATIONS, use line 5.b. (combined monthly available income) to find the applicable income level under COMBINED GROSS INCOME, then use line 6 (number of children) to determine the basic child support obligation under the appropriate column at the applicable income level.

Line 7.b. (Virginia Code §§ 20-108.2(E) and 63.2-1900) — Insert costs for "health care coverage" when actually being paid by a parent, to the extent such costs are directly allocable to the child or children, and which are the extra costs of covering the child or children beyond whatever coverage the parent providing the coverage would otherwise have. "Health care coverage" means any plan providing hospital, medical or surgical care coverage for dependent children provided such coverage is available and can be obtained by a person obligated under Virginia law for support of a dependent child or the child's caretaker at a reasonable cost (such as through employers, unions or other groups without regard to service delivery mechanism). This item should also include the cost of any dental care coverage for the child or children paid by a parent.

Lines 7.c. (Virginia Code § 20-108.2(F)) — Insert actual cost or the amount required to provide quality child care, whichever is less. If applicable, allocate ratably between employment-related child care and other child care based on custodian's activities while child care is being provided.

Line 12(a) — If amounts paid to or for the child who is the subject of the order and derived by the child from the parent's entitlement to disability insurance benefits have been included in a parent's gross income, that amount should be subtracted from that parent's child support obligation.

Line 12 (b-c) (Virginia Code § 20-108.1(B)) — If applicable, describe adjustment to child support for factors not addressed in guidelines calculation, then show amount to be added to or subtracted from each party-parent's child support obligation (use plus and minus signs appropriately).

Line 13 — If additional items are entered in lines 12 (a-c), add and subtract such items from line 10 and enter the totals on this line. In cases involving split custody, the amount of child support to be calculated using these guidelines shall be the difference between the amounts owed by each parent as a noncustodial parent, computed in accordance with these guidelines, with the noncustodial parent owing the larger amount paying the difference to the other parent.

For the purpose of applying these provisions, split custody shall be limited to those situations where each parent has physical custody of a child or children born of the parents, born of either parent and adopted by the other parent or adopted by both parents. For the purposes of calculating a child support obligation where split custody exists, a separate family unit exists for each parent, and child support for that family unit shall be calculated upon the number of children in that family unit who are born of the parents, born of either parent and adopted by the other parent or adopted by both parents. Where split custody exists, a parent is a custodial parent to the children in that parent's family unit and is a noncustodial parent to the children in the other parent's family unit.

CHILD SUPPORT GUIDELINES
WORKSHEET — SHARED CUSTODY
Commonwealth of Virginia   Va. Code § 20-108.2

Case No.: ....

....   v.   ....

                                                                                                          DATE

I. GUIDELINE CALCULATION

A. INCOME

	Mother	Father	Combined
Monthly Gross Income (see instructions on Page 2)	(1) $.	(2) $.	
Adjustments for spousal support payments (see instructions on Page 2)	(3) $.	(4) $.	
Adjustments for support of child(ren) (see instructions on Page 2)	(5) $.	(6) $.	
Deductions from Monthly Gross Income allowable by law (see instructions on Page 2)	(7) -$.	(8) -$.	
Available Gross Income	(9) $.	(10) $.	= (11) $.
Percentage of Combined Gross Income	(12) $. ....%	(13) $.	= 100%

B. CHILD SUPPORT NEEDS

Number of children for whom support is sought	(14) .
Child support from guideline table — apply lines (11) and (14) to table	(15) $.
Total shared support — line (15) x 1.40	(16) $.

	Mother	Father	
Total days in year each parent has custody	(17) .	(18) .	= 365
Each parent's custody share	(19) . ...%	(20) . ... %	= 100%

C. EACH PARENT'S SUPPORT OBLIGATION TO OTHER PARENT

1. Father's obligation to Mother

	Mother	Father
Basic support to Mother — lines (19) x (16)		(21) $. .
Health care coverage __PAID__ by Mother (if any)		(22) $. .
Work-related child care of Mother (if any)		(23) $. .
Total — lines (21) + (22) + (23)		(24) $. .
Father's obligation — lines (24) x (13) =		(25) $. .

2. Mother's obligation to Father

	Mother	Father
Basic support to Father — lines (20) x (16)	(26) $.	
Health care coverage __PAID__ by Father (if any)	(27) $.	
Work-related child care of Father (if any)	(28) $.	
Total — lines (26) + (27) + (28)	(29) $.	
Mother's obligation — lines (29) x (12) =	(30) $.	

D. NET MONTHLY CHILD SUPPORT PAYABLE FROM ONE PARENT TO THE OTHER PARENT

Shared custody child support guideline amount — difference between lines (25) and (30) = (31)   (31) $.   0

(32) Payable to [ ] Mother [ ] Father (see instructions on Page 2)

II. ADJUSTMENTS (IF ANY) TO SHARED CUSTODY CHILD SUPPORT GUIDELINE AMOUNT

A. ADJUSTMENT ITEMS

	Mother	Father
1. Credit for benefits received by or for the child derived from the parent's entitlement to disability insurance benefits to the extent that such derivative benefits are included in a parent's gross income	(33) $.	(34) $.
2.	$.	$.
3.	$.	$.
Total adjustments	(35) $.	(36) $.

Net adjustment (difference between lines (35) and (36)   (37) $.   0

(38) Owed to [ ] Mother [ ] Father (see instructions on Page 2)

B. TOTAL ADJUSTED SUPPORT (see instructions on Page 2)   (39) $.

(40) Payable to [ ] Mother [ ] Father

FORM DC-640 (PAGE ONE OF TWO) 07/04 PDF

CHILD SUPPORT GUIDELINES WORKSHEET INSTRUCTIONS

General — Use monthly financial information rounded to the nearest dollar in making these calculations. To convert data to monthly figures,

- multiply weekly financial data by 4.33
- multiply bi-weekly financial data by 2.167
- multiply semi-monthly financial data by 2
- divide annual financial data by 12

Amounts of $.50 or more should be rounded up to the nearest dollar; amounts less than $.50 should be rounded *down* to the nearest dollar.

Lines 1 and 2 — Gross income is defined by Virginia Code § 20-108.2(C).

    a. Gross income "shall mean all income from all sources, and shall include, but not be limited to, income from salaries, wages, commissions, royalties, bonuses, dividends, severance pay, pensions, interest, trust income, annuities, capital gains, social security benefits, worker's compensation benefits, disability insurance benefits, veterans' benefits, spousal support, rental income, gifts, prizes or awards. If a parent's gross income includes disability insurance benefits, it shall also include any amounts paid to or for the child who is the subject of the order and derived by the child from the parent's entitlement to disability insurance benefits."

    b. Gross income "shall not include benefits from public assistance programs as defined in Virginia Code § 63.2-100 [Temporary Assistance to Needy Families, auxiliary grants to the aged, blind and disabled, medical assistance, energy assistance, food stamps, employment services, child care, general relief] federal Supplemental Security benefits, child support received, or income received by the payor from secondary employment income not previously included in "gross income," where the payor obtained the income to discharge a child support arrearage established by a court or administrative order and the payor is paying the arrearage pursuant to the order."

Lines 3 and 4 — If spousal support is paid by a party pursuant to an existing court or administrative order or written agreement, regardless of whether it is being paid to the other party or to a person not a party to this proceeding, subtract that amount under the payor's column. If spousal support is being received by a party pursuant to an existing court or administrative order or written agreement, regardless of whether it is being paid by the other party to this proceeding, add the amount under the payee's column. Use plus and minus signs appropriately. If a party is not paying or receiving spousal support, insert "none" in the appropriate column(s).

Lines 5 and 6 - When a party is paying child support payments pursuant to an existing court or administrative order or written agreement for a child or children who are not the subject of the proceeding, subtract this amount from gross income. When a party has a child or children who are not the subject of the proceeding in their household or primary physical custody, subtract the amount as shown on the Schedule of Monthly Basic Child Support Obligations that represents that party's support obligation for that child or children based solely on that party's income as the total income available. If these provisions are inapplicable, insert "none" in the appropriate column(s). There is only a presumption that these amounts will be deducted from gross income.

Line 7 and 8 (Virginia Code § 20-108.2(C)) — If either parent has income from self-employment, a partnership or a closely-held business, subtract reasonable business expenses under the column of the party with such income. Include one-half of self-employment tax paid, if applicable. If none, insert "none."

NOTE: Any adjustments to gross income shall not create or reduce a support obligation to an amount which seriously impairs the custodial parent's ability to maintain minimal adequate housing and provide other basic necessities for the child.

Line 15 — Using Virginia Code § 20-108.2(B) SCHEDULE OF MONTHLY BASIC CHILD SUPPORT OBLIGATIONS, use line (11) (combined monthly available income) to find the applicable income level under COMBINED GROSS INCOME, then use line (14) (number of children) to determine the basic child support obligation under the appropriate column at the applicable income level.

Line 22 and 27 — **(Virginia Code §§ 20-108.2(E) and 63.2-1900)** — Insert costs for "health care coverage" when actually paid by a parent, to the extent such costs are directly allocable to the child or children, and which are the extra costs of covering the child or children beyond whatever coverage the parent providing the coverage would otherwise have. "Health care coverage" means any plan providing hospital, medical or surgical care coverage for dependent children provided such coverage is available and can be obtained by a person obligated under Virginia law for support of a dependent child or the child's caretaker at a reasonable cost (such as through employers, unions or other groups without regard to service delivery mechanism). This item should also include the cost of any dental care coverage for the child or children paid by a parent.

Lines 23 and 28 (Virginia Code § 20-108.2(F)) — Any child-care costs incurred on behalf of the child or children due to employment of the custodial parent shall be added to the basic child support obligation. Child-care costs shall not exceed the amount required to provide quality care from a licensed source.

Line 32 — If Line (25) is <u>larger</u> than Line (30), check Mother on Line (32). If Line (25) is <u>smaller</u> than Line (30), check Father on Line (32).

Lines 33 and 34 — If amounts paid to or for the child who is the subject of the order and derived by the child from the parent's entitlement to disability insurance benefits have been included in a parent's gross income, that amount should be subtracted from that parent's child support obligation.

Line 38 — If Line (35) is <u>larger</u> than Line (36), check Mother on Line (38). If Line (35) is <u>smaller</u> than Line (36), check Father on Line (38).

Lines 39 and 40 — If Lines (31) and (37) are owed to the same party, put the sum of the amounts in these lines on Line (39) and, in Line (40), check the party checked on line (32). If Lines (31) and (37) are owed to different parties, put the difference between the amounts in these lines on Line (39) and, in Line (40), check the party to whom the larger of the amounts in Lines (31) and (37) are owed.

FEDERAL POVERTY GUIDELINES (Notice Date: February 13, 2004)								
Household Size	1	2	3	4	5	6	7	8
Guideline plus 50%	$ 13,965	$ 18,735	$ 23,505	$ 28,275	$ 33,045	$ 37,815	$ 42,585	$ 47,355
(Add $4,770 for each additional member in households of more than eight.)								

CHILD SUPPORT GUIDELINES
WORKSHEET — SPLIT CUSTODY
Commonwealth of Virginia   Va. Code § 20-108.2

Case No.: _____

_____ v. _____   _____

DATE

	MOTHER	FATHER
1. Monthly Gross Income (see instructions on Page 2)	$	$
2. Adjustments for spousal support payments (see instructions on Page 2)	$	$
3. Adjustments for support of child(ren) (see instructions on Page 2)	$	$
4. Deductions from Monthly Gross Income allowable by law (see instructions on Page 2)	-$	$
5. a. Available monthly income	$	$

5. b. Combined monthly available income

   (combine both available monthly income figures from line 5.a.)   _____

6. Percent obligation of each party (divide "available monthly income" on line Line 5.a. by line 5.b.)   %_____   %_____

7. Number of children for which that person is the noncustodial parent.   _____   _____

	MOTHER	FATHER
8. a. Monthly basic child support obligation for number of children listed above (from schedule — see instructions on Page 2)	$	$
b. Monthly amount allowable for health care coverage paid by other parent (see instructions on Page 2)	$	$
c. Monthly amount allowable for employment-related child care expense paid by other parent (see instructions on Page 2)	$	$
9. Total monthly child support obligation of each parent (add lines 8.a., 8.b., and 8.c. for each parent)	$	$
10. Total monthly child support obligation of each party (multiply line 6 by line 9)	$	$

	MOTHER	FATHER
11. Adjustments (if any) to Child Support Guidelines Calculation (see instructions on Page 2)		
a. Credit for benefits received by or for the child derived from the parent's entitlement to disability insurance benefits to the extent that such derivative benefits are included in a parent's gross income	-$	-$
b. _____	$	$
c. _____	$	$
12. Each party's adjusted obligation to other party	$	$
13. Net payment	$	$

CHILD SUPPORT GUIDELINES WORKSHEET INSTRUCTIONS

For the purpose of applying this provision, split custody shall be limited to those situations where each parent has physical custody of a child or children born of the parents, born of either parent and adopted by the other parent or adopted by both parents. For the purposes of calculating a child support obligation where split custody exists, a separate family unit exists for each parent, and child support for that family unit shall be calculated upon the number of children in that family unit who are born of the parents, born of either parent and adopted by the other parent or adopted by both parents. Where split custody exists, a parent is a custodial parent to the children in that parent's family unit and is a noncustodial parent to the children in the other parent's family unit.

General — Use monthly financial information rounded to the nearest dollar in making these calculations. To convert data to monthly figures,

- multiply weekly financial data by 4.33
- multiply bi-weekly financial data by 2.167
- multiply semi-monthly financial data by 2
- divide annual financial data by 12

Amounts of $.50 or more should be rounded up to the nearest dollar; amounts less than $.50 should be rounded down to the nearest dollar.

Line 1 — Gross income is defined by Virginia Code § 20-108.2(C).

a. Gross income "shall mean all income from all sources, and shall include, but not be limited to, income from salaries, wages, commissions, royalties, bonuses, dividends, severance pay, pensions, interest, trust income, annuities, capital gains, social security benefits, worker's compensation benefits, disability insurance benefits, veterans' benefits, spousal support, rental income, gifts, prizes or awards. If a parent's gross income includes disability insurance benefits, it shall also include any amounts paid to or for the child who is the subject of the order and derived by the child from the parent's entitlement to disability insurance benefits."

b. Gross income "shall not include benefits from public assistance programs as defined in Virginia Code § 63.2-100 [Temporary Assistance to Needy Families, auxiliary grants to the aged, blind and disabled, medical assistance, energy assistance, food stamps, employment services, child care, general relief] federal Supplemental Security benefits, child support received, or income received by the payor from secondary employment income not previously included in "gross income," where the payor obtained the income to discharge a child support arrearage established by a court or administrative order and the payor is paying the arrearage pursuant to the order."

Line 2 — If spousal support is being paid by a party pursuant to an existing court or administrative order or written agreement, regardless of whether it is being paid to the other party or to a person not a party to this proceeding, subtract that amount under the payor's column. If spousal support is being received by a party pursuant to an existing court or administrative order or written agreement, regardless of whether it is being paid by the other party to this proceeding, add the amount under the payee's column. Use plus and minus signs appropriately. If a party is not paying or receiving spousal support, insert "none" in the appropriate column(s).

Line 3 — When a party is paying child support payments pursuant to an existing court or administrative order or written agreement for a child or children who are not the subject of the proceeding, subtract this amount from gross income. When a party has a child or children who are not the subject of the proceeding in their household or primary physical custody, subtract the amount as shown on the Schedule of Monthly Basic Child Support Obligations that represents that party's support obligation for that child or children based solely on that party's income as the total income available. If these provisions are inapplicable, insert "none" in the appropriate column(s). **There is only a presumption that these amounts will be deducted from gross income.**

Line 4 (Virginia Code § 20-108.2(C)) — If either parent has income from self-employment, a partnership or a closely-held business, subtract reasonable business expenses under the column of the party with such income. Include one-half of any self-employment tax paid, if applicable. If none, insert "none."

Line 5.a. — As applicable, add to and subtract from line 1 the figures in lines 2, 3 and 4 and enter the total for each column.

NOTE: Any adjustments to gross income shall not create or reduce a support obligation to an amount which seriously impairs the custodial parent's ability to maintain minimal adequate housing and provide other basic necessities for the child.

Line 8.a. — Using Virginia Code § 20-108.2(B) SCHEDULE OF MONTHLY BASIC CHILD SUPPORT OBLIGATIONS, use line 5.b. (combined monthly available income) to find the applicable income level under COMBINED GROSS INCOME, then use line 7 (number of children) to determine the basic child support obligation under the appropriate column at the applicable income level.

Line 8.b. (Virginia Code §§ 20-108.2(E) and 63.2-1900) — Insert costs for "health care coverage" when actually being paid by a parent, to the extent such costs are directly allocable to the child or children, and which are the extra costs of covering the child or children beyond whatever coverage the parent providing the coverage would otherwise have. "Health care coverage" means any plan providing hospital, medical or surgical care coverage for dependent children provided such coverage is available and can be obtained by a person obligated under Virginia law for support of a dependent child or the child's caretaker at a reasonable cost (such as through employers, unions or other groups without regard to service delivery mechanism). This item should also include the cost of any dental coverage for the child or children paid by a parent.

Lines 8.c. (Virginia Code § 20-108.2(F)) — Insert actual cost or the amount required to provide quality child care, whichever is less. If applicable, allocate ratably between employment-related child care and other child care based on custodian's activities while child care is being provided.

Line 11 (a-c) (Virginia Code § 20-108.1(B)) If amounts paid to or for the child who is the subject of the order and derived by the child from the parent's entitlement to disability insurance benefits have been included in a parent's gross income, that amount should be subtracted from that parent's child support obligation. If applicable, describe adjustment to child support for factors not addressed in guidelines calculation, then show amount to be added to or subtracted from each party-parent's child support obligation (use plus and minus signs appropriately).

Line 12 — If additional items are entered in lines 11 (a-c), add and subtract such items from line 10 and enter the totals on this line. In cases involving split custody, the amount of child support to be calculated using these guidelines shall be the difference between the amounts owed by each parent as a noncustodial parent, computed in accordance with these guidelines, with the noncustodial parent owing the larger amount paying the difference to the other parent.

VIRGINIA:

IN THE CIRCUIT COURT FOR _____ **COUNTY.**

_____,

Plaintiff,

v.   **CASE NO.** _____

_____,

Defendant.

<u>**COMPLAINT FOR DIVORCE**</u>

COMES NOW the Plaintiff, and as for his or her Complaint for Divorce, respectfully states as follows:

1.   The parties hereto were lawfully married on _____, _____ in _____:

2.   There were no children born or adopted of the marriage.

3.   Both parties hereto are over the age of eighteen (18) years. Neither party is an active duty member of the Armed Forces of the United States.

4.   The Plaintiff and Defendant are both domiciliaries and residents of the Commonwealth of Virginia and have been for more than six (6) months prior to the filing of this suit. The parties last cohabited as husband and wife in _____.

5.   The parties did separate and cease cohabiting together as husband and wife on _____, _____, with the intent to terminate the marriage. The parties have remained separate and apart without any cohabitation and without interruption since the aforesaid date, constituting a period now in excess of one year.

6.   The parties have entered into a written Property Settlement Agreement dated _____, _____, which Agreement resolves all matters of property and support between them.

WHEREFORE, Plaintiff respectfully prays that the Court:

A. grant him or her a divorce from the Defendant pursuant to Section 20-91(A)(9) of the Code of Virginia on the ground of having lived separate and apart for a period in excess of one year;

B. Affirm, ratify and approve the parties' Agreement dated _____, _____ and incorporate, but not merge it, into the final decree of divorce, if any, that the Court grants;

C. grant him or her such other relief as the needs of the case may require and to which he or she shows him or herself entitled.

_____

Plaintiff's signature

_____

Plaintiff's name

_____
_____

Plaintiff's address

_____

Plaintiff's telephone number

COVER SHEET FOR FILING CIVIL ACTIONS
COMMONWEALTH OF VIRGINIA

Case No. ....
(CLERK'S OFFICE USE ONLY)*

.... Circuit Court

.... v./*In re:* ....
PLAINTIFF(S)   DEFENDANT(S)

....

I, the undersigned [ ] plaintiff [ ] attorney for plaintiff hereby notify the Clerk of Court that I am filing the following civil action. (Please indicate by checking box that most closely identifies the claim being asserted or relief sought.)

[ ] Accounting
[ ] Administrative Appeal
[ ] Adult Protection
[ ] Aid and Guidance
[ ] Annexation
[ ] Annulment
[ ] Appeal Decision of ABC Board
[ ] Appeal Decision of Board of Zoning
[ ] Appeal Decision of Comp Board
[ ] Appeal Decision of Employment Commission
[ ] Appeal Decision of Local Government
[ ] Appeal Decision of Marine Resources Commission
[ ] Appeal Decision of Voter Registration
[ ] Appointment of Church Trustee, Substitute Fiduciaries
[ ] Approval of Right to be Eligible to Vote
[ ] Asbestos Litigation
[ ] Attachment
[ ] Bond Forfeiture Appeal
[ ] Child Abuse and Neglect - Unfounded Complaint
[ ] Civil Contempt
[ ] Claim Impleading Third Party Defendant
[ ] Complaint - (Miscellaneous)
[ ] Compromise Settlement
[ ] Condemnation
[ ] Confessed Judgment
[ ] Concealed Handgun Permit Denial
[ ] Conservator of Peace
[ ] Construe Will

[ ] Contract Action
[ ] Contract Specific Performance
[ ] Correct/Erroneous State/Local Taxes
[ ] Counterclaim
[ ] Court Appointment of Guardian (Competency)
[ ] Cross Claim
[ ] Custody/Visitation/Support/ Equitable Distribution
[ ] Declaratory Judgment
[ ] Declare Death
[ ] Delinquent Taxes
[ ] Detinue
[ ] Divorce
[ ] Ejectment
[ ] Encumber/Sell Real Estate
[ ] Enforce Vendor's Lien
[ ] Escheat
[ ] Establish Boundaries
[ ] Expunge
[ ] Forfeiture of U.S. Currency
[ ] Freedom of Information
[ ] Garnishment
[ ] General Tort Liability (other than motor vehicle)
[ ] Grievance Procedures
[ ] Guardian Appointment
[ ] Impress/Declare a Trust
[ ] Injunction
[ ] Interdiction
[ ] Interrogatory
[ ] Intentional Tort
[ ] Judgment Lien-Bill to Enforce
[ ] Judicial Review

[ ] Landlord/Tenant
[ ] Mechanics Lien
[ ] Medical Malpractice
[ ] Motor Vehicle Tort
[ ] Name Change
[ ] Order to Sever
[ ] Partition
[ ] Petition
[ ] Product Liability
[ ] Quiet Title
[ ] Referendum Elections
[ ] Reformation of Trust
[ ] Reinstatement of Driving Privileges
[ ] Reinstatement (General)
[ ] Removal
[ ] Separate Maintenance
[ ] Standby Guardian/ Conservator
[ ] Termination of Mineral Rights
[ ] Unlawful Detainer
[ ] Vehicle Confiscation
[ ] Will Contested
[ ] Writ of Certiorari
[ ] Writ of Habeas Corpus
[ ] Writ of Mandamus
[ ] Writ of Prohibition
[ ] Writ of Quo Warranto
[ ] Wrongful Death
[ ] Other

....

[ ] Damages in the amount of $ .... are claimed.

....
DATE

[ ] PLAINTIFF   [ ] DEFENDANT   [ ] ATTORNEY FOR [ ] PLAINTIFF
                                                    [ ] DEFENDANT

....
PRINT NAME

....
ADDRESS /TELEPHONE NUMBER OF SIGNATOR

FORM CC-1416 (MASTER) PAGE ONE 1/06

* See reverse side for Civil Action Type Codes
- for Clerk's Office Use Only

DIVORCE Case Cover Sheet

To be filed with the Complaint and any Cross-Bill of Complaint in ALL divorce cases

Date Filed: _____   Case Number: _____

PLEASE COMPLETE ALL SHADED AREAS

PARTIES

PLAINTIFF	DEFENDANT	SERVICE DATE/TYPE

ATTORNEYS

PLAINTIFF ATTORNEY	DEFENSE ATTORNEY:
BAR ID:	BAR ID:
	ANSWER DATE:
	CROSS-BILL DATE:
FIRM:	FIRM:
Name:	Name:
Street:	Street:
City: State: Zip	City: State: Zip
Phone Number: ( )	Phone Number: ( )

Check all that apply):

❐ TOTALLY UNCONTESTED (custody, support and property issues resolved OR no custody, property or support issues)	❐ CONTESTED PROPERTY OR SUPPORT ISSUES	❐ CONTESTED CUSTODY ISSUES
❐ ORE TENUS (planning to file a Request for Ore Tenus hearing)		

REQUESTED SERVICE:

❐ SHERIFF   ❐ SPECIAL PROCESS SERVER   ❐ ACCEPTANCE

❐ PUBLICATION   ❐ WAIVER   ❐ NO SERVICE AT THIS TIME

VIRGINIA:

IN THE CIRCUIT COURT FOR THE COUNTY OF _____

_____,   )

Plaintiff,   )

)

)

v.   )   **CASE NO.** _____

)

)

_____,   )

Defendant.   )

ACCEPTANCE OF SERVICE

COMES NOW the defendant, _____ who hereby accepts Service of Process of the Complaint with attached Subpoena in Chancery in this matter.

_____

Defendant

COMMONWEALTH OF VIRGINIA:

COUNTY OF _____ to-wit:

ACKNOWLEDGED, SUBSCRIBED and **SWORN** to before me by _____, this ____ day of _____, 200_____.

My Commission Expires: _____

_____

Notary Public

**ACCEPTANCE/WAIVER OF SERVICE OF PROCESS AND
WAIVER OF FUTURE SERVICE OF PROCESS
AND NOTICE**
COMMONWEALTH OF VIRGINIA

Case No. ....

.... Circuit Court

.... v. ....
PLAINTIFF   DEFENDANT

I, the undersigned party named below, swear under oath/affirm the following:

1.   I am a party   ☐ plaintiff ☐ defendant in the above-styled suit.

2.   I have received a copy of the following documents on this date:

☐ Complaint filed on ....
DATE

☐ Summons with copy of Complaint filed on .... attached
DATE

☐ Other – Describe: .... filed on ....
DATE

I understand that my receipt of these copies and my signature below constitute
☐ the acceptance of service of process of these copies, or
☐ a waiver of service of process and notice which may be prescribed by law.

3.   I agree to voluntarily and freely waive any future service of process and notice as checked below in this case:
☐ a.   any further service of process.
☐ b.   notice of the appointment of a commissioner in chancery and hearings held by such commissioner in chancery, if a commissioner in chancery is appointed.
☐ c.   notice of the taking of depositions.
☐ d.   notice of the filing of any reports by a commissioner in chancery or of the filing of depositions.
☐ e.   notice of entry of any order, judgment or decree, including the final decree of divorce.
I understand that, by waiving service of process, I am giving up my right to be notified of the events described immediately above.

....   _____
DATE   ☐ DEFENDANT   ☐ PLAINTIFF

TO DEFENDANT: Notify the Court in writing of any changes of your address while this case is pending.
State of.., ☐ City ☐ County of..
Subscribed and sworn to/affirmed before me this day by the above-named party.

....   _____
DATE   ☐ CLERK   ☐ DEPUTY CLERK

_____   My commission expires: ....
NOTARY PUBLIC

FORM CC-1406 (MASTER) 1/06 PDF
VA. CODE §§ 8.01-327; 20-99.1:1
Rules 3:5, 3:8

CC-1406 – ACCEPTANCE OF SERVICE OF PROCESS
AND WAIVER OF NOTICE

DATA ELEMENTS

1.   Court case number. (If not known, inquire with the clerk of court.)

2.   Name of court.

3.   Name of plaintiff.

4.   Name of defendant.

5.   Check appropriate box to identify person accepting/waiving process.

6.   Check appropriate box for applicable service. If document is not a Subpoena in Chancery or Bill of Complaint, check box below Bill of Complaint and enter description of document received. See Using This Form, 2(a).

7.   Check appropriate box to indicate acceptance or waiver of process.

8.   Check appropriate box for which the defendant has waived future service of process.

9.   Date defendant is accepting process and/or waiving process.

10.   Signature of person accepting process or counsel in proceeding. Check appropriate title box. See Using This Form, 2(c).

11.   Enter name of state, check applicable box and enter the city or county name where affirmation is taken. Not filled out online.

12.   Date of defendant/plaintiff affirmation. Not filled out online.

13.   Signature of person taking affirmation, if clerk or deputy clerk. Check the appropriate title box. Not filled out online.

14.   Notary public. Not filled out online.

15.   Date Notary Public's commission expires. Not filled out online.

VIRGINIA:
IN THE CIRCUIT COURT OF THE [CITY] _____ [COUNTY] OF _____

_____,
Plaintiff,

v.   **CASE NO.** _____

_____,
Defendant.

AFFIDAVIT

I, the undersigned, swear/affirm as follows:

1. I am [name], [address], [telephone number]. I am a private process server in this suit.
2. I am not a party to or otherwise interested in the subject matter in controversy in this case.
3. I am 18 years of age or older.
4. I served [name of person served with papers], upon whom service of process was to be made, with copies of the Bill of Complaint, filed on _____, _____, with Subpoena in Chancery attached, and the [here, identify other papers served, for example, "Notice to Take Depositions, filed on _____, _____"], as shown below:
   a. Date of Service: _____
   b. Place of Service (address): _____
   c. Method of Service: (Check one)
      (1) _____ By personal service;
      (2) _____ Being unable to make personal service, a copy was delivered to a family member (not a temporary sojourner or guest) age 16 or older at the usual place of abode of the person to be served after giving information of its purport. The name, age of recipient, and relation of recipient to party served are:

_____

      (3) _____ Being unable to make personal service, a copy was posted on front door or such other door as appears to be the main entrance of the usual place of abode (other authorized recipient not found).

_____   _____
         Date   [Name of process server]

COMMONWEALTH OF VIRGINIA
[CITY] [COUNTY] of _____

Subscribed and sworn to/affirmed before me this _____ day of _____, _____, by [name of process server].

_____   _____
         Date   Notary Public
                                             My commission expires: _____

VIRGINIA:

    IN THE CIRCUIT COURT OF THE [CITY] [COUNTY] OF _____

_____,

Plaintiff,

v.   **CASE NO.** ____

_____,

Defendant.

REQUEST FOR ORDER OF PUBLICATION

    The clerk will please enter an order of publication in this matter. Plaintiff's Affidavit in Support of Order of Publication is filed herewith.

_____

Plaintiff's name

Address: _____

_____

_____

Telephone: _____

VIRGINIA:

IN THE CIRCUIT COURT OF THE [CITY] [COUNTY] OF _____

_____,

Plaintiff,

v.   **CASE NO. ____**

_____,

Defendant.

AFFIDAVIT IN SUPPORT OF ORDER OF PUBLICATION

[Name of plaintiff], being duly sworn, deposes and says:
1. [Name of plaintiff] is the Plaintiff in the above-styled divorce suit.
2. The above-named Defendant's last known address [was [address]] [is not known].
3. The Defendant's present whereabouts are unknown.
4. The Plaintiff has used due diligence to attempt to locate the Defendant without effect.

_____

[Name of Plaintiff]

COMMONWEALTH OF VIRGINIA

[CITY] [COUNTY] of _____, to-wit:

Subscribed and sworn to/affirmed before me this _____ day of _____, _____, by [name of plaintiff].

_____

Notary Public
My commission expires: _____

VIRGINIA:

IN THE CIRCUIT COURT OF THE [CITY] [COUNTY] OF _____

_____,

Plaintiff,

v.   **CASE NO. ____**

_____,

Defendant.

AFFIDAVIT IN SUPPORT OF ORDER OF PUBLICATION

[Name of plaintiff], being duly sworn, deposes and says:

1.   [Name of plaintiff] is the Plaintiff in the above-styled divorce suit.
2.   The Defendant is not a resident of the Commonwealth of Virginia.
3.   The above-named Defendant's last known address was [address outside of Virginia].

_____

[Name of Plaintiff]

COMMONWEALTH OF VIRGINIA

[CITY] [COUNTY] of _____, to-wit:

Subscribed and sworn to/affirmed before me this _____ day of _____, ____, by [name of plaintiff].

_____

Notary Public
My commission expires: _____

VIRGINIA:

   IN THE CIRCUIT COURT OF THE [CITY] [COUNTY] OF _____

_____,

Plaintiff,

v.   **CASE NO.** ____

_____,

Defendant.

AFFIDAVIT IN SUPPORT OF ORDER OF PUBLICATION

[Name of plaintiff], being duly sworn, deposes and says:

   1.   [Name of plaintiff] is the Plaintiff in the above-styled divorce suit.

   2.   The above-named Defendant's last known address was [address],which is located within the [City] [County] of _____, Virginia.

   3.   Plaintiff sought service of process on the Defendant at [his] [her] last known residence, and the Sheriff of _____, Virginia has filed a return of service stating that the process has been in [his] [her] hands for 21 days and that [he] [she] has been unable to make service of process.

   4.   The Defendant's present whereabouts are unknown.

_____

[Name of Plaintiff]

COMMONWEALTH OF VIRGINIA

[CITY] [COUNTY] of _____, to-wit:

Subscribed and sworn to/affirmed before me this _____ day of _____, _____, by [name of plaintiff].

_____

Notary Public

My commission expires: _____

VIRGINIA:
IN THE CIRCUIT COURT OF _____ **COUNTY**

_____,   )
Plaintiff,   )
)
)
v.   )   **CASE NO.** _____
)
)
_____,   )
Defendant.   )

AFFIDAVIT FOR SERVICE BY PUBLICATION

Comes now _____, Plaintiff seeking service on _____, the defendant by ORDER OF PUBLICATION, AND who under oath deposes and states under oath that the Defendant in this cause,

❏ Is a non-resident individual, other than a non-resident individual fiduciary who has appointed a statutory agent;
OR

❏ Cannot be found, and that diligence has been used without effect to ascertain the location of the party to be served;
OR

❏ Cannot be served with court process, and that a return has been filed by the Sheriff which shows that the process has been in his or her hands for twenty-one (21) days and the Sheriff has been unable to make service;
OR

❏ OTHER:

and the last known mailing address of the Defendant is as follows:

Name: _____
Address: _____
_____

OTHER INFORMATION:

_____
Signature of Plaintiff

_____
Counsel for Plaintiff

TO BE COMPLETED BY A NOTARY PUBLIC/OR DEPUTY CLERK

In the Commonwealth/State of

In the County of

Subscribed and sworn to before me by_____ this _____ day of _____, _____.
_____   My Commission Expires:
Notary Public/Deputy Clerk

VIRGINIA
IN THE CIRCUIT COURT OF _____ COUNTY

_____   CASE NO.
Plaintiff

VS

_____
Defendant

ORDER OF PUBLICATION

The reason for this cause is   _to obtain a divorce_

An affidavit having been made and filed showing that the Defendant in the above-entitled cause is

☐   *Is a non-resident individual, other than a non-resident individual fiduciary who has appointed a statutory agent;*

OR

☐   *Cannot be found, and that diligence has been used without effect to ascertain the location of the party to be served;*

OR

☐   *Cannot be served with court process, and that a return has been filed by the Sheriff which shows that the process has been in his or her hands for twenty-one (21) days and the Sheriff has been unable to make service;*

OR

☐   *OTHER:* _____

and last known mailing address of the Defendant is as follows:
Name   _____
Address   _____

TO BE COMPLETED BY CLERK'S OFFICE

Upon consideration, this Order of Publication is granted and it is ORDERED that the above named Defendant shall appear her on or before _____ day of _____, _____ after proper publication of this Order, to protect his/her interest in this cause.

Entered: _____   *TESTE:* _____
                                        BY: _____
                                                DEPUTY CLERK

Signature of Complainant or Counsel for Complainant
*Address:*_____

Phone Number: _____

VIRGINIA:

IN THE CIRCUIT COURT OF _____ **COUNTY**

_____,   )

Plaintiff,   )

)

)

v.   )   **CASE NO.** _____

)

)

_____,   )

Defendant.   )

REQUEST FOR ORE TENUS HEARING

I, _____ [ ] Plaintiff, [ ] Defendant, [ ] Counsel for Plaintiff, [ ] Counsel for Defendant (check one), hereby request that this matter be set for an _Ore Tenus_ hearing as all issues in this case are totally uncontested. I have received and read the Fairfax Circuit Court's _Ore Tenus_ Hearing Instructions and agree to fully comply with them.

_____

NAME

Attachments:

1. Property Settlement Agreement: [ ]   Address:
2. Final Decree: [ ] _____
3. Other: [ ] _____   _____

                                                                      _____

                                                                      _____

                                                              Daytime Phone No: (_____) _____

                                                              VSB# (If Attorney): _____

CERTIFICATE OF SERVICE

I hereby certify that if notice is required by either Rule 1:12 of the Rules of the Supreme Court Virginia of Virginia Code Section 20-99 of 20-99.1:1, a true copy of this pleading and all attachments have been served on opposing counsel of record.

_____

(Print name and sign)

H-41

COMMONWEALTH OF VIRGINIA – REPORT OF DIVORCE OR ANNULMENT
Department of Health – Division of Vital Records – Richmond

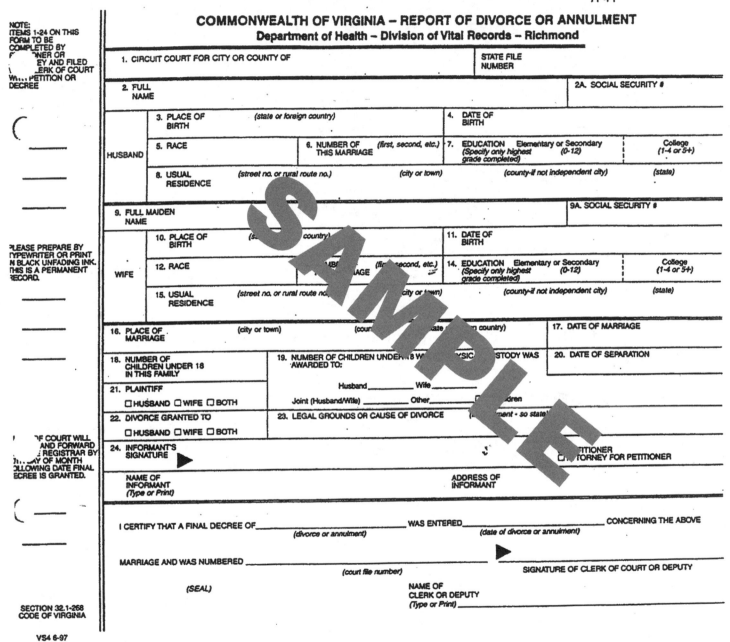

NOTE:
ITEMS 1-24 ON THIS FORM TO BE COMPLETED BY PETITIONER OR ATTORNEY AND FILED WITH CLERK OF COURT WITH PETITION OR DECREE

PLEASE PREPARE BY TYPEWRITER OR PRINT IN BLACK UNFADING INK. THIS IS A PERMANENT RECORD.

CLERK OF COURT WILL COMPLETE AND FORWARD TO STATE REGISTRAR BY 10th DAY OF MONTH FOLLOWING DATE FINAL DECREE IS GRANTED.

SECTION 32.1-268 CODE OF VIRGINIA

VS4 6-97

1. CIRCUIT COURT FOR CITY OR COUNTY OF
STATE FILE NUMBER

2. FULL NAME
2A. SOCIAL SECURITY #

HUSBAND
3. PLACE OF BIRTH (state or foreign country)
4. DATE OF BIRTH
5. RACE
6. NUMBER OF THIS MARRIAGE (first, second, etc.)
7. EDUCATION Elementary or Secondary (Specify only highest grade completed) (0-12) | College (1-4 or 5+)
8. USUAL RESIDENCE (street no. or rural route no.) (city or town) (county-if not independent city) (state)

9. FULL MAIDEN NAME
9A. SOCIAL SECURITY #

WIFE
10. PLACE OF BIRTH (state or foreign country)
11. DATE OF BIRTH
12. RACE
13. NUMBER OF THIS MARRIAGE (first, second, etc.)
14. EDUCATION Elementary or Secondary (Specify only highest grade completed) (0-12) | College (1-4 or 5+)
15. USUAL RESIDENCE (street no. or rural route no.) (city or town) (county-if not independent city) (state)

16. PLACE OF MARRIAGE (city or town) (county or state or foreign country)
17. DATE OF MARRIAGE

18. NUMBER OF CHILDREN UNDER 18 IN THIS FAMILY
19. NUMBER OF CHILDREN UNDER 18 WHOSE PHYSICAL CUSTODY WAS AWARDED TO: Husband _____ Wife _____ Joint (Husband/Wife) _____ Other _____ Children
20. DATE OF SEPARATION

21. PLAINTIFF ☐ HUSBAND ☐ WIFE ☐ BOTH

22. DIVORCE GRANTED TO ☐ HUSBAND ☐ WIFE ☐ BOTH
23. LEGAL GROUNDS OR CAUSE OF DIVORCE (if judgment - so state)

24. INFORMANT'S SIGNATURE ▶
☐ PETITIONER ☐ ATTORNEY FOR PETITIONER

NAME OF INFORMANT (Type or Print)
ADDRESS OF INFORMANT

I CERTIFY THAT A FINAL DECREE OF _____ (divorce or annulment) WAS ENTERED _____ (date of divorce or annulment) CONCERNING THE ABOVE

MARRIAGE AND WAS NUMBERED _____ (court file number) ▶

(SEAL)

SIGNATURE OF CLERK OF COURT OR DEPUTY

NAME OF CLERK OR DEPUTY (Type or Print) _____

(An original of this document must be obtained directly from the court.)

VIRGINIA:
IN THE CIRCUIT COURT OF _____ **COUNTY**

_____,   )
Plaintiff,   )
)
)
v.   )   **CASE NO.** _____
)
)
_____,   )
Defendant.   )

DECREE OF REFERENCE

THIS CAUSE came on upon the Complaint for Divorce filed duly herein; upon process service of the Complaint for Divorce upon the Defendant; upon this cause having matured for a hearing; and upon motion of the Plaintiff for referral of this cause to a Commissioner in Chancery; and

IT APPEARING TO THE COURT that this cause has matured for the appointment of and reference to a Commissioner in Chancery; it is, accordingly

ADJUDGED, ORDERED and **DECREED** that this cause hereby is referred to _____ _____, a Commissioner in Chancery for this Court, for the purpose of taking evidence of the parties and their witnesses, and reporting to this Court findings, conclusions of law recommendations in regard to the allegations contained in the pleadings.

ENTERED this _____ day of _____, 20_____.

_____
                                              JUDGE

WE ASK FOR THIS:
Counsel

[Certificate of Service]

VIRGINIA:

IN THE CIRCUIT COURT OF _____ COUNTY

_____   )

Plaintiff,   )

v.   )   CASE NO. _____

_____   )

Defendant   )

AGREED DECREE OF REFERENCE

The parties, by their respective counsel, request this Court to appoint _____ to be the Commissioner in Chancery in this cause.

Further, the undersigned represent that:

1. They have familiarized themselves with the General Order for Commissioners Hearings in Divorce Cases, dated March 11, 1996.

2. The above named person is a Commissioner in Chancery for this Court.

3. This Commissioner does not have a conflict with either party or counsel.

4. This Commissioner has agreed to serve in this matter.

5. A copy of this Decree of Reference will be transmitted to the Commissioner.

6. The cause will be set for the Commissioner's Hearing no closer to the trial date than Sixty days, to allow for the Report to be filed and any Exceptions taken.

WHEREFORE, it appearing that this cause should be referred to a Commissioner in Chancery in accordance with the stipulations set forth above, it is:

ADJUDGED, ORDERED and DECREED that _____ is hereby appointed the Commissioner in Chancery in this matter.

ENTERED this ___ day of _____, 20___.

_____
JUDGE

SEEN & AGREED   SEEN & AGREED

_____   _____
Counsel for Plaintiff   Counsel for Defendant

VIRGINIA:

IN THE CIRCUIT COURT FOR THE COUNTY OF _____

_____,	)
Plaintiff,	)
	)
	)
v.	) **CASE NO.** _____
	)
	)
_____,	)
Defendant.	)

FINAL DECREE OF DIVORCE

THIS MATTER CAME ON upon the Complaint filed by the Plaintiff upon the filing of an Answer by the Defendant; upon the signing of an Acceptance of Service; upon the taking of depositions of the Plaintiff and his or her witness before a Notary Public; and the filing of a transcript of said depositions herein; and

IT APPEARING unto the Court

1. That the parties herein were married on _____, _____, in _____;

2. That there were no children born or adopted of the marriage;

3. That the Plaintiff and Defendant last cohabited as husband and wife in _____;

4. That both parties are bona fide residents and domicillaries of the Commonwealth of Virginia and have been so for more than six months prior to the institution of this suit;

5. That both parties are over the age of eighteen years and neither party is an active member of the Armed Forces of the United States;

6. That the parties have lived separate and apart, without any cohabitation and without interruption, for a period of more than one year, with the intent to permanently terminate the marital relationship;

7. That the parties entered into a Property Settlement Agreement dated _____, _____, which Agreement settles all issues of property and support;

8. That there is no child or spousal support payable by one party to the other, nor are there any health insurance obligations in this Decree, hence the provisions of Virginia Code §20-60.3 do not apply.

WHEREFORE, it is this ___ day of _____, _____:

ORDERED that the Plaintiff, _____ be and hereby is granted a divorce *a vinculo matrimonii* from the Defendant _____ on the ground of having lived separate and apart for a period of at least one year, pursuant to Section 20-91.A.(9) of the Code of Virginia 1950, as amended; and it is further

ORDERED that the parties' Agreement dated _____, _____ is hereby approved, ratified, and affirmed, and incorporated into this Decree to the extent of this Court's jurisdiction, but said Agreement is not merged in this Decree and the Agreement shall remain binding on and enforceable by the parties separately from this Decree; and it is further

ORDERED that the Clerk of this Court shall cause a copy of this Decree to issue to counsel of record for Complainant and to the Defendant; and

THIS CAUSE IS FINAL and should be removed from the docket.

ENTERED this _____ day of _____, 200_____.

_____
Judge

I ASK FOR THIS:

Plaintiff's signature _____
Plaintiff's name _____
Plaintiff's address _____
Plaintiff's telephone number _____

SEEN AND _____:

Defendant's signature _____
Defendant's name _____
Defendant's address _____
Defendant's telephone number _____

VIRGINIA:
IN THE CIRCUIT COURT FOR THE COUNTY OF _____

_____,)
Plaintiff,   )
)
)
)
v.   )   **CASE NO.** _____
)
)
_____,)
Defendant.   )

FINAL DECREE OF DIVORCE

THIS MATTER CAME ON upon the Complaint filed by the Plaintiff upon the filing of an Answer by the Defendant; upon the signing of an Acceptance of Service; upon the taking of depositions of the Plaintiff and his or her witness before a Notary Public; and the filing of a transcript of said depositions herein; and

WHEREUPON, pursuant to Virginia Code §20-60.3, the parties are hereby notified of the following provisions of Virginia law and the parties hereby represent to this Court that the information provided below is true information:

NOTICES and INFORMATION:

1. Support payments may be withheld as they become due pursuant to §20-79.1 or §20-79.2, from income as defined in §63.1-250, without further amendments of this Order or having to file an application for services with the Department of Social Services.

2. Support payments may be withheld pursuant to Chapter 13 (§63.1-249, et seq.) of Title 63.1 without further amendments to the order upon application for services with the Department of Social Services.

3. A duty of support is owed for the following children of the parties:

Name	Date of Birth	Resides With
_____	_____	_____
_____	_____	_____
_____	_____	_____
_____	_____	_____

4. The following is true information regarding the parties subject of this Order:

Person Responsible for paying child support is the _____.

MOTHER: _____

    Date of Birth: _____

    SSN: (see separate private memorandum)

    Driver's License #: _____

    State of Issuance: _____

    Resid. Address: _____

    Home Phone #: _____

    Employment: _____

    Work Address: _____

    Work Phone #: _____

FATHER:

    Date of Birth: _____

    SSN: (see separate private memorandum)

    Driver's License #: _____

    State of Issuance: _____

    Resid. Address: _____

    Home Phone #: _____

    Employment: _____

    Work Address: _____

    Work Phone #: _____

5. A petition may be filed for the suspension of any license, certificate, registration, or other authorization to engage in a profession, trade, business, or occupation issued by the Commonwealth of Virginia to a person responsible for support as provided in §63.1-263.1, upon a delinquency for a period of ninety days or more or in an amount of $5,000 or more.

Neither party holds any such license, certificate, registration, or authorization. [OR put in who holds what license]

6. The Order of this Court as to the amount and terms of the child support and spousal support are as set forth in the support provisions of this Decree.

7. a. The Order of this Court as to health care coverage for spouse and children and any policy information are set forth in the health care provision of this Order.

b. This Order does not contain any provision for extraordinary medical expenses to be paid by or reimbursed to a party pursuant to subsection D and G3 of §10-108.2.

8. There are no support arrearages as of the date of entry of this Decree.

9. If child support payments have been ordered, then, unless the Court orders otherwise for good cause shown, the parties shall give each other and this Court at least thirty days' advance written notice of any change in address, and shall give notice of any change of telephone number within thirty days after the change. The parties shall give these notices to each other and, when payments are to be made through the Department of Social Services (DSS), to the DSS.

10. If child support payments are ordered to be paid through the (DSS), the obligor shall keep the DSS informed of his or her current employer's name, address, and telephone number. If payments are made directly to the obligee then the obligor shall keep this Court informed of his or her current employer's name, address, and telephone number.

11. The separate amounts due to each person under this Order for child support or the affirmation of a separation agreement are set forth in the support provision of this Order.

12. In determination of a support obligation, the support obligation as it becomes due and unpaid creates a judgment by operation of law.

13. The Department of Social Services may, pursuant to Chapter 13 (§63.1-249, et seq.) of Title 63.1 and in accordance with §20-108.2 and §63.1-252.2, initiate a review of the amount of support ordered by any court.

WHEREUPON, in appearing to this Court:

1. That the parties herein were married on _____, _____, in _____;

2. That there were _____ children born of the marriage;

3. That the Plaintiff and Defendant last cohabitated as husband and wife in _____;

4. That both parties are bona fide residents and domicillaries of the Commonwealth of Virginia and have been so for more than six months prior to the institution of this suit;

5. That both parties are over the age of eighteen years and neither party is an active member of the Armed Forces of the United States;

6. that the parties have lived separate and apart, without any cohabitation and without interruption since _____, _____, constituting a period of more than one year, with the intent to permanently terminate the marital relationship;

7. That the parties entered into a Property Settlement Agreement dated _____, _____, which Agreement settles all issues of property and support;

8. That the Plaintiff is entitled to a divorce a vinnculo matrimonii pursuant to Virginia Code §20-91(A)(9), therefore, it is:

ORDERED as follows:

1. Divorce: That the Plaintiff is hereby granted a Final Decree of Divorce, a vinculo matrimonii, from the Defendant pursuant to Virginia Code 20-91(A)(9), based on the fact that the parties have lived separate and apart, without any cohabitation and without interruption, for a period in excess of one year; and

2. Agreement: That the Property Settlement Agreement of the parties dated _____, _____, is hereby ratified and affirmed and is incorporated into, but is not merged into, this Final Decree of Divorce pursuant to Virginia Code 20-109.1` and the parties are ordered to comply with all provisions thereof.

3. Custody: [Specify the basic custody/visitation provisions of the PSA.] Pursuant to Virginia Code §20-124.5, either party who intends to relocate his or her residence shall give a thirty-day advance written notice of any such intended relocation and of any intended change of address, said notice being given to both the other party and to this Court.

4. Child Support: _____ shall pay to _____, as child support, the sum of $_____ per _____, beginning _____, 200_____ and to be paid _____, until further order of this Court.

       (1) This support amount set forth above [ ] Does [ ] Does Not include any payment for extraordinary medical expenses to be paid by or reimbursed to a party pursuant to subsection D and G 3 of §20-108.2 OR

          In addition to the support amount set forth above, _____ shall pay or reimburse to _____, for the extraordinary medical expenses of _____ as follows: _____.

       (2) Support shall be paid for any child until the child reaches the age of eighteen, and shall continue to be paid for a child who is (i) a full-time high school student, (ii) not self-supporting, and (iii) living in the home of the parent seeking or receiving child support, until the child reaches the age of nineteen or graduates from high school,, whichever occurs first.

       (3) That said support shall be payable directly by the _____ to the _____ and shall NOT be by Income Deduction order.

5. Spousal Support: [Specify any spousal support provision of the PSA]

6. Health Care: That the _____ shall provide health insurance for the minor children so long as such insurance coverage is available under the terms of his or her employer provided health insurance policy. The health insurance carrier is _____, and said insurance is provided as a benefit of the Defendant's employment with _____.

Health insurance [is] [is not] required by this Order for a spouse or former spouse.

7. Arrearages: There are no support arrearages as of the date of this Order.

THIS CAUSE IS FINAL.

ENTERED this _____ day of _____, 200_____.

_____
                JUDGE

WE ASK FOR THIS: **SEEN and AGREED:**

Counsel for Plaintiff   Counsel for Defendant

VIRGINIA

IN THE CIRCUIT COURT OF _____ **COUNTY**

_____,   )
Plaintiff,   )
)
v.   )   **CASE NO.** _____
)
_____,   )
Defendant.   )

AFFIDAVIT REGARDING MILITARY SERVICE

The undersigned, _____, deposes and states this _____ Day of _____:

1. I am the Plaintiff in the above-captioned divorce case.
2. I am married to the Defendant.
3. The Defendant is not in the military service of the Army of the United States, the United States Navy, the Marine Corps, the Coast Guard, the Air Force, nor is he or she an officer of the Public Health Service detailed by proper authority for duty either with the Army or the Navy.

Plaintiff's signature _____

Plaintiff's name _____

Plaintiff's address _____

_____

_____

Plaintiff's telephone number _____

STATE OF _____)

COUNTY OF _____) to wit:

I HEREBY CERTIFY that before me the undersigned Notary Public, personally appeared _____, known to me to be the person whose name is subscribed above, and signed the foregoing document and swore that the contents of the foregoing document are true.

WITNESS my hand and official seal this ____ day of _____, _____.

_____
Notary Public
My commission expires:_____

Summary of District of Columbia Divorce Laws

This appendix summarizes the most important laws concerning divorce in the District of Columbia. You can use this summary to find a quick answer to a question or as a starting point for future research.

1. FILING.
(a) the Complaint is filed in the "Superior Court of the District of Columbia, Family Court";
(b) it is titled a "Complaint for Divorce" or "Complaint for Legal Separation";
(c) it is filed by the "Plaintiff";
(d) the other spouse is the "Defendant";
(e) it is filed at 500 Indiana Avenue, NW, 5th Floor; and
(f) the final papers are called the "Findings of Fact, Conclusions of Law, and Judgment of Absolute Divorce." *District of Columbia* Rules.

2. RESIDENCY. One party must have been a resident for six months immediately prior to filing for divorce. Military personnel are considered residents if they have been stationed in DC for six months. *District of Columbia Code; Title 16, Chapter 9, Section 902.*

3. GROUNDS FOR ABSOLUTE DIVORCE.
(a) mutual and voluntary separation for six months;
(b) involuntary separation for one year. *District of Columbia Code; Title 16, Chapter 9, Sections 904(a), 905, and 906.*

4. GROUNDS FOR LEGAL SEPARATION.
(a) mutual and voluntary separation (no minimum duration);
(b) involuntary separation for one year;

(c) adultery; and,
(d) cruelty. *District of Columbia Code; Title 16, Chapter 9, Section 904(b).*

5. MEDIATION AND PARENTING CLASSES. The court has started a pilot program of sending cases to a mediator. In child custody cases, the court may order either or both spouses to attend parenting classes. *District of Columbia Code; Title 16, Chapter 9, Sections 911(2)d.*

6. UNCONTESTED DIVORCE. Upon written request, the Court will schedule a brief hearing before a Commissioner, where at least one party testifies, to obtain a divorce. *District of Columbia* Rules.

7. CHILD CUSTODY. The court may award sole or joint custody based on the best interests of the child, without regard to spouse's sex or sexual orientation, race, color, national origin, or political affiliations. The following factors shall also be considered:
(a) the preference of the child, if the child is of sufficient age and capacity;
(b) the wishes of the parents;
(c) the child's adjustment to his or her home, school, and community;

(d) the mental and physical health of all individuals involved;

(e) the relationship of the child with parents, siblings, and other significant family members;

(f) the willingness of the parents to share custody and make shared decisions;

(g) the prior involvement of the parent in the child's life;

(h) the geographical proximity of the parents;

(i) the sincerity of the parent's request;

(j) the age and number of children;

(k) the demands of parental employment;

(l) the impact on any welfare benefits;

(m) any evidence of spousal or child abuse;

(n) financial capability of providing custody; and,

(o) the benefit to the parties. There is a rebuttable presumption that joint custody is in the best interests of the child; unless child abuse, neglect, parental kidnapping or other intrafamily violence has occurred. The court may order the parents to submit a written parenting plan for custody. *District of Columbia Code; Title 16, Chapter 9, Sections 911 and 914.*

8. CHILD SUPPORT. Either parent may be ordered to pay reasonable child support in accordance with the child support guidelines in Title 16, Chapter 9, Section 916.1 and 916.2 of the DC Code. The guidelines provide that the judge may exercise discretion and increase or decrease the recommended child support by 3% based on the facts of the case. Greater variations from the child support guidelines are based on the following factors:

(a) the child's needs are exceptional;

(b) the non-custodial parent's income is substantially less than the custodial parent's income;

(c) a property settlement between the parents provides resources for the child above the minimum support requirements;

(d) the non-custodial parent provides support for other dependents and the guideline amounts would cause hardship;

(f) the non-custodial parent needs a temporary reduction (of no longer than 12 months) in support payments to repay a substantial debt;

(g) the custodial parent provides medical insurance coverage;

(h) the custodial parent receives child support payments for other children and the custodial parent's household income is substantially greater than that of the non-custodial parent; and,

(i) any other extraordinary factors. Child support may be ordered to be paid through the Clerk of the Superior Court. District of Columbia Code; Title 16, Chapter 9, Sections 911 and 916.

9. ALIMONY. Either party may be awarded rehabilitative or indefinite alimony. The court must consider:

(1) ability of the party seeking alimony to be wholly or partly self-supporting;

(2) time necessary for the party seeking alimony to gain sufficient education or training to enable that party to secure suitable employment;

(3) standard of living that the parties established during their marriage, but giving consideration to the fact that there will be two households to maintain;

(4) duration of the marriage;

(5) circumstances which contributed to the estrangement of the parties;

(6) age of each party;

(7) physical and mental condition of each party;

(8) ability of the party from whom alimony is sought to meet his or her needs while meeting the needs of the other party; and,

(9) financial needs and financial resources of each party, including:

(A) income;

(B) income from assets, both marital and non-marital;

(C) potential income which may be imputed to non-income producing assets of a party;

(D) any previous award of child support in this case;

(E) the financial obligations of each party;

(F) the right of a party to receive retirement benefits; and,

(G) the taxability or non-taxability of income. *District of Columbia Code; Title 16, Chapter 9, Section 16-913.*

10. EQUITABLE DISTRIBUTION OF PROPERTY. If there is no Separation Agreement, each party keeps his or her non-marital property (acquired before the marriage or acquired during the marriage by gift from a third party or inheritance) and any increase in such separate property and any property acquired in exchange for such separate property. All other property, regardless of how title is held, is marital property. The court will distribute it based on:

(1) the duration of the marriage;

(2) the age, health, occupation, amount, and sources of income, vocational skills, employability, assets, debts, and needs of each of the parties;

(3) provisions for the custody of minor children;

(4) whether the distribution is in lieu of or in addition to alimony;

(5) each party's obligation from a prior marriage or for other children;

(6) the opportunity of each party for future acquisition of assets and income;

(7) each party's contribution as a homemaker or otherwise to the family unit;

(8) each party's contribution to the education of the other party which enhanced the other party's earning ability;

(9) each party's increase or decrease in income as a result of the marriage or duties of homemaking and child care;

(10) each party's contribution to the acquisition, preservation, appreciation, dissipation, or depreciation in value of the

assets which are subject to distribution, the taxability of these assets, and whether the asset was acquired or the debt incurred after separation;

(11) the effects of taxation on the value of the assets subject to distribution; and,

(12) the circumstances which contributed to the estrangement of the parties

District of Columbia Code; Title 16, Chapter 9, Section 910.

11. NAME CHANGE. Upon request, the birth name or previous name may be restored. *District of Columbia Code; Title 16, Chapter 9, Section 915.*

12. PREMARITAL AGREEMENTS. The agreement must be in writing and signed by both parties and is enforceable without consideration. An agreement is not enforceable if the party can prove that

(a) the agreement was not voluntarily executed or

(b) the agreement was unconscionable when executed and before the execution the party was not provided a fair and reasonable disclosure of the property or financial obligations of the other party, the party did not voluntarily waive any right to the disclosure of these obligations, and the party did not have adequate knowledge regarding these obligations. If a provision of the agreement modifies or eliminates spousal support and that causes the party to be eligible for public assistance, the court may require the party to provide support to the extent to avoid that eligibility. If the marriage is determined to be void, the agreement is enforceable only to the extent necessary to avoid an inequitable result, unless the agreement expressly provides that it shall be enforceable in the event the marriage is determined to be void. *District of Columbia Code, Title 16, Chapter 30, Sections 142, 146, and 147.*

Child Support Guidelines in the District of Columbia

The **CHILD SUPPORT GUIDELINES WORKSHEET** is used to calculate the proper amount of child support. The guidelines are presumptively correct and must be followed by the commissioner or judge, unless there are some special circumstances that would justify deviation from the guidelines.

Child support is calculated as a percentage of the noncustodial parent's annual income. The following tables establish a basic order for children 0-6 years of age and then add a percentage to that basic order if the children are older.

CHART 1
CHILD SUPPORT ORDER FORMULA
FOR THE SUPERIOR COURT
ONE CHILD
AGES 0-6

ANNUAL GROSS INCOME OF NONCUSTODIAL PARENT	CHILD SUPPORT ORDER
0 -- $7,500	Discretion--Minimum $50/month
$7,501 -- 15,000	20% of Gross Income
15,001 -- 25,000	21% of Gross Income
25,001 -- 50,000	22% of Gross Income
50,001 -- 75,000	23% of Gross Income

AGES 7-12

ANNUAL GROSS INCOME OF NONCUSTODIAL PARENT	CHILD SUPPORT ORDER
0 -- $7,500	Discretion--Minimum $50/month
$7,501 -- 15,000	20% of Gross Income + 10% of Basic Order (22%)
15,001 -- 25,000	21% of Gross Income + 10% of Basic Order (23.1%)
25,001 -- 50,000	22% of Gross Income + 10% of Basic Order (24.2%)
50,001 -- 75,000	23% of Gross Income + 10% of Basic Order (25.3%)

AGES 13-21

ANNUAL GROSS INCOME OF NONCUSTODIAL PARENT	CHILD SUPPORT ORDER
0 -- $7,500	Discretion--Minimum $50/month
$7,501 -- 15,000	20% of Gross Income + 15% of Basic Order (23%)
15,001 -- 25,000	21% of Gross Income + 15% of Basic Order (24.15%)
25,001 -- 50,000	22% of Gross Income + 15% of Basic Order (25.3%)
50,001 -- 75,000	23% of Gross Income + 15% of Basic Order (26.45%)

CHART 2
CHILD SUPPORT ORDER FORMULA
FOR THE SUPERIOR COURT
TWO CHILDREN
AGES 0-6 (oldest child)

ANNUAL GROSS INCOME OF NONCUSTODIAL PARENT		CHILD SUPPORT ORDER
0 -- $7,500		Discretion--Minimum $50/month
$7,501 -- 15,000		26% of Gross Income
15,001 -- 25,000		27% of Gross Income
25,001 -- 50,000		28% of Gross Income
50,001 -- 75,000		29% of Gross Income

AGES 7-12 (oldest child)

ANNUAL GROSS INCOME OF NONCUSTODIAL PARENT		CHILD SUPPORT ORDER
0 -- $7,500		Discretion--Minimum $50/month
$7,501 -- 15,000		26% of Gross Income + 10% of Basic Order (28.6%)
15,001 -- 25,000		27% of Gross Income + 10% of Basic Order (29.7%)
25,001 -- 50,000		28% of Gross Income + 10% of Basic Order (30.8%)
50,001 -- 75,000		29% of Gross Income + 10% of Basic Order (31.9%)

AGES 13-21 (oldest child)

ANNUAL GROSS INCOME OF NONCUSTODIAL PARENT		CHILD SUPPORT ORDER
0 -- $7,500		Discretion--Minimum $50/month
$7,501 -- 15,000		26% of Gross Income + 15% of Basic Order (29.9%)
15,001 -- 25,000		27% of Gross Income + 15% of Basic Order (31.05%)
25,001 -- 50,000		28% of Gross Income + 15% of Basic Order (32.2%)
50,001 -- 75,000		29% of Gross Income + 15% of Basic Order (33.35%)

CHART 3
CHILD SUPPORT ORDER FORMULA
FOR THE SUPERIOR COURT
THREE CHILDREN
AGES 0-6 (oldest child)

ANNUAL GROSS INCOME OF NONCUSTODIAL PARENT	CHILD SUPPORT ORDER
0 -- $7,500	Discretion--Minimum $50/month
$7,501 -- 15,000	30% of Gross Income
15,001 -- 25,000	31% of Gross Income
25,001 -- 50,000	32% of Gross Income
50,001 -- 75,000	33% of Gross Income

AGES 7-12 (oldest child)

ANNUAL GROSS INCOME OF NONCUSTODIAL PARENT	CHILD SUPPORT ORDER
0 -- $7,500	Discretion--Minimum $50/month
$7,501 -- 15,000	30% of Gross Income + 10% of Basic Order (33.0%)
15,001 -- 25,000	31% of Gross Income + 10% of Basic Order (34.1%)
25,001 -- 50,000	32% of Gross Income + 10% of Basic Order (35.2%)
50,001 -- 75,000	33% of Gross Income + 10% of Basic Order (36.3%)

AGES 13-21 (oldest child)

ANNUAL GROSS INCOME OF NONCUSTODIAL PARENT	CHILD SUPPORT ORDER
0 -- $7,500	Discretion--Minimum $50/month
$7,501 -- 15,000	30% of Gross Income + 15% of Basic Order (34.5%)
15,001 -- 25,000	31% of Gross Income + 15% of Basic Order (35.65%)
25,001 -- 50,000	32% of Gross Income + 15% of Basic Order (36.8%)
50,001 -- 75,000	33% of Gross Income + 15% of Basic Order (37.95%)

CHART 4
CHILD SUPPORT ORDER FORMULA
FOR THE SUPERIOR COURT
FOUR OR MORE CHILDREN
AGES 0-6 (oldest child)

ANNUAL GROSS INCOME OF NONCUSTODIAL PARENT	CHILD SUPPORT ORDER
0 -- $7,500	Discretion--Minimum $50/month
$7,501 -- 15,000	32% of Gross Income
15,001 -- 25,000	33% of Gross Income
25,001 -- 50,000	34% of Gross Income
50,001 -- 75,000	35% of Gross Income

AGES 7-12 (oldest child)

ANNUAL GROSS INCOME OF NONCUSTODIAL PARENT	CHILD SUPPORT ORDER
0 -- $7,500	Discretion--Minimum $50/month
$7,501 -- 15,000	32% of Gross Income + 10% of Basic Order (35.2%)
15,001 -- 25,000	33% of Gross Income + 10% of Basic Order (36.3%)
25,001 -- 50,000	34% of Gross Income + 10% of Basic Order (37.4%)
50,001 -- 75,000	35% of Gross Income + 10% of Basic Order (38.5%)

AGES 13-21 (oldest child)

ANNUAL GROSS INCOME OF NONCUSTODIAL PARENT	CHILD SUPPORT ORDER
0 -- $7,500	Discretion--Minimum $50/month
$7,501 -- 15,000	32% of Gross Income + 15% of Basic Order (36.8%)
15,001 -- 25,000	33% of Gross Income + 15% of Basic Order (37.95%)
25,001 -- 50,000	34% of Gross Income + 15% of Basic Order (39.1%)
50,001 -- 75,000	35% of Gross Income + 15% of Basic Order (40.25%)

District of Columbia Resources

The following information provides some additional resources for District of Columbia legal clinics, domestic shelters, and family law websites.

LEGAL CLINICS

**American University—
Domestic Violence Clinic**
4801 Massachusetts Avenue
Suite 417
Washington, DC 20016
202-274-4140
www.wcl.american.edu/clinical/domestic.cfm

**American University—
Women and the Law Clinic**
4801 Massachusetts Avenue, NW
Washington, DC 20016
202-274-4140
www.wcl.american.edu/clinical/women.cfm

**Asian Pacific American Legal
Resource Center**
735 15th Street, NW
Suite 315
Washington, DC 20005
202-393-3572
www.charityadvantage.com/apalrc

AYUDA
1736 Columbia Road, NW
Washington, DC 20009
202-387-2870
www.ayudainc.org

**Catholic University Families and
the Law Clinic**
3602 John McCormack Road
Catholic University Campus
Washington, DC 20001
202-319-6788

Child Support Services Division
441 4th Street, NW
Suite 550N
Washington, DC 20024
202-724-6529

Children's Law Center
901 15th Street, NW
Suite 500
Washington, DC 20005
202-467-4900
www.childrenslawcenter.org

**Counsel for Child Abuse and Neglect—
D.C. Superior Court**
500 Indiana Avenue, NW.
Room 4416
Washington, DC 20001
202-879-1406
www.dccourts.gov/dccourts/superior/
family/ccan.jsp

**D.C. Lawyer Referral Service—
Bar Association of the
District of Columbia**
1819 H Street, NW
12ᵗʰ Floor
Washington, DC 20006
202-296-7845
www.badc.org/html/lawref.htm

**DC Bar Pro Bono Program Free
Custody Clinic**
500 Indiana Avenue, NW
Washington, DC 20001
202-737-4700 ext. 292

**DC Bar Pro Bono Program Free
Divorce Clinic**
500 Indiana Avenue, NW
Washington, DC 20001
202-737-4700 ext. 292

**Domestic Violence Intake—
D.C. Superior Court**
500 Indiana Avenue, NW
Room 4235
Washington, DC 20001
202-879-0152

**Domestic Violence Intake—
Greater Southeast Hospital**
1328 Southern Avenue, SE
Room 311
Washington, DC 20032
202-561-3000

**Domestic Violence Legal Empowerment
and Appeals Project**
2000 G Street, NW
Washington, DC 20052
202-994-2278

Family Court Self-Help Center
500 Indiana Avenue, NW
Room JM 570
Washington, DC 20001

**Georgetown University Law Center
Domestic Violence Clinic**
600 New Jersey Avenue, NW
Room 334
Washington, DC 20001
202-662-9640

**Legal Aid Society of the
District of Columbia**
666 11ᵗʰ Street, NW
8ᵗʰ Floor
Washington, DC 20001
202-628-1161
www.legalaiddc.org

**Legal Aid Society of the District of
Columbia—SE Intake**
1901 Mississippi Avenue, SE
Washington, DC 20020
202-436-3077
www.legalaiddc.org

**Legal Information Helpline
District of Columbia**
1250 H Street
6ᵗʰ Floor
Washington, DC 20005
202-626-3499
202-626-3492

Neighborhood Legal Services Program
701 4ᵗʰ Street, NW
Washington, DC 20001
202-682-2700

**Neighborhood Legal Services Program—
Southeast**
1213 Good Hope Road, SE
Washington, DC 20001
202-678-2000

Office of Bar Counsel
515 5ᵗʰ Street, NW
Building A
Room 127
Washington, DC 20001
202-638-1501

Office of People's Counsel
1133 15ᵗʰ Street, NW
Suite 500
Washington, DC 20005
202-727-3071
www.opc-dc.gov

University Legal Services
220 I Street, NE
Suite 130
Washington, DC 20002
202-547-0198
www.uls-dc.org

**Women Empowered Against Violence
    (WEAVE)**
1111 16th Street, NW
Suite 200
Washington, DC 20036
202-452-9550 ext. 103
www.weaveincorp.com

DOMESTIC VIOLENCE
SHELTERS

DC Coalition Against Domestic Violence
P. O. Box 76069
Washington, DC 20013
202-783-5332

D.C. Hotline
P.O. Box 57194
Washington, DC 20037
202-223-0020
202-223-2255

House of Imagene
P.O. Box 1493
Washington, DC 20013
202-797-7460

House of Ruth—Herspace
651 10th Street, NE
Washington, DC 20002
202-347-0737
Hotline/Crisis: 202-347-2777

Mary House
4303 13th Street, NE
Washington, DC 20017
202-635-0534

My Sister's Place
5 Thomas Circle
4th Floor
Washington, DC 20005
202-986-1476
Hotline/Crisis: 202-529-5991

Whitman-Walker Clinic Victim Services
1407 S Street, NW
Washington, DC 20009
202-797-4447

FAMILY LAW WEBSITES

About Divorce in the District of Columbia
http://divorcesupport.about.com

District of Columbia Cases
www.divorcesource.com/research/edj/
    states/dc.shtml

**District of Columbia
Child Support Calculator**
www.alllaw.com/calculators/childsupport/dc

**District of Columbia
Child Support Guidelines Statute**
www.supportguidelines.com/glines/dc_cs.html

District of Columbia Divorce Laws
www.divorcenet.com/states/
    district_of_columbia

District of Columbia Family Court
www.dccourts.gov/dccourts/superior

Divorce Law Info
www.divorcelawinfo.com/DC/flc.htm

District of Columbia Blank Forms

This section contains the forms you will use to file your divorce case; obtain service of process on your spouse; obtain an order of default, if applicable; calculate child support, if applicable; and, conclude your case with a divorce hearing. Make copies of these forms and amend them to fit your specific situation.

TABLE OF FORMS

SUPERIOR COURT OF THE DISTRICT OF COLUMBIA
FAMILY COURT

Jacket No. _____   **FINANCIAL STATEMENT**   Date _____

_____ V. _____

NAME:	SOCIAL SECURITY NO.:	OCCUPATION:

NAME AND ADDRESS OF CURRENT EMPLOYER:	I claim _____ exemptions for withholding tax purposes.

INCOME INFORMATION*

1. Monthly gross wages .... $_____

2. Less Mandatory Monthly Deductions:
   - Federal Income Tax............$_____
   - State Income Tax .... _____
   - Retirement:
     - FICA...................... _____
     - Social Security .... _____
   - Medical Insurance............... _____
   - Other........................$_____
   - TOTAL......................$_____

3. Monthly Net Wages .... $_____
   (Subtract Line 2 form line 1)

4. Monthly income from all other sources (e.g., part-time or overtime wages, fees rents, dividends, commissions, unemployment compensation, disability, social security, retirement, interest, bonuses, etc.) .... $_____

5. Less Other Mandatory Monthly Deductions:
   - Federal Income Tax............$_____
   - State Income Tax .... _____
   - Retirement:
     - FICA...................... _____
     - Social Security .... _____
   - Medical Insurance............... _____
   - Other........................ _____
   - TOTAL......................$_____

6. Monthly Net Income from all other sources .... $_____
   (Subtract Line 5 form Line 4)

7. Total Monthly Net Disposable Income..................... $_____
   (Add Lines 3 and 6)

8. Total Monthly Gross Income..............$_____
   (Add Lines 1 and 4)

SUMMARY

9. Total Monthly Net Disposable Income..................... $_____

10. Less Total Monthly Expenses .... $_____

11. Difference: .... $_____

AVERAGE MONTHLY EXPENSES

	Wife/Husband	Children
Housing, etc.		
Rent/Mortages	$_____	$_____
Utilities	_____	_____
Taxes	_____	_____
Food		
Groceries/Household Supplies	_____	_____
Meals Out	_____	_____
Automobile		
Payment	_____	_____
Gas/Oil....................	_____	_____
Repairs....................	_____	_____
Insurance..................	_____	_____
Tags	_____	_____
Life Insurance	_____	_____
(List beneficiaries)		
_____	_____	_____
_____	_____	_____
_____	_____	_____
Health Insurance (not .... listed as income deduction)	_____	_____
School		
Tuition	_____	_____
Supplies/Fees	_____	_____
Child Care Expenses		
To allow for employment/ education	_____	_____
To allow for recreation	_____	_____
Lessons (e.g. music, dance, art) .	_____	_____
Allowance	_____	_____
Clothing/Uniforms	_____	_____
Dry Cleaning/Laundry	_____	_____
Medical Expenses .... (Unpaid by insurance)	_____	_____
Charitable Contributions	_____	_____
Recreation	_____	_____
Vacations	_____	_____
Miscellaneous:		
_____	_____	_____
_____	_____	_____
Periodic Payments Required on Bills:		
_____	_____	_____
_____	_____	_____
Total Monthly Expenses	_____	_____

*NOTE: If you are paid weekly, multiply your weekly gross wages by 4.3 to arrive at yur monthly gross wage. If you are paid every two weeks multiply your bi-weekly gross wages by 2.15 to arrive at yur monthly gross wage.

Form FDX101-731 Apr. 89   **PLEASE ATTACH LATEST WAGE STATEMENTS SHOWING YOUR DEDUCTIONS**

LIABILITIES

Type of Debt	To Whom Owned	Date Incurred	Total Amt. of Debt	Amt. Paid to Date	Balance Due
		Total Liabilities			

ASSETS
(List as separately or jointly owned with spouse)

	Separate	Joint
Cash		
Automobiles		
Bank Accounts		
Bonds		
Notes		
Real Estate		
Stocks		
Personal Property		
Total Assets		

SUMMARY

	Separate	Joint
Total Assets		
Less Total Liabilities		
Net Worth		

I certify that this statement indicates my current financial situation to the best of my knowledge.

Subscribed and sworn to before me this _____ day of _____, _____

_____
(Deputy Clerk or Notary Public)

9-2591 wd-321

Child Support Guideline Calculator

(All figures are per year. Please do not enter dollar signs or commas in the fields.)

Non-Custodial Parent

Gross Income:

Other Child Support Paid Per Year:

Additional Health Insurance Paid for Children Per Year:

Custodial Parent

Gross Income:

Child Care Cost Per Year:

Children

(1) Total Number of biological or adopted Children in the non-custodial parent's household who are being supported by the non-custodial parent plus
(2) the number of children in this case whom support is sought by petitioner:

Age of the Oldest Child Supported by the Non-Custodial Parent:

Number of Children (in this case only) Living With the Custodial Parent:

Age of the Oldest Child Living With the Custodial Parent:

Submit

District of Columbia Courts
(202) 879-1010
TTY TDD Directory

Telephone Directory by Topic | Site Map | D.C. Government Web Site

Feedback | Accessibility | Privacy & Security | Terms & Conditions

Moultrie Courthouse
500 Indiana Ave., N.W.
Washington, D.C. 20001

COURT OF THE DISTRICT OF COLUMBIA
FAMILY COURT
Domestic Relations Branch

_____

PRINT YOUR NAME

_____

STREET ADDRESS

_____

CITY, STATE AND ZIP CODE

☐ SUBSTITUTE ADDRESS: CHECK BOX IF YOU
HAVE WRITTEN SOMEONE ELSE'S ADDRESS BECAUSE
YOU FEAR HARASSMENT OR HARM.

PLAINTIFF,

v.

_____

PRINT YOUR SPOUSE'S NAME

_____

STREET ADDRESS

_____

CITY, STATE AND ZIP CODE

DEFENDANT.

DR   _____

Related Cases:

_____

_____

_____

COMPLAINT FOR ABSOLUTE DIVORCE
Action Involving Child Support   ◯ yes   ◯ no

I, _____, am the Plaintiff in this case and state that
          PRINT YOUR NAME

1. This Court has the authority to decide my request for divorce and related issues because
[CHECK ALL THAT APPLY]

☐ I have been a resident of the District of Columbia for more than six months immediately before filing this Complaint.

☐ My spouse has been a resident of the District of Columbia for more than six months immediately before filing this Complaint.

2. My spouse and I were married [CHECK ONE]

◎ by ceremony on _____ , in _____ .
DATE   CITY AND STATE

◎ by common law on or about _____ , in _____ .
DATE   CITY AND STATE

3. My spouse and I separated on or about _____ .
DATE

4. I state the following about the separation: [CHECK ONE]

◎ The separation has been **mutual and voluntary, and** has continued without interruption or cohabitation for a period of more than **six months** immediately before filing this Complaint.

◎ The separation has continued without interruption or cohabitation for a period of more than **one year** immediately before filing this Complaint.

5. I state the following with regard to my married name: [CHECK ONE]

◎ I did not change my name when I married my spouse.

◎ I changed my name when I married my spouse. I do not wish to return to a former name.

◎ I changed my name when I married my spouse and I now wish to return to my birth name or another legal name I used before my marriage. I have no illegal or fraudulent reason for making this request. The former name I want restored is

_____ .
PRINT THE FORMER NAME YOU WOULD LIKE THE COURT TO RESTORE

328

Marital Property & Marital Debt

6. I state the following about property from my marriage: [CHECK ONE]

☒ My spouse and I have no marital property.

☒ My spouse and I may have marital property, but I am not asking the Court to divide or distribute it.

☒ My spouse and I have a written agreement resolving all of our marital property issues and I am not asking the Court to divide or distribute any marital property.

☒ My spouse and I have marital property that I am asking the Court to divide or distribute, and I have completed and attached the additional information required on Attachment A, which I incorporate into this Complaint.

☒ I am not sure if my spouse and I have marital property.

7. I state the following about debt from my marriage: [CHECK ONE]

☒ My spouse and I have no marital debt.

☒ My spouse and I may have marital debt, but I am not asking the Court to assign responsibility for it.

☒ My spouse and I have a written agreement resolving all of our marital debt issues and I am not asking the Court to assign responsibility for it.

☒ My spouse and I have marital debt that I am asking the Court to assign responsibility for, and I have completed and attached the additional information required on Attachment A, which I incorporate into this Complaint.

☒ I am not sure if my spouse and I have marital debt.

Alimony

8. I state the following about my need for temporary financial support from my spouse until the time the Court grants this request for divorce: [CHECK ONE]

☒ I need temporary financial support and will file a separate motion ("Motion for Temporary Alimony") asking the Court to grant this request.

☒ I do not want temporary financial support at this time.

9. I state the following about alimony: [CHECK ONE]

    ☐ I need alimony from my spouse and I believe my spouse has the ability to pay alimony to me.

    ☐ I do not want my spouse to pay alimony to me.

Custody

---

10. I state the following about our child(ren) who are under the age of 18: [CHECK ONE]

    ☐ My spouse and I do not have any children together (through birth or adoption) who are under the age of 18.

    ☐ My spouse and I do have children together (through birth or adoption) who are under the age of 18, but I am not asking the court to decide custody at this time.

    ☐ My spouse and I do have children together (through birth or adoption) who are under the age of 18, and we have a written agreement about custody; I am not asking the court to decide custody at this time.

    ☐ My spouse and I do have children together (through birth or adoption) who are under the age of 18, and I am asking the court to decide custody. I have completed and attached the additional information required on Attachment B, which I incorporate into this Complaint.

Child Support

---

11. My spouse has the legal obligation to contribute to the support of our child(ren) who are 21 years old or younger or who are adult disabled children.

12. I state the following about my request for child support: [CHECK ONE]

    ☐ My spouse and I do not have any children together (through birth or adoption), or our children together are over the age of 21 years and are not adult disabled children.

    ☐ My spouse and I do have children together (through birth or adoption) who are under the age of 21 or who are adult disabled children, but I am not asking the Court to award child support at this time.

○ My spouse and I do have children together (through birth or adoption) who are under the age of 21 or who are adult disabled children, and we have an agreement regarding child support; that agreement is consistent with the Child Support Guideline of the District of Columbia and/or it is fair and just.

○ My spouse and I do have children together (through birth or adoption) who are under the age of 21 or who are adult disabled children, and I am asking the Court to award child support, *and* I have completed and attached the additional information required on Attachment C, which I incorporate into this Complaint.

Attachments

13. **I have included the following attachment(s):**

☐ No attachments
☐ Attachment A (Marital Property and/or Marital Debt)
☐ Attachment B (Child Custody)
☐ Attachment C (Child Support)

Request for Relief

I RESPECTFULLY REQUEST that [CHECK ALL THAT APPLY]

☐ The Court grant me an Absolute Divorce.

☐ The Court divide marital property and/or assign marital debt in a manner that is equitable, just and reasonable.

☐ The Court award alimony in a manner that is fair and equitable.

☐ The Court award custody in the best interests of the child(ren).

☑ The Court hold a hearing on my request for child support within 45 days of filing and issue a Notice of Hearing and Order Directing Appearance ("NHODA") to the other parent with the date and time of the hearing.

☐ The Court award child support according to the Child Support Guideline of the District of Columbia and other applicable laws, including:
      ☐ current child support (support starting today and continuing into the future)
      ☐ retroactive child support (support for time before today)
      ☐ medical support

☐ The Court ◉ *include* our Settlement Agreement as a part of its order.
◉ *not include* our Settlement Agreement as a part of its order.

☐ The Court restore me to my former name.

I ALSO REQUEST that the Court award any other relief it considers fair and proper.

[CHECK ONE]

◉ I *do not* know of any proceedings in the District of Columbia or in any state or territory involving the same claim or subject matter as this case.

◉ I *do* know of proceedings in the District of Columbia or in any state or territory involving the same claim or subject matter as this case, as listed on the first page of this Complaint ("Related Cases").

Respectfully Submitted,

_____
SIGN YOUR NAME

_____
STREET ADDRESS

_____
CITY, STATE AND ZIP CODE

_____
TELEPHONE NUMBER

☐ SUBSTITUTE ADDRESS: CHECK BOX IF YOU HAVE WRITTEN SOMEONE ELSE'S ADDRESS BECAUSE YOU FEAR HARASSMENT OR HARM.

I, _____, solemnly swear or affirm under criminal penalties for the making of a false statement that I have read the foregoing Complaint for Absolute Divorce and that the factual statements made in it are true to the best of my personal knowledge, information and belief.

_____
SIGN YOUR NAME

_____
DATE

_____
PRINT YOUR NAME

RULE 4
CERTIFICATE OF SERVICE

WHEN YOU FILE YOUR COMPLAINT, THE FAMILY COURT CENTRAL INTAKE CENTER WILL GIVE YOU A **SUMMONS** THAT YOU MUST SERVE ON THE OTHER PARTY WITH A COPY OF YOUR COMPLAINT.

YOU MUST SERVE THE OTHER PARTY BEFORE THE SUMMONS EXPIRES IN 60 DAYS.

IF YOU ARE UNABLE TO SERVE THE OTHER PARTY WITHIN THE 60 DAYS, YOU CAN ASK THE FAMILY COURT CENTRAL INTAKE CENTER TO GIVE YOU ANOTHER SUMMONS. THE SECOND SUMMONS IS CALLED AN "ALIAS SUMMONS." YOU **MUST** ASK FOR THE ALIAS SUMMONS **BEFORE** THE FIRST SUMMONS EXPIRES.

HERE ARE THE WAYS YOU CAN SERVE YOUR COMPLAINT AND THE SUMMONS:

- **by having someone else,** who is over 18 years old and not a party to the case (NOT you), **hand it to the other party;** or

- **by having someone else,** who is over 18 years old and not a party to the case (NOT you), **leave a copy at the other party's home** with a person of suitable age and discretion who lives there; or

- **by mailing it to the other party** by certified mail, return receipt requested.

> IF THE RETURN RECEIPT ("GREEN CARD") COMES BACK TO YOU, FILE IT WITH THE FAMILY COURT CENTRAL INTAKE CENTER BY ATTACHING IT TO AN "AFFIDAVIT OF RETURN OF SERVICE BY CERTIFIED MAIL."

AFTER YOU SERVE THE OTHER PARTY, YOU MUST COMPLETE THE CERTIFICATE OF SERVICE PORTION FOUND AT THE BOTTOM OF THE SUMMONS AND FILE IT WITH THE FAMILY COURT CENTRAL INTAKE CENTER.

GOVERNMENT OF THE DISTRICT OF COLUMBIA
DEPARTMENT OF HEALTH
CERTIFICATE OF DIVORCE,
DISSOLUTION OF MARRIAGE OR ANNULMENT

D–

COURT IDENTIFICATION
(Court File Number)

108–

FILE NUMBER

TYPE IN PERMANENT INK

PINK—COURT COPY

YELLOW—STATISTICAL COPY

WHITE—VITAL RECORDS PERMANENT FILE

HUSBAND

HUSBAND—NAME	FIRST	MIDDLE	LAST
1.			

USUAL RESIDENCE — STREET ADDRESS	CITY, TOWN OR LOCATION	
2a.	2b.	

COUNTY	STATE	DATE OF BIRTH (Mo, Day, Yr.)
2c.	3.	4.

WIFE

WIFE—NAME	FIRST	MI	LAST	MAIDEN NAME
5a.				5b.

USUAL RESIDENCE — STREET ADDRESS	CITY, TOWN OR LOCATION	
6a.		

COUNTY	TE	DATE OF BIRTH (Mo, Day, Yr.)
6c.		8.

DATE OF THIS MARRIAGE (Mo, Day, Yr.)	CHILDREN UNDER 18 IN THIS FAMILY (Specify)	PLAINTIFF CHECK	HUSBAND	WIFE	BOTH	OTHER (Specify)
9.	10.	11.				

ATTORNEY FOR PLANTIFF—NAME (Type or Print)	ADDRESS OF ATTORNEY—STREET OR R.F.D. NO.	CITY OR TOWN	STATE	ZIP
12.	13.			

DECREE

THIS DECREE IS GRANTED ON (MONTH DAY YEAR.) ONLY COURT RECORDS CAN INDICATE THE DATE ON WHICH A DECREE BECOMES FINAL.	TYPE OF DECREE CHECK	DIVORCE	DISSOLUTION	ANNULMENT
	15.			
14.	TITLE OF COURT 16. SUPERIOR COURT OF THE DISTRICT OF COLUMBIA			

SIGNATURE OF CERTIFYING OFFICIAL	TITLE OF OFFICIAL
17.	18. CLERK OF THE COURT

INFORMATION FOR STATISTICAL PURPOSES ONLY

HUSBAND

RACE—HUSBAND Specify (e.g., White, Black, American Indian, etc.)	NUMBER OF THIS MARRIAGE Specify (First, second, etc.)	WIFE	RACE—WIFE Specify (e.g., White, Black, American Indian, etc.)	NUMBER OF THIS MARRIAGE Specify (First, second, etc.)
19.	20.		21.	22.

DHS-1601 (7/97)   THIS CERTIFICATE IS TO BE FILED WITH THE CLERK OF THE COURT WITH THE PETITION   97-0960 PM5

(An original of this document must be obtained directly from the court.)

SUPERIOR COURT OF THE DISTRICT OF COLUMBIA
FAMILY COURT

_____

PRINT PETITIONER'S/PLAINTIFF'S NAME

PETITIONER/PLAINTIFF,

v.

_____   Case No. _____

PRINT RESPONDENT'S/DEFENDANT'S NAME

RESPONDENT/DEFENDANT.

REQUEST TO PROCEED WITHOUT PRE-PAYMENT OF COSTS
(*In Forma Pauperis*)

I, _____, am the   ⚪ PLAINTIFF/PETITIONER
     PRINT YOUR NAME   ⚪ DEFENDANT/RESPONDENT   in this case.

I respectfully ask this Court to allow me to pursue this case without pre-paying fees or costs and without giving security for them. In support of this request, I state the following:

1. I am not able to pay the costs of this case or to give security for it without substantial hardship to myself or to my family.

2. The issues I want to present to the Court are set out in the attached document(s):
[CHECK ALL THAT APPLY]

    ☐ Complaint
    ☐ Counterclaim
    ☐ Petition
    ☐ Motion
    ☐ Subpoena

3. I state the following about my income: [CHECK ALL THAT APPLY]

☐ **I receive the following public benefits, *and the law presumes that I am eligible to proceed without pre-payment of costs*:**

    ☐ Temporary Assistance to Needy Families (TANF)
    ☐ Program on Work, Employment, and Responsibility (POWER)
    ☐ General Assistance for Children (GAC)
    ☐ Supplemental Security Income or Social Security Disability (SSI or SSDI)
    ☐ Interim Disability Assistance (IDA)
    ☐ Food Stamps

☐ **I am employed** and I state the following about my employment:

    ☐ I earn $_____ per month.

    ☐ My employer is _____.

    ☐ My employer's address is _____.

☐ **I am not employed** and I state the following about the last time I was employed:

    ○ I have never been employed.

    ○ I was last employed on _____ and earned $_____ per month.
                   DATE

☐ In the past 12 months, I have received the following **other income**:

    ☐ I have received $_____ from _____.

    ☐ I have received $_____ from _____.

4. I state the following about my property:

☐ I do not have any cash, savings or checking accounts.

☐ I do not own any automobiles, real estate, stocks, bonds, or other valuable property.

☐ I have $_____ in cash, including money in savings or checking accounts.

☐ I own the following vehicles, real estate, stock, bonds, or other valuable property:

_____

_____

_____

[LIST THE PROPERTY AND AMOUNT OF MONEY IT IS WORTH]

5. I state the following about my debt:

◯ I do not owe any money.

◯ I owe the following amounts of money:

$ AMOUNT OWED	OWED TO	$ AMOUNT PAID EACH MONTH

6. The following persons are dependent upon me for support:

NAME	RELATIONSHIP

I RESPECTFULLY REQUEST that the Court grant my Request to Proceed without Pre-Payment of Costs.

Respectfully Submitted,

_____
SIGN YOUR NAME

_____
STREET ADDRESS

_____
CITY, STATE AND ZIP CODE

_____
TELEPHONE NUMBER

☐ SUBSTITUTE ADDRESS: CHECK BOX IF YOU HAVE WRITTEN SOMEONE ELSE'S ADDRESS BECAUSE YOU FEAR HARASSMENT OR HARM.

338

I, _____, solemnly swear or affirm under criminal penalties for the making of a false statement that I have read the foregoing Request for Permission to Proceed Without Pre-Payment of Costs and Supporting Affidavit and that the factual statements made in it are true to the best of my personal knowledge, information and belief.

_____
SIGN YOUR NAME

_____
DATE

_____
PRINT YOUR NAME

POINTS AND AUTHORITIES IN SUPPORT OF
REQUEST TO PROCEED WITHOUT PRE-PAYMENT OF COSTS

In support of my Request to Proceed Without Pre-Payment of Costs, I refer to:

1.   Super. Ct. Dom. Rel. R. 7(b)(1)(A) and 54(f).

2.   D.C. Code §§ 15-712, 13-340(a), and 16-918(a).

**SUPERIOR COURT OF THE DISTRICT OF COLUMBIA
FAMILY COURT**

_____

PRINT PETITIONER'S/PLAINTIFF'S NAME

PETITIONER/PLAINTIFF,

v.

_____

PRINT RESPONDENT'S/DEFENDANT'S NAME

RESPONDENT/DEFENDANT.

Case No. _____

ORDER

Upon consideration of ⚪ PLAINTIFF'S ⚪ DEFENDANT'S Request for Permission to Proceed Without Pre-Payment of Costs, any and all supporting argument and documentation provided, and the record herein, it is this _____ day of _____, 20_____ hereby ORDERED that

_____ **The request is GRANTED.**

_____ **The request is DENIED.**

SO ORDERED.

_____   _____

DATE   JUDGE'S SIGNATURE

**COURT OF THE DISTRICT OF COLUMBIA
FAMILY COURT
Domestic Relations Branch**

_____

PRINT PLAINTIFF'S NAME

PLAINTIFF,

v.

DR _____

_____

PRINT DEFENDANT'S NAME

DEFENDANT.

**RULE 4(c)(2)
AFFIDAVIT OF RETURN OF SERVICE BY CERTIFIED MAIL**

I, _____, am the ⊙ PLAINTIFF   in this case.

     PRINT YOUR NAME   ⊙ DEFENDANT

1. On _____**, I sent to the other party by certified mail, return-receipt requested, a copy of my**

    ⊙ Summons and Complaint for Absolute Divorce
    ⊙ Summons and Complaint for Legal Separation
    ⊙ Summons and Complaint for Annulment of Marriage
    ⊙ Summons and Complaint for Custody and/or Visitation
    ⊙ Notice of Motion and Motion to Modify Custody and/or Visitation
    ⊙ Notice of Motion and Motion for Contempt

2. I received the return-receipt ("green card") from the U.S. Postal Service. It was signed

by _____ **and dated** _____.

    NAME OF PERSON WHO SIGNED THE RECEIPT   DATE SIGNED

3.   **I reviewed the return receipt ("green card")** and **state that**

 ☉ The other party signed the return receipt ("green card").

 ☉ A person of suitable age and discretion who lives at the home of the other party signed the return receipt ("green card").

 ☉ I do not know if the person who signed the signed the return receipt ("green card") is a person of suitable age and discretion who lives at the home of the other party.

 ☉ I do not know who signed the return receipt ("green card").

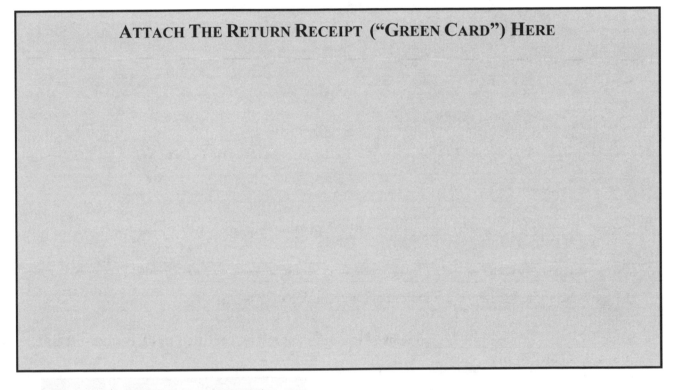

ATTACH THE RETURN RECEIPT ("GREEN CARD") HERE

I, _____, solemnly swear or affirm under criminal penalties for the making of a false statement that I have read this Affidavit of Return of Service by Certified Mail and that the factual statements made in it are true to the best of my personal knowledge, information and belief.

_____   _____
SIGN YOUR NAME   DATE

_____
PRINT YOUR NAME

COURT OF THE DISTRICT OF COLUMBIA
FAMILY COURT
Domestic Relations Branch

_____

PRINT YOUR NAME

PLAINTIFF,

v.

_____

PRINT THE OTHER PARTY'S NAME

DEFENDANT.

DR   _____

Judge   _____

MOTION TO SERVE BY PUBLICATION OR POSTING

I, _____, am the Plaintiff in this case.

PRINT YOUR NAME

1.   I have attempted to serve the Defendant with notice of this case.

2.   I have been unable to find the Defendant.

3.   I believe that the Defendant is a non-resident of the District of Columbia or that the Defendant has been absent from the District of Columbia for at least six months.

4.   I believe the Defendant cannot be found because I have made diligent efforts to discover the whereabouts of the Defendant. My efforts include looking for information about the Defendant's current address, last known address and last known employer; information from other people who know the Defendant; information about the Defendant from jails, prisons and the military; and other efforts.

[YOU MUST TRY YOUR BEST TO COMPLETE STEPS 1 – 17]

Information About the Defendant's Current Address

[YOU MUST TRY TO COMPLETE EACH OF THE FOLLOWING STEPS]

1. ☐ I do not know the Defendant's current home address or telephone number.

2. ☐ I last had contact with the Defendant on _____
   PRINT DATE OF LAST CONTACT

3. ☐ My last contact with the Defendant was

   ◉ in person at _____
   PRINT ADDRESS OR PLACE WHERE YOU LAST HAD CONTACT

   ◉ by telephone at _____
   IF YOU CALLED THE DEFENDANT, PRINT THE NUMBER YOU CALLED

4. ◉ The Defendant and I have never lived together.
   OR
   ◉ The Defendant and I last lived together on _____ at this address:
   PRINT DATE

   _____
   STREET ADDRESS

   _____
   CITY   STATE   ZIP

Information About the Defendant's Last Known Address & Telephone

[YOU MUST TRY TO COMPLETE EACH OF THE FOLLOWING STEPS]

5. ☐ The Defendant's last known home address is

_____
STREET ADDRESS

_____
CITY   STATE   ZIP

6. ☐ I mailed the Summons and Complaint to the Defendant at the last known address by "certified mail, return receipt requested" on_____
PRINT DATE

    ☑ The post office sent the return receipt to me unsigned or marked "not found."

    ☑ The post office never sent the return receipt to me.

7. ☐ The Defendant's last known telephone number is _____
PRINT THE TELEPHONE NUMBER

8. ☐ I called the Defendant's last known telephone number on _____
PRINT DATE YOU CALLED

9. ☐ When I called the last known telephone number, this is what happened:

_____

_____

10. ☐ I called "411" and asked for the Defendant's telephone number on _____
PRINT DATE

    ☑ The "411" operator told me there was no listing for the Defendant.

    ☑ The "411" operator gave me this telephone number: _____
PRINT NUMBER FROM "411"

When I called the number from "411," this is what happened:

_____

_____

Information About the Defendant's Last Known Employer

[YOU MUST TRY TO COMPLETE EACH OF THE FOLLOWING STEPS]

11. ☐ The Defendant's last known employer is

_____
COMPANY NAME

_____
STREET ADDRESS

_____
CITY   STATE   ZIP

12. ☐ I contacted the Defendant's last known employer on _____
PRINT DATE YOU CONTACTED EMPLOYER

13. ☐ When I spoke to the last known employer, this is what happened:

_____

_____

Information From Other People Who Know the Defendant

[YOU MUST TRY TO COMPLETE EACH OF THE FOLLOWING STEPS]

14. ☐   I tried to contact the Defendant's relatives or friends in person, by telephone or by mail.

The person I contacted was…	The contact was…	This is what happened…
name: relationship to Defendant:	☐ in person ☐ by telephone ☐ by mail ☐ on this date:	
name: relationship to Defendant:	☐ in person ☐ by telephone ☐ by mail ☐ on this date:	
name: relationship to Defendant:	☐ in person ☐ by telephone ☐ by mail ☐ on this date:	
name: relationship to Defendant:	☐ in person ☐ by telephone ☐ by mail ☐ on this date:	
name: relationship to Defendant:	☐ in person ☐ by telephone ☐ by mail ☐ on this date:	

Information From Jails and Prisons About the Defendant

[YOU MUST TRY TO COMPLETE EACH OF THE FOLLOWING STEPS]

15. ☐ I called these jails and prisons to find out if the Defendant is incarcerated or on parole.

Jail or Prison	Contact	This is what happened…
Bureau of Prisons Inmate Locator Service 320 First St NW, Rm 524 Washington, DC 20534 (202) 307-3126 *or* www.bop.gov (Click on "Inmate Locator" on left side of screen) Search by name, Register #, DCDC #, FBI # or INS #.	○ I called on this date: *or* ○ I searched the website, printed the search results and am attaching a copy to this Motion.	☐ The Bureau of Prisons told me:
Correctional Treatment Facility (202) 698-3000 Search by last name, PDID #, or DCDC #.	☐ I called on this date:	☐ The Correctional Treatment Facility told me:
District of Columbia Jail Records Office (202) 673-8257 Search by full name & DOB, PDID # or DCDC #.	☐ I called on this date:	☐ The DC Jail told me:
US Parole Commission (301) 492-5990 Search by full name and/or REG #.	☐ I called on this date:	☐ The US Parole Commission told me:

Information From the Military About the Defendant

[YOU MUST TRY TO COMPLETE EACH OF THE FOLLOWING STEPS]

16. ☐ I sent a letter to all the branches of the military to find out if the Defendant is in the military. I am attaching copies of the letters I sent and any replies that I got.

YOU MUST INCLUDE A STAMPED SELF-ADDRESSED ENVELOPE WITH EACH LETTER. THE LOCATOR SERVICES ARE FREE TO IMMEDIATE FAMILY MEMBERS; ALL OTHERS MUST INCLUDE A CHECK OR MONEY ORDER FOR **$3.50** MADE OUT TO "TREASURER OF THE U.S."

Branch of Military	Contact	This is what happened...
US Army Worldwide Locator ATTN: AHRC-ERP US Army Enlisted Records & Evaluation Center 8899 East 56th St Indianapolis, IN 46249-5301 **NOTE: ENCLOSE $3.50 IF YOU ARE NOT AN IMMEDIATE FAMILY MEMBER**	☐ I wrote a letter and I am attaching a copy of my letter to this Motion.	○ I got a letter back from the Army and I am attaching a copy to this Motion. ○ The Army never replied to my letter.
US Navy Worldwide Locator Bureau of Naval Personnel PERS 312F 5720 Integrity Drive Millington, TN 38055-3120 (901) 874-3351 **NOTE: ENCLOSE $3.50 IF YOU ARE NOT AN IMMEDIATE FAMILY MEMBER**	☐ I wrote a letter and I am attaching a copy of my letter to this Motion.	○ I got a letter back from the Navy and I am attaching a copy to this Motion. ○ The Navy never replied to my letter.
US Air Force Worldwide Locator HQ AFMPC/RMIQL 550 C Street West, Suite 50 Randolph AFB, TX 78150-4752 (210) 652-5775 **NOTE: ENCLOSE $3.50 IF YOU ARE NOT AN IMMEDIATE FAMILY MEMBER**	☐ I wrote a letter and I am attaching a copy of my letter to this Motion.	○ I got a letter back from the Air Force and I am attaching a copy to this Motion. ○ The Air Force never replied to my letter.

Marine Corps Worldwide Locator HQ US Marine Corps Personnel Mgmt Support Branch MMSB-10 2008 Elliot Road, Suite 201 Quantico, VA 22134-5030 (703) 640-3942 or (703) 640-3943 NOTE: ENCLOSE $3.50 IF YOU ARE NOT AN IMMEDIATE FAMILY MEMBER	☐ I wrote a letter and I am attaching a copy of my letter to this Motion.	◯ I got a letter back from the Marine Corps and I am attaching a copy to this Motion. ◯ The Marine Corps never replied to my letter.
Coast Guard Personnel Command (CGPC-ADM-3) 2100 Second Street NW Washington, DC 20593-0001 (202) 267-1340 NOTE: ENCLOSE $3.50 IF YOU ARE NOT AN IMMEDIATE FAMILY MEMBER	☐ I wrote a letter and I am attaching a copy of my letter to this Motion.	◯ I got a letter back from the Coast Guard and I am attaching a copy to this Motion. ◯ The Coast Guard never replied to my letter.
National Oceanic and Atmospheric Administration (NOAA) Commissioned Personnel Center 1315 East-West Highway Room 12100 Silver Spring, MD 20910 (301) 713-3444 NOTE: THIS IS FREE FOR EVERYONE	☐ I wrote a letter and I am attaching a copy of my letter to this Motion.	◯ I got a letter back from the NOAA and I am attaching a copy to this Motion. ◯ The NOAA never replied to my letter.
Public Health Service Office of Commissioned Corps 1101 Wootton Parkway, Suite 100 Rockville, MD 20852 (240) 453-6000 NOTE: THIS IS FREE FOR EVERYONE	☐ I wrote a letter and I am attaching a copy of my letter to this Motion.	◯ I got a letter back from the Public Health Service and I am attaching a copy to this Motion. ◯ The Public Health Service never replied to my letter.

Other Information About Your Search for the Defendant

[YOU MUST TRY TO COMPLETE EACH OF THE FOLLOWING STEPS]

17. ☐ I also tried to find the Defendant by doing these other things:

_____

_____

_____

Request to Post Notice in Clerk's Office Instead of in the Newspaper

[COMPLETE THIS SECTION ONLY IF YOU CANNOT AFFORD TO PUBLSH A NOTICE IN THE NEWSPAPER]

IF THE JUDGE GRANTS THIS MOTION, THERE ARE TWO WAYS TO NOTIFY THE DEFENDANT ABOUT THIS CASE:

* **PUBLICATION** MEANS THAT YOU WILL PAY A NEWSPAPER TO PUBLISH A NOTICE.

* **POSTING** MEANS THAT A NOTICE WILL BE POSTED AT THE COURTHOUSE. POSTING IS FREE, BUT IT IS ONLY FOR PEOPLE WHO CANNOT AFFORD TO PUBLISH A NOTICE IN THE NEWSPAPER.

If I have to pay to publish a notice in the newspaper, it will cause me a substantial hardship because:

☐ I have already been allowed to file this case without paying any fees (IFP).

or

☐ I cannot afford to pay to publish a notice in the newspaper for the following reasons [EXPLAIN WHY YOU CANNOT AFFORD TO PUBLISH A NOTICE IN THE NEWSPAPER, INCLUDING DETAILED INFORMATION ABOUT YOUR INCOME AND EXPENSES]:

_____

_____

_____

_____

Request for Relief

I RESPECTFULLY REQUEST that [CHECK ALL THAT APPLY]

☐ the Court allow me to serve the Defendant by publishing a notice in the newspaper.

☐ the Court allow me to serve the Defendant by posting a notice in the Domestic Relations Clerk's Office.

☐ Other _____

_____

_____

I ALSO REQUEST that the Court award any other relief it considers fair and proper.

I   ⊙ Do   request an oral hearing in front of the judge on this motion.
    ⊙ Do Not

Respectfully Submitted,

_____
SIGN YOUR NAME

_____
STREET ADDRESS

_____
CITY, STATE AND ZIP CODE

_____
TELEPHONE NUMBER

☐ SUBSTITUTE ADDRESS: CHECK BOX IF YOU HAVE WRITTEN SOMEONE ELSE'S ADDRESS AND PHONE NUMBER BECAUSE YOU FEAR HARASSMENT OR HARM.

I, _____, solemnly swear or affirm under criminal penalties for the making of a false statement that I have read the foregoing Motion to Serve by Publication or Posting and that the factual statements made in it are true to the best of my personal knowledge, information and belief.

_____   _____
SIGN YOUR NAME   DATE

_____
PRINT YOUR NAME

POINTS AND AUTHORITIES IN SUPPORT OF MOTION

In support of this Motion to Serve by Publication or Posting, I refer to:

1. Super. Ct. Dom. Rel. R. 4(g) and 7(b).

2. D.C. Code §§ 13-336, 13-338-40 and 16-4601.07(a).

3. Bearstop v. Bearstop, 377 A.2d 405 (D.C. 1977); Cruz v. Sarmiento, 737 A.2d 1021 (D.C. 1999).

4. The record in this case.

5. The attached supporting document(s).

[LIST ANY DOCUMENTS THAT YOU ARE ATTACHING]

_____

_____

_____

_____

_____

_____

_____

_____

_____

_____

_____

_____

_____

_____

_____

_____

_____

_____

_____

_____   _____
                    Attorney   *Address*

ORDER PUBLICATION — ABSENT DEFENDANT _____

Superior Court of the District of Columbia
FAMILY COURT
DOMESTIC RELATIONS BRANCH

_____
                              Plaintiff

            vs.   Jacket No._____

_____
                              Defendant

The object of this suit is_____

_____

_____

_____

_____

_____

_____

On motion of the plaintiff, it is this _____ day of _____

20___, ordered that the defendant _____

_____

_____

cause_____h_____appearance to be entered herein on or before the fortieth day, exclusive of Sundays and

legal holidays, occurring after the day of the first publication of this order; otherwise the cause will be pro-

ceeded with as in case of default. Provided, a copy of this order is published once a week for three suc-

cessive weeks in the Washington Law Reporter, and the _____.

before said day.

Attest:
                                    _____
                                                          Judge

Clerk of the Superior Court
of the District of Columbia

        By_____
                    Deputy Clerk

SUPERIOR COURT OF THE DISTRICT OF COLUMBIA
FAMILY COURT
DOMESTIC RELATIONS BRANCH

_____)	
Your Name)	
)	
_____)	CASE NO. _____
Address)	
)	
_____)	
City, State, Zip)	

           Plaintiff,

vs.

_____)

Defendant's Name   )

_____)

Address   )

_____)

City, State, Zip   )

           Defendant.   )

POINTS AND AUTHORITIES
IN SUPPORT OF MOTION TO ALLOW
SERVICE BY PUBLICATION

1. Plaintiff has been unable to serve Defendant, _____,
    despite diligent efforts.

2. Plaintiff will not be able to continue with this case if this Motion is denied.

3. D.C. Code Sec. 16-4505(a) (4) (1989)

4. D.C. Code Secs. 13-336(a) (2) & 13-340 (a) (1989)

5. SCR-Dom Rel. 4 (j)

6. Bearstop vs. Bearstop, 337 A.2d 405 (D.C. 1977)

SUPERIOR COURT OF THE DISTRICT OF COLUMBIA
FAMILY DIVISION
DOMESTIC RELATIONS BRANCH

PRAECIPE

Jacket No.: _____   Date: _____

Social File No.: _____

_____

(Plaintiff)   *vs.*

_____

(Defendant or Respondent)

The Clerk of said Court will please enter a default and set an ex parte hearing.

Attorney's Name: (Please Print)	Attorney's Name: (Please Print)
Address: ☐ Plaintiff ☐ Government	Address: ☐ Defendant ☐ Respondent
Attorney's Signature:	Attorney's Signature:

Registration No.	Telephone No.	Registration No.	Telephone No.

COURT OF THE DISTRICT OF COLUMBIA
FAMILY COURT
Domestic Relations Branch

_____

PRINT YOUR NAME

PLAINTIFF,

v.

_____   DR   _____

PRINT THE OTHER PERSON'S NAME

DEFENDANT.

AFFIDAVIT IN SUPPORT OF DEFAULT

I, _____, am the Plaintiff in this case and state that

         PRINT YOUR NAME

1. The Defendant was served with the Summons and Complaint in this case on _____.

                                                              DATE

2. Proof of service was filed in the Clerk's office on _____.

                                                                 DATE

3. An Affidavit in Compliance with the Servicemembers Civil Relief Act of 2003 is being filed with this Affidavit in Support of Default.

4. The Defendant has not filed an Answer with me or with the Court, and has not otherwise appeared in this case.

5. The time for Defendant to file an Answer in this case has expired, and the Court has not given an extension of time.

I RESPECTFULLY REQUEST that the Clerk enter a default judgment against the Defendant in this case.

Respectfully Submitted,

_____
YOUR SIGNATURE

_____
STREET ADDRESS

_____
CITY, STATE AND ZIP CODE

_____
TELEPHONE NUMBER

☐ SUBSTITUTE ADDRESS: CHECK BOX IF YOU ARE
USING SOMEONE ELSE'S ADDRESS BECAUSE YOU FEAR
HARASSMENT OR HARM.

I, _____, solemnly swear or affirm under criminal penalties for the making of a false statement that I have read the foregoing Affidavit in Support of Default and that the factual statements made in it are true to the best of my personal knowledge, information and belief.

_____   _____
SIGN YOUR NAME   DATE

_____
PRINT YOUR NAME

COURT OF THE DISTRICT OF COLUMBIA
FAMILY COURT
Domestic Relations Branch

_____

PRINT YOUR NAME

PLAINTIFF,

v.

_____   DR   _____

PRINT THE OTHER PERSON'S NAME

DEFENDANT.

AFFIDAVIT IN COMPLIANCE WITH THE SERVICEMEMBERS CIVIL RELIEF ACT

I, _____, am the Plaintiff in this case and state that

    PRINT YOUR NAME

1. I am making this Affidavit to comply with the provisions of the Servicemembers Civil Relief Act, 50 U.S.C. App. § 520 (2003).

2. With regard to the Defendant's military service, I state that [CHECK ONE]

    ☐ I *do* have personal knowledge that the Defendant is *not* currently in the armed forces of the United States Army, Navy, Air Force, Marine Corps or Coast Guard, and is *not* a commissioned officer of the National Oceanic and Atmospheric Administration or the Public Health Service. Further, to the best of my information and belief, the Defendant has *not* received notice of induction or notice to report for military service. [CHECK THIS BOX IF YOU *KNOW FOR SURE* THAT THE DEFENDANT IS NOT IN THE SERVICE]

    ☐ I *do not* have personal knowledge of Defendant's service obligations, **but I have asked** the United States Army, Navy, Air Force, Marine Corps, Coast Guard, National Oceanic and Atmospheric Administration and Public Health Service whether the Defendant is enlisted **and** each has confirmed that Defendant is **not** enlisted for service in its armed forces or commissioned division.

Respectfully Submitted,

_____

SIGN YOUR NAME

_____

STREET ADDRESS

_____

CITY, STATE AND ZIP CODE

_____

TELEPHONE NUMBER

☐ SUBSTITUTE ADDRESS: CHECK BOX IF YOU HAVE WRITTEN SOMEONE ELSE'S ADDRESS BECAUSE YOU FEAR HARASSMENT OR HARM.

I, _____, solemnly swear or affirm under criminal penalties for the making of a false statement that I have read the foregoing Affidavit in Compliance with the Servicemembers Civil Relief Act and that the factual statements made in it are true to the best of my personal knowledge, information and belief.

_____   _____

SIGN YOUR NAME   DATE

_____

PRINT YOUR NAME

Information From the Military About the Defendant

[YOU MUST TRY TO COMPLETE EACH OF THE FOLLOWING STEPS]

☐ I sent a letter to all the branches of the military to find out if the Defendant is in the military. I am attaching copies of the letters I sent and any replies that I got.

YOU MUST INCLUDE A STAMPED SELF-ADDRESSED ENVELOPE WITH EACH LETTER. THE LOCATOR SERVICES ARE FREE TO IMMEDIATE FAMILY MEMBERS; ALL OTHERS MUST INCLUDE A CHECK OR MONEY ORDER FOR **$3.50** MADE OUT TO "TREASURER OF THE U.S."

Branch of Military	Contact	This is what happened...
US Army Worldwide Locator ATTN: AHRC-ERP US Army Enlisted Records & Evaluation Center 8899 East 56th St Indianapolis, IN 46249-5301 NOTE: ENCLOSE **$3.50** IF YOU ARE NOT AN IMMEDIATE FAMILY MEMBER	☐ I wrote a letter and I am attaching a copy of my letter to this Motion.	○ I got a letter back from the Army and I am attaching a copy to this Motion. ○ The Army never replied to my letter.
US Navy Worldwide Locator Bureau of Naval Personnel PERS 312F 5720 Integrity Drive Millington, TN 38055-3120 (901) 874-3351 NOTE: ENCLOSE **$3.50** IF YOU ARE NOT AN IMMEDIATE FAMILY MEMBER	☐ I wrote a letter and I am attaching a copy of my letter to this Motion.	○ I got a letter back from the Navy and I am attaching a copy to this Motion. ○ The Navy never replied to my letter.
US Air Force Worldwide Locator HQ AFMPC/RMIQL 550 C Street West, Suite 50 Randolph AFB, TX 78150-4752 (210) 652-5775 NOTE: ENCLOSE **$3.50** IF YOU ARE NOT AN IMMEDIATE FAMILY MEMBER	☐ I wrote a letter and I am attaching a copy of my letter to this Motion.	○ I got a letter back from the Air Force and I am attaching a copy to this Motion. ○ The Air Force never replied to my letter.

Marine Corps Worldwide Locator HQ US Marine Corps Personnel Mgmt Support Branch MMSB-10 2008 Elliot Road, Suite 201 Quantico, VA 22134-5030 (703) 640-3942 or (703) 640-3943 NOTE: ENCLOSE $3.50 IF YOU ARE NOT AN IMMEDIATE FAMILY MEMBER	☐ I wrote a letter and I am attaching a copy of my letter to this Motion.	⭕ I got a letter back from the Marine Corps and I am attaching a copy to this Motion. ⭕ The Marine Corps never replied to my letter.
Coast Guard Personnel Command (CGPC-ADM-3) 2100 Second Street NW Washington, DC 20593-0001 (202) 267-1340 NOTE: ENCLOSE $3.50 IF YOU ARE NOT AN IMMEDIATE FAMILY MEMBER	☐ I wrote a letter and I am attaching a copy of my letter to this Motion.	⭕ I got a letter back from the Coast Guard and I am attaching a copy to this Motion. ⭕ The Coast Guard never replied to my letter.
National Oceanic and Atmospheric Administration (NOAA) Commissioned Personnel Center 1315 East-West Highway Room 12100 Silver Spring, MD 20910 (301) 713-3444 NOTE: THIS IS FREE FOR EVERYONE	☐ I wrote a letter and I am attaching a copy of my letter to this Motion.	⭕ I got a letter back from the NOAA and I am attaching a copy to this Motion. ⭕ The NOAA never replied to my letter.
Public Health Service Office of Commissioned Corps 1101 Wootton Parkway, Suite 100 Rockville, MD 20852 (240) 453-6000 NOTE: THIS IS FREE FOR EVERYONE	☐ I wrote a letter and I am attaching a copy of my letter to this Motion.	⭕ I got a letter back from the Public Health Service and I am attaching a copy to this Motion. ⭕ The Public Health Service never replied to my letter.

Rule 55 (DEFAULT)

Superior Court of the District of Columbia

FAMILY DIVISION
DOMESTIC RELATIONS BRANCH

_____ *Plaintiff*

   vs.

_____ *Defendant*

Jacket No. _____

DEFAULT

It appearing that the above-named defendant has failed to plead or otherwise defend this action though duly served with summons and copy of the complaint on the _____ day of _____ 20____, and an affidavit on behalf of the plaintiff having been filed, it is the_____ day of _____, 20____, declared that_____

_____

_____

defendant herein is in default.

Witness, the Honorable Chief Judge of the Superior Court and the seal of said Court.

Clerk of the Superior Court
of the District of Columbia

By _____

Deputy Clerk

SUPERIOR COURT OF THE DISTRICT OF COLUMBIA
FAMILY COURT

Domestic Relations Office
Paternity and Support Office
Juvenile and Neglect Office
Mental Health and Retardation Office

Counsel for Child Abuse and Neglect

PRAECIPE

Jacket No. : _____   Date: _____

Social File No.: _____

_____
(Plaintiff or Petitioner)

vs.

_____
(Defendant or Respondent)

The Clerk of said Court will please note:	that this matter is uncontested as

to all issues; please set a hearing date as soon as possible.

Attorney's Name: (Please Print)	Attorney's Name: (Please Print)
[X] Plaintiff or Petitioner	[X] Defendant
[ ] Government	[ ] Respondent
Mailing Address:	Mailing Address:
E-Mail Address:	E-Mail Address:
Attorney's Signature:	Attorney's Signature:
Registration No. Telephone No. Fax No.	Registration No. Telephone No. Fax No.

Form FD-358/Apr.02

White – Legal Record Copy   Yellow – Copy

SUPERIOR COURT OF THE DISTRICT OF COLUMBIA

WASHINGTON, D. C. 20001

CONSENT TO HAVE PROCEEDINGS CONDUCTED BY HEARING COMMISSIONER

_____   Case Number:
            Plaintiff
    v.

_____
            Defendant

Consent Granted.   Pursuant to SCR-Civ. 73 and the Initial Order signed by Chief Judge Ugast, dated October 1, 1992, plaintiff(s)/ defendant(s) hereby consent to have all proceedings in the above captioned case conducted by a hearing commissioner rather than a judge.   It is understood that this consent constitutes a waiver of jury trial.   It is further understood that this consent may be withdrawn only upon leave of the Presiding Judge of the Civil Division, or that Judge's designee, for good cause shown.

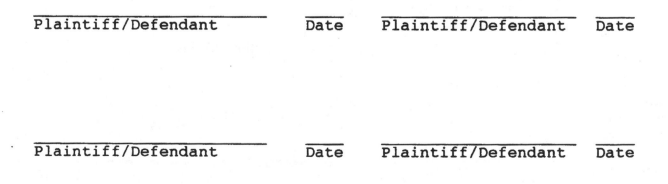

_____   ____   _____   ____
Plaintiff/Defendant   Date   Plaintiff/Defendant   Date

_____   ____   _____   ____
Plaintiff/Defendant   Date   Plaintiff/Defendant   Date

12/01

SUPERIOR COURT OF THE DISTRICT OF COLUMBIA
FAMILY COURT
DOMESTIC RELATIONS BRANCH

_____	)
(YOUR NAME)	)
_____	)
(STREET ADDRESS)	)
_____	)
(CITY, STATE, ZIP CODE)	)
	)
Soc. Sec. No._____	)
	)
PLAINTIFF,	)
VS.	) CASE NO. _____
	)
_____	)
(YOUR SPOUSE'S NAME)	)
_____	)
(STREET ADDRESS)	)
_____	)
(CITY, STATE, ZIP CODE)	)
	)
Soc. Sec. No._____	)
	)
DEFENDANT.	)

FINDINGS OF FACT, CONCLUSIONS OF LAW AND JUDGMENT OF ABSOLUTE DIVORCE

This matter was heard on the _____ day of

_____, 20____, upon the pleadings filed herein. Upon the

evidence adduced, the court makes the following:

FINDINGS OF FACT

1. The _____ is and has been a bona fide resident of the
    (PLAINTIFF/DEFENDANT)

District of Columbia for more than six (6) months next preceding the filing of the complaint
herein.

2. The plaintiff and defendant were lawfully married to each other on

_____ in _____.
(MONTH DAY, YEAR)   (CITY, STATE)

3. Since _____, 20_____, the plaintiff and defendant
          (MONTH, DAY)   (YEAR)

have continuously lived separate and apart from each other without cohabitation.

4. The plaintiff and the defendant together are the parents of the following _____
                                                     (#)

child(ren) born or adopted prior to or during the marriage:

NAME	SOCIAL SECURITY NUMBER	BIRTH DATE
		___/___/___
		___/___/___
		___/___/___
		___/___/___
		___/___/___
		___/___/___

5. The following prior orders have been issued regarding custody, visitation, and child

support:

_____
_____
_____
_____
_____

6. The minor child(ren) are in the care and custody of the _____,
                                                       (PLAINTIFF/DEFENDANT)

who is a fit and proper person to have custody of the minor child(ren).

7.   The _____ shall have reasonable rights of visitation with the
          (PLAINTIFF/DEFENDANT)

parties' minor child(ren). The following is additional information about visitation:

_____

_____

_____

8.   The _____,who is financially able to do so, will pay
          (PLAINTIFF/DEFENDANT)
$_____ every _____ for the support of their minor
    (amount)   (mo./wk./two weeks)

child(ren).

9.   There are no property rights to be adjucicated between the plaintiff and defendant.

10.   There is no reasonable prospect of reconciliation of this marriage.

11.   The_____ requests restoration of his/her former name,
          (PLAINTIFF/DEFENDANT)
_____. This request is not made for any illegal
    (BIRTH NAME OR PRIOR NAME)
or fraudulent reason.

CONCLUSIONS OF LAW

Based upon the foregoing Findings of Fact, the court concludes as a matter of law that the

plaintiff is entitled to a Judgment of Absolute Divorce from the defendant on the ground of

mutual and voluntary separation without cohabitation for six months next preceding the

commencement of this action.

JUDGMENT

WHEREFORE, it is by the court this _____ day of _____, 20____,

ORDERED, ADJUDGED AND DECREED:

1. That the plaintiff, _____, be and hereby
(YOUR FULL MARRIED NAME)

is awarded an Absolute Divorce from the defendant, _____
(YOUR SPOUSE'S FULL MARRIED NAME)

on the ground of separation without cohabitation for one year next preceding the commencement

of this action;

PROVIDED, HOWEVER, that this Judgment shall not become effective to dissolve

the bonds of matrimony until the time allowed for taking an appeal has expired or until the final

disposition of any appeal so taken.

2. That the _____ be and hereby is awarded
(PLAINTIFF/DEFENDANT)

permanent custody of the parties' minor child(ren), namely,

_____

_____, with reasonable

rights of visitation reserved to the _____. The following
(PLAINTIFF/DEFENDANT)

information is provided about visitation: _____

_____

_____

_____

_____

4

3. That the _____ be and is hereby ordered
               (PLAINTIFF/DEFENDANT)

to pay to the _____ the amount of $ _____
               (PLAINTIFF/DEFENDANT)   (AMOUNT)

every _____ toward the support of the parties' minor children beginning
         (week/month/two weeks)

on _____, 20_____.
         (MONTH/DAY/YEAR)

All payments are to be made payable to the "Clerk, D.C. Superior Court" and must include this case number. Payments are to be made through the Financial Clerk of the Family Division, Room 4335A, 500 Indiana Avenue, N.W., Washington, D.C. 20001. The Clerk shall forward all payments to the _____.
                                                              (PLAINTIFF/DEFENDANT)

4. That both parties must notify the Court within ten days of any change of

employer or income. If the non-custodial parent is in arrears in an amount equal to 30 days

of support payments, the support payments shall be withheld from his/her employment income or

from any other income. Once withholding begins, all payments must be made through the Court

Registry. Any other payments shall be considered a gift and shall not offset the duty to support.

Any withholding order entered herein may be changed if any party moves for a reapportionment

of periodic arrears payments to reflect a change in the non-custodial parents' ability to pay.

5. That the _____ be and hereby is restored to the use of
               (PLAINTIFF/DEFENDANT)
his/her former name, _____.
                          (BIRTH NAME OR PRIOR NAME)

_____
JUDGE/COMMISSIONER
D.C. SUPERIOR COURT

Copies to:

_____
(YOUR NAME)

_____
(STREET ADDRESS)

_____
(CITY, STATE, ZIP)

_____
(YOUR SPOUSE'S NAME)

_____
(STREET ADDRESS)

_____
(CITY, STATE, ZIP)

COURT OF THE DISTRICT OF COLUMBIA
FAMILY COURT
Domestic Relations Branch

_____

PRINT PLAINTIFF'S NAME

PLAINTIFF,   DR _____

v.

_____   Judge _____

PRINT DEFENDANT'S NAME

DEFENDANT.

JOINT WAIVER OF APPEAL OF DIVORCE ORDER/JUDGMENT

Plaintiff and Defendant each state that:

1. I have reviewed the Divorce Order/Judgment that will be entered in this case.

2. I understand that either party has the right to appeal the Divorce Order/Judgment for up to 30 days after the order has been entered on the court docket.

3. I understand that the divorce is not considered final until this time to appeal has expired unless we both agree to waive our right to appeal.

Knowing this, both parties sign below to show that we give up our right to appeal.

Respectfully Submitted,

_____   _____
PLAINTIFF'S SIGNATURE   DATE

_____   _____
DEFENDANT'S SIGNATURE   DATE

Index

D

E

Earnings Withholding Order, 175

education, 104, 144, 177, 178, 184, 186, 203

emails, 20

emotional divorce, 5

employees, 14, 37

employer, 14, 74, 81, 85, 166, 172, 175

employment, 40, 109, 135, 137, 146, 178, 179

equitable distribution, 181, 184, 201

equity, 3, 34, 42, 158, 181, 204

ex parte order, 15, 89

exceptions with a judicial decision, 105, 106, 190, 191, 201

exhibits, 77, 118, 124, 127

expenses, 7, 9, 13, 14, 19, 23, 28, 34, 36, 41, 59, 76, 88, 151, 153, 154, 155, 156, 157, 158, 163, 164, 165, 166, 167, 168, 169, 170, 172, 173, 178

F

family, 3, 5, 10, 11, 16, 19, 20, 27, 50, 53, 54, 58, 63, 101, 103, 107, 122, 137, 146, 158, 161, 171, 178, 183, 184, 185, 187, 193, 198, 201, 202, 205, 208

FICA, 164, 166

financial statements, 19, 59, 92, 100, 124, 129, 131, 163, 164, 165, 167, 169, 171, 173

Findings of Fact, Conclusions of Law and Judgment of Absolute Divorce, 100, 111

flexibility, 25, 36

former name, 3, 64, 65

fraud, 4

friends, 5, 10, 73, 75, 81, 93, 101, 138, 183

furniture, 58, 123, 124, 165, 181, 183, 184, 202, 208

G

good faith, 81

grandparents, 134, 143

grounds, 3, 4, 30, 33, 47, 49, 50, 51, 52, 53, 54, 55, 58, 61, 62, 64, 67, 91, 93, 95, 96, 99, 104, 105, 108, 122, 123, 129, 179, 182, 197, 199, 200, 202, 207

fault, 39, 51, 138, 177, 185

no-fault, 51

Guidelines for Effective Parenting, 39, 139, 141, 144, 147, 149

H

harassment, 59, 62, 109

health, 36, 37, 40, 122, 135, 137, 151, 152, 156, 166, 168, 178, 184, 185, 186, 196, 198, 203

hearing, 4, 15, 16, 23, 30, 70, 71, 77, 88, 89, 90, 92, 93, 94, 96, 97, 98, 100, 102, 103, 104, 105, 106, 107, 108, 109, 110, 111, 113, 115, 116, 117, 118, 119, 122, 123, 190, 191, 199, 200, 202, 205, 207

hearsay, 127

holidays, 36, 88, 123, 141, 142, 145, 146, 147, 148, 149, 153

I

income, 19, 23, 27, 36, 58, 59, 63, 131, 149, 151, 152, 154, 155, 156, 157, 158, 159, 160, 161, 162, 163, 164, 165, 166, 167, 170, 172, 173, 177, 179, 180, 182, 186, 193, 194, 198

inheritance, 14, 42, 125, 182, 206

injunctions, 15

R

S